AMERICA'S
TEST KITCHEN

also by **america's test kitchen**

**FOR A FULL LISTING OF
ALL OUR BOOKS:**

CooksIllustrated.com

AmericasTestKitchen.com

praise for **america's test kitchen titles**

Selected as the Cookbook Award Winner of 2021 in the Health and Nutrition category

INTERNATIONAL ASSOCIATION OF CULINARY PROFESSIONALS (IACP) ON *THE COMPLETE PLANT-BASED COOKBOOK*

"An exhaustive but approachable primer for those looking for a 'flexible' diet. Chock-full of tips, you can dive into the science of plant-based cooking or just sit back and enjoy the 500 recipes."

MINNEAPOLIS STAR TRIBUNE ON *THE COMPLETE PLANT-BASED COOKBOOK*

"In this latest offering from the fertile minds at America's Test Kitchen the recipes focus on savory baked goods. Pizzas, flatbreads, crackers, and stuffed breads all shine here . . . Introductory essays for each recipe give background information and tips for making things come out perfectly."

BOOKLIST (STARRED REVIEW) ON *THE SAVORY BAKER*

"A mood board for one's food board is served up in this excellent guide . . . This has instant classic written all over it."

PUBLISHERS WEEKLY (STARRED REVIEW) ON *BOARDS: STYLISH SPREADS FOR CASUAL GATHERINGS*

"Reassuringly hefty and comprehensive, *The Complete Autumn and Winter Cookbook* by America's Test Kitchen has you covered with a seemingly endless array of seasonal fare . . . This overstuffed compendium is guaranteed to warm you from the inside out."

NPR ON *THE COMPLETE AUTUMN AND WINTER COOKBOOK*

"Here are the words just about any vegan would be happy to read: 'Why This Recipe Works.' Fans of America's Test Kitchen are used to seeing the phrase, and now it applies to the growing collection of plant-based creations in *Vegan for Everybody*."

THE WASHINGTON POST ON *VEGAN FOR EVERYBODY*

Selected as the Cookbook Award Winner of 2021 in the General category

INTERNATIONAL ASSOCIATION OF CULINARY PROFESSIONALS (IACP) ON *MEAT ILLUSTRATED*

"Another flawless entry in the America's Test Kitchen canon, Bowls guides readers of all culinary skill levels in composing one-bowl meals from a variety of cuisines."

BUZZFEED BOOKS ON *BOWLS*

Selected as the Cookbook Award Winner of 2021 in the Single Subject category

INTERNATIONAL ASSOCIATION OF CULINARY PROFESSIONALS (IACP) ON *FOOLPROOF FISH*

"The book's depth, breadth, and practicality makes it a must-have for seafood lovers."

PUBLISHERS WEEKLY (STARRED REVIEW) ON *FOOLPROOF FISH*

"*The Perfect Cookie* . . . is, in a word, perfect. This is an important and substantial cookbook . . . If you love cookies, but have been a tad shy to bake on your own, all your fears will be dissipated. This is one book you can use for years with magnificently happy results."

HUFFPOST ON *THE PERFECT COOKIE*

"The book offers an impressive education for curious cake makers, new and experienced alike. A summation of 25 years of cake making at ATK, there are cakes for every taste."

THE WALL STREET JOURNAL ON *THE PERFECT CAKE*

"The go-to gift book for newlyweds, small families, or empty nesters."

ORLANDO SENTINEL ON *THE COMPLETE COOKING FOR TWO COOKBOOK*

"If you're one of the 30 million Americans with diabetes, *The Complete Diabetes Cookbook* by America's Test Kitchen belongs on your kitchen shelf."

PARADE.COM ON *THE COMPLETE DIABETES COOKBOOK*

"True to its name, this smart and endlessly enlightening cookbook is about as definitive as it's possible to get in the modern vegetarian realm."

MEN'S JOURNAL ON *THE COMPLETE VEGETARIAN COOKBOOK*

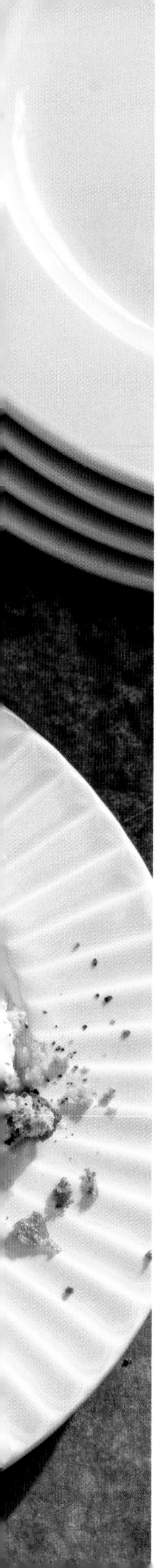

THE COMPLETE
small plates
COOKBOOK

300+
Shareable Tapas,
Meze, Bar Snacks,
Dumplings,
Salads, and More

AMERICA'S TEST KITCHEN

Library of Congress Cataloging-in-Publication Data

Names: America's Test Kitchen (Firm), author.
Title: The complete small plates cookbook : 300+ shareable tapas, meze, bar snacks, dumplings, salads, and more / America's Test Kitchen.
Description: Boston, MA : America's Test Kitchen, [2023] | Includes index.
Identifiers: LCCN 2022048116 (print) | LCCN 2022048117 (ebook) | ISBN 9781954210370 | ISBN 9781954210387 (ebook)
Subjects: LCSH: Appetizers. | Snack foods. | LCGFT: Cookbooks.
Classification: LCC TX740 .C648 2023 (print) | LCC TX740 (ebook) | DDC 641.81/2--dc23/eng/20221024
LC record available at https://lccn.loc.gov/2022048116
LC ebook record available at https://lccn.loc.gov/2022048117

21 Drydock Avenue, Boston, MA 02210

Printed in Canada
10 9 8 7 6 5 4 3 2 1

Distributed by
Penguin Random House Publisher Services
Tel: 800.733.3000

pictured on front cover Pan-Seared Scallops with Asparagus-Citrus Salad (page 294), Carciofi alla Giudia (page 233), Baguette with Radishes, Butter, and Herbs (page 327)

pictured on back cover Sweet Glazed Peaches (page 373), Chicken Satay (page 303), Grilled Onion, Pear, and Prosciutto Flatbread (page 336)

editorial director, books Adam Kowit

executive food editor Dan Zuccarello

deputy food editor Leah Colins

executive managing editor Debra Hudak

project editors Kaumudi Marathé and Sara Zatopek

test cooks Olivia Counter, Jacqueline Gochenouer, Eric Haessler, Hisham Hassan, José Maldonado, and Patricia Suarez

contributing editor Cheryl Redmond

design director Lindsey Timko Chandler

associate art director Kylie Alexander

photography director Julie Bozzo Cote

senior photography producer Meredith Mulcahy

senior staff photographers Steve Klise and Daniel J. van Ackere

staff photographer Kevin White

additional photography Joseph Keller and Carl Tremblay

food styling Joy Howard, Sheila Jarnes, Catrine Kelty, Chantal Lambeth, Gina McCreadie, Kendra McNight, Ashley Moore, Christie Morrison, Marie Piraino, Elle Simone Scott, Kendra Smith, and Sally Staub

project manager, publishing operations Katie Kimmerer

senior print production specialist Lauren Robbins

production and imaging coordinator Amanda Yong

production and imaging specialists Tricia Neumyer and Dennis Noble

copy editor Rebecca Springer

proofreader Vicki Rowland

indexer Elizabeth Parson

chief creative officer Jack Bishop

executive editorial directors Julia Collin Davison and Bridget Lancaster

contents

welcome to **america's test kitchen**

This book has been tested, written, and edited by the folks at America's Test Kitchen, where curious cooks become confident cooks. Located in Boston's Seaport District in the historic Innovation and Design Building, it features 15,000 square feet of kitchen space, including multiple photography and video studios. It is the home of *Cook's Illustrated* magazine and *Cook's Country* magazine and is the workday destination for more than 60 test cooks, editors, and cookware specialists. Our mission is to empower and inspire confidence, community, and creativity in the kitchen.

We start the process of testing a recipe with a complete lack of preconceptions, which means that we accept no claim, no technique, and no recipe at face value. We simply assemble as many variations as possible, test a half-dozen of the most promising, and taste the results blind. We then construct our own recipe and continue to test it, varying ingredients, techniques, and cooking times until we reach a consensus. As we like to say in the test kitchen, "We make the mistakes so you don't have to." The result, we hope, is the best version of a particular recipe, but we realize that only you can be the final judge of our success (or failure). We use the same rigorous approach when we test equipment and taste ingredients.

All of this would not be possible without a belief that good cooking, much like good music, is based on a foundation of objective technique. Some people like spicy foods and others don't, but there is a right way to sauté, there is a best way to cook a pot roast, and there are measurable scientific principles involved in producing perfectly beaten, stable egg whites. Our ultimate goal is to investigate the fundamental principles of cooking to give you the techniques, tools, and ingredients you need to become a better cook. It is as simple as that.

To see what goes on behind the scenes at America's Test Kitchen, check out our social media channels for kitchen snapshots, exclusive content, video tips, and much more. You can watch us work (in our actual test kitchen) by tuning in to *America's Test Kitchen* or *Cook's Country* on public television or on our websites. Listen to *Proof*, *Mystery Recipe*, and *The Walk-In* (AmericasTestKitchen.com/podcasts), to hear engaging, complex stories about people and food. Want to hone your cooking skills or finally learn how to bake—with an America's Test Kitchen test cook? Enroll in one of our online cooking classes. And you can engage the next generation of home cooks with kid-tested recipes from America's Test Kitchen Kids.

However you choose to visit us, we welcome you into our kitchen, where you can stand by our side as we test our way to the best recipes in America.

Join Our Community of Recipe Testers
Our recipe testers provide valuable feedback on recipes under development by ensuring that they are foolproof in home kitchens. Help the America's Test Kitchen book team investigate the how and why behind successful recipes from your home kitchen.

facebook.com/AmericasTestKitchen
instagram.com/TestKitchen
youtube.com/AmericasTestKitchen
tiktok.com/@TestKitchen
twitter.com/TestKitchen
pinterest.com/TestKitchen

AmericasTestKitchen.com
CooksIllustrated.com
CooksCountry.com
OnlineCookingSchool.com
AmericasTestKitchen.com/kids

getting started

introduction

Grazing on several small plates is the creative approach to eating that so many of us enjoy these days, tasting our way through little dishes of interesting food. It's flavorful, it's fun, and it works for so many occasions, from weeknight dinners to entertaining. Taking our cue from the popular restaurant trend, we hand-selected the vibrant recipes in this book to bring small plates home.

The Complete Small Plates Cookbook celebrates the versatility and appeal of small plates dining. We thought outside the plate that consists of a main protein and two sides and instead experimented with preparing multiple smaller dishes. We picked recipes that creatively come together to offer variety as well as ease. A big part of the appeal comes from choosing different kinds of food that harmonize in taste and texture. The small plates model works well whether you're having a family meal, a cocktail party, or are dining solo.

What's a small plate? Varied and interesting food that goes beyond cheese and crackers and the usual appetizers to include different flavors, textures, and compositions. Think multicultural bar snacks that range from a handful of spiced almonds or roasted chickpeas to pigs in blankets to Indian pakoras and karaage, Japanese fried chicken. And shareable salads that are more than lettuce and tomatoes and include grains, beans, and fruit and that also serve as a first layer on which to place skewers of meat or seafood, fritters, or grain cakes. Everyday carrots might not seem like a candidate for an interesting small plate until you roast them with shallots and drape them with garlicky chermoula. You can elevate them even further by serving them on a bed of farro.

So, how to start? The book is organized into flexible food categories such as dips and spreads; cheese and eggs; vegetables; proteins; and dumplings and savory breads. The recipes are ordered from smallest to small, light to hearty, and simpler to more complex in preparation and presentation. Chapters also include spreads of bonus recipes that easily add interest and help to complete a meal: quick pickles, slow-cooker dips, grilled vegetables, cold shrimp dishes, even one-bite fruit desserts.

You'll discover that small plates deliver big results. This kind of cooking is achievable and lower stress, especially if you follow the game plan with each recipe. It lightens your prep load because you can totally experiment with dishes as you make smaller amounts, make some things ahead, add some store-bought items, and create complexly flavored and interesting meal mash-ups.

So check out the 300 recipes in the book and start turning small plates into rich and rewarding meals your way. You can't go wrong.

The Game Plan

Most of the recipes in this book are accompanied by one or more tips meant to help you plan your menu and present your dishes with panache. These suggestions fall into three areas:

Head Start: Instructions for making all or part of a dish at least a few hours—but often a day or more—in advance.

Finish Line: Ways to level up your presentation game, such as by adding a garnish or choosing an interesting way to serve the dish.

Perfect Pair: Other recipes we think are particularly good complements to the dish.

sorting out small plates

Making a satisfying array of small plates is all about putting the right pieces together. But how do you know what those pieces should be, or how many of them you need? Instead of thinking in terms of mains and sides, we find it helpful to think about what each plate is contributing to the whole—perhaps a hit of intense flavor, a different texture, staying power, or even color—and combine them to create a varied and pleasing spread.

Flavor, texture, and color are relatively easy to judge, but it can be harder to interpret small plates portion sizes and determine which dishes will fill you up and which will leave you wanting more. To help, we classified every recipe in the book into one of these three categories:

Nibbles: These are the smallest bites, such as toasted nuts, roasted chickpeas, olives, pickles, and cheese. Little more than a mouthful, they're a great way to add flavor and textural interest and round out a meal, but they don't stand very well on their own—unless you're enjoying them as a snack or as part of a light, nibbles-only menu featuring many different kinds (see page 7 for more information).

Little Bites: More substantial than a bite-size nibble, these versatile dishes are still relatively light (think vegetables drizzled with a sauce, salads, shrimp, or meatballs). Adding a few to a menu is a great way to surround an anchor dish as well as incorporate complementary flavors.

Heartier Bites: The largest of our small plates, these generally feature more substantial food, such as chicken wings, vegetarian proteins, or whole grains. They may also be more complex dishes like those typically found on restaurant menus, such as chicken or beef lettuce cups, scallop skewers with asparagus citrus salad, and crispy lentils and herbs. These heartier bites are generally the most filling and can often serve as the anchor dish around which the rest of a meal comes together.

creating a small plates menu

As you start to think about how you want to mix and match the different shareable recipes in the book, consider these three questions:

What's the Occasion?

Whether you are looking to prepare a party, weeknight dinner, or sit-down brunch, the hundreds of recipes in the book offer endless combinations of dishes for different occasions. You might offer a spread of only nibbles and little bites for a night of board games or add several heartier bites for a grazing cocktail party. To help you envision how to combine multiple small plates into a cohesive whole, consult our cooking strategies (pages 6–7) and menus (pages 10–13).

How Much Food to Serve?

A lot of what makes a small plate a small plate—and a nibble a nibble, and so on—comes down to portion size. While our classes of recipes are meant to serve as a helpful guide for menu planning, they're not set in stone. You might find as you experiment with these recipes, that what we consider a little bite works as a heartier bite if you're serving larger portions to fewer people, or even as a nibble if cut into smaller pieces or served on toothpicks. Play with portion sizes to find what works best for your occasion.

For a group of four, one heartier bite and a couple of little bites or nibbles may be plenty. For a larger gathering of eight, you'll want to serve more than one hearty bite to ensure everyone feels satisfied. See our sample menus (pages 10–13) to get a sense of how to combine dishes with different yields.

And remember, not every plate needs to be homemade. Keep some meal-friendly store-bought items in your pantry or refrigerator to provide reinforcements if you find you need more food pronto (see page 8).

How Much Time Do You Have?

The possibilities of how to combine dishes are limitless, but the bottom line is you're still going to have to prepare all of the food you want to serve, so you want to be realistic about how much to take on. To help you figure that out, every recipe lists both the hands-on active time and total time involved in making it. You can also consult the Head Start feature included with the recipes to find information on how to make part or all of the recipe in advance. And lastly, consult the Appendix (pages 395–397) for a handy reference listing of all of the recipes in the book that can be made ahead.

five cooking strategies

There's no single way to prepare a small plates meal or spread. The number of people and the style of your gathering will impact what dishes—and how many of them—you'll want to serve (see page 5 for more information). When it comes to choosing what small plates to make, there are several different strategies you can use. We've included our top five favorites, with scenarios that illustrate how each of them might look in practice.

Strategy: Make Everything Ahead

The easiest way to enjoy a stress-free small-plates experience is to give yourself nothing to do in the kitchen at the time you plan to eat them. Rely on prepared foods (such as store-bought dips, crackers, and cheeses) and recipes that can be made at least a day ahead of time (see pages 395–397).

You'll be cool as a cucumber if you plan to serve only room-temperature or chilled dishes. That could mean a dip with crudités, store-bought crackers, a fresh salad, a cold protein such as shrimp (see pages 260–267) or poke (page 269), a refreshing make-ahead cocktail, and nibbles like olives or cheese. Since everything either comes from the refrigerator or pantry or is store-bought, the kitchen work will naturally happen ahead of time.

Strategy: Cook a Centerpiece Dish

One step more involved than making absolutely everything ahead is to plan to cook just one killer recipe the day you want to serve it. This keeps the last-minute cooking to a minimum while allowing you to enjoy a fresh-cooked dish. Pick one recipe that needs to be prepared right before it's served and served hot (perhaps a meaty anchor plate), then surround it with dishes that can be served at room temperature. As always, you can round out your small plates with make-ahead and store-bought additions. Try out this strategy with a traditional brunch. Pick a day-of dish to make—think egg-based dishes like Breakfast Buttercups (page 147) or Egg Roulade with Spinach and Gruyére (page 144) to act as the centerpiece. Then add Quick Giardiniera (page 76), bruschetta (pages 330–331), and/or assorted cheeses to your offerings.

Strategy: Make It Meze

A meze-inspired spread is a deconstructed meal that offers a selection of small plates. It is a relatively easy way to pull diverse dishes together, as there is no right or wrong way to do it. Instead of a succession of plates, everything is set out at once to be enjoyed communally. It frees you from worrying "Do these dishes go together?" It's a no-plan plan.

A meze spread could focus on Mediterranean ingredients such as olives, fresh fruits and vegetables, hummus, pita, eggs, and cheese. Or it might take a more eclectic approach to flavors. Just make sure the menu reflects varied ingredients. For example, if you have one chickpea dish, such as roasted chickpeas, don't plan to serve hummus too. Go with another dip such as Muhammara (page 103) instead.

Strategy: Stick to Nibbles

While serving a heartier anchor dish and some lighter-but-still-substantial bites makes sense for many occasions, there are many times when it's just fine to make a meal entirely out of nibbles.

Whether you're in the mood to make a casual solo dinner of snacks or organize a cocktail party, it's an opportunity to keep things simple by serving tiny bites. Have an assortment of finger foods, such as nuts, cheese, roasted chickpeas, skewers, chilled shrimp, and a dip or two at the ready to keep yourself and/or guests grazing happily all night long.

Strategy: Cook Outdoors

If you fire up the grill, you can use it to cook two or three components for multiple small plates. A protein and a simple vegetable (see pages 230–231) can be grilled side by side. Or stagger the cooking and load up the grill with smoky polenta (page 52) after your Gambas a la Plancha are done (page 260). You can serve a cold beverage (pages 382–392) to help everyone stay cool while you cook. To fill out your menu, plan to make some salads and a chilled dessert or two indoors ahead of time.

getting a head start

No matter the scope of your small plates cooking, here are some test kitchen tips to help you get a leg up. Preparing some recipes in advance and getting your pantry and fridge organized makes serving multiple small plates easier. Here are ideas for what you can prepare in the month, week, days, or hours before go time. For a complete list of recipes that you can make ahead and/or freeze, see pages 395–397.

Stock Your Freezer and Pantry (up to 1 month ahead)

Making a small plate such as Gougères (page 324) and stashing it in your freezer means you are ready for anything. Stocking your freezer with indispensable frozen components such as puff pastry, shrimp, and biscuits means you can cook something wonderful with no notice. Having some well-chosen ingredients in your pantry or fridge means you can freestyle on the fly. Superhero ingredients include nuts, olives, pickles, salsa, roasted red peppers, preserves, and tinned fish. Chocolate and dried fruit make an instant dessert plate.

Make or Buy Things That Keep (up to 1 week ahead)

Cook and refrigerate grains for use in salads or other dishes. Make and refrigerate dips and spreads such as hummus or tapenade or make a special sauce. Shop for perishable foods such as fresh produce.

Prep Ahead (1 or 2 days ahead)

Organize and prep ingredients ahead. Many fruits and vegetables can be chopped and refrigerated in an airtight container for at least a day or two without loss of quality. Prepare salad greens: After washing and drying greens, loosely roll the leaves inside paper towels and store in a zipper-lock bag, leaving the bag slightly open. See page 395 for dishes that can be made a few days ahead and refrigerated until needed.

Gather Serving Items (hours ahead)

Shop your house to put together an interesting collection of cute bowls, Mason jars, and other serving pieces. We find that thinking about and labeling serving dishes in advance is time well spent. Assemble more delicate dishes, such as salads with leafy greens or fresh fruit. Take out cheeses at least an hour ahead for maximum flavor.

At the Last Minute

Cook any dishes, such as meat or fried foods, that cannot be prepared ahead. Reheat frozen or refrigerated premade dishes and dress preassembled salads. Check out the Finish Line feature for presentation and garnish ideas.

serving small plates

Change It Up

Using a different garnish—oil, spices, lemon wedges—or dipping sauce can alter the look and flavor of a dish, so you can use a recipe you like on different occasions for various menus and keep it fresh.

Dress Up a Dip

Top hummus or other dips with dukkah or another topping to match a theme or maybe suit vegetarian/vegan guests. Make a large batch of hummus and top separate bowls of it with Baharat Beef Topping, Baharat-Spiced Plant-Based Topping, and/or Crispy Mushroom and Sumac Topping (pages 100–101) to appeal to meat eaters and vegetarians alike. You can also dress up the table by using ingredients from the recipes—carrots, apples, or berries—as decoration. If you intend to serve fruit, wash, drain, and arrange it in a pretty bowl as an edible centerpiece.

Put It to Bed

Use a simple salad (see pages 154–155) as a bed for hearty proteins. Not only do you combine two flavorful dishes but you add vibrant color to the table. Think of a dish such as Pan-Seared Scallops with Asparagus-Citrus Salad (page 294). It combines the sweetness of scallops with their beautiful brown sear, and the color and crunch of asparagus accentuates the tart-sweet juiciness of citrus.

Piece Out

Dishes such as socca (page 50), Spanish Tortilla (page 148), or Baguette with Radishes, Butter, and Herbs (page 327) are often cut into big wedges or thick slices to make a full-size individual portion. For a small bite, cut them into bite-size slices, squares, or wedges so they can serve more people.

Encourage Grazing

While you may have most of your spread set out on one table, place olives, nuts, and other nibbles in bowls or ramekins around the room so guests can easily find something to munch on.

menu ideas

We created these sample menus to help start you thinking about various ways to put small plates together. They take into consideration occasion, serving size, number of dishes, and cooking time. Make-ahead recipes are marked with a *.

◀ **The Easiest Get-Together**

A casual gathering for 6

Caprese Skewers (page 34)
Marinated Manchego * (page 127)
Baguette with Radishes, Butter, and Herbs (page 327)
Prosciutto-Wrapped Figs with Gorgonzola (page 42)
Tomato Salad (page 154)
Dark chocolate and fresh or dried fruit

Weeknight Dinner

A sit-down meal for 4

Pork and Ricotta Meatballs * (page 278)
Skillet-Roasted Brussels Sprouts with Chorizo and Manchego (page 245)
Naan with Artichokes, Pesto, and Goat Cheese (page 334)
Raspberry Mini Cheesecakes * (page 374)

Make It for More:

Add these recipes and invite the neighbors for a sit-down meal for 8

Beet Muhammara * (page 103) with crackers
Feta cheese with pita chips
Sangria for a Crowd (page 392)

Weekend Brunch ▶

A sit-down meal for 6

Breakfast Buttercups (page 147)

Bruschetta with Whipped Feta and Roasted Red
  Pepper Topping (page 331)

Cantaloupe Salad with Olives and Red Onion
  (page 172)

Nut Financiers * (page 360)

Make It for More:

Add these recipes to create a buffet for 10

Smoked Salmon Deviled Eggs (page 129)

Strawberries with Balsamic Vinegar (page 371)

Berbere-Spiced Bloody Marys * (page 388) x 2

Meatless Monday

A sit-down meal for 4

Chilled Marinated Tofu * (page 41)

Butternut Squash Steaks with Honey-Nut
  Topping (page 246)

Espinacas con Garbanzos * (page 256)

Individual Summer Berry Puddings * (page 377)

Tinned Fish Party

An improvised light dinner for 6

Cans of tuna, sardines, mussels, mackerel, and smoked salmon (1 can per person)

Sourdough, dark bread, and/or crackers

Lemon wedges, salted butter, raw shallots and/or radishes, mustard, and capers or cornichons

Stuffed Pickled Cherry Peppers * (page 83)

Herb Salad (page 155)

Vegetable Meze

A grazing meal for 6

Frico Friabile * (page 124)

Marinated Eggplant with Capers and Mint * (page 209)

Red Lentil Kibbeh (page 287)

Butternut Squash and Apple Fattoush * (page 185)

Kamut with Carrots and Pomegranate * (page 195)

Turkish Stuffed Apricots (page 370)

California Dreamin' in the Backyard

Stand-up light food and drinks for 6

Orange-Fennel Almonds (page 33)

Whipped Feta Dip * (page 88) with crudités

Fresh Fig Salad (page 174)

Chickpea Cakes * (page 284) on Bibb lettuce with Romesco Sauce (page 15)

Sweet Glazed Peaches (page 373)

Wine, beer, and canned cocktail

Grilled Surf and Turf

An outdoor gathering for 8 to 10

Chunky Guacamole * (page 92) and tortilla chips

Grilled Polenta with Charred Scallion and Gorgonzola Topping * (page 52)

Arrosticini (page 317)

Gambas a la Plancha (page 260)

Grilled plum tomatoes (see page 231)

Fingerling Potato Salad with Sun-Dried Tomato Dressing * (page 186)

Chocolate Cream Pies in a Jar * (page 381)

Sangria for a Crowd (page 392)

Everything Fried

Dinner in the kitchen for 6

Fried Pickles (page 38)

Fritto Misto di Mare (page 275)

Carciofi alla Guidia * (page 233)

Patatas Bravas (page 210)

Apple-Fennel Rémoulade * (page 162)

Homemade Labneh * (page 91) and berries

Indian Tea Party

A sit-down nosh for 6

Orange-Cardamom Spiced Nuts (page 33)

Pakoras (page 49) with Cilantro-Mint Chutney (page 18)

Naan with Ricotta, Sun-Dried Tomatoes, and Olive Tapenade (page 334)

Gajarachi Koshimbir (page 160)

Pine Nut Macaroons * (page 363)

Masala Chai * (page 387)

Open House ▶

Finger food and drinks for 16

Easy Cheese Straws * (page 321)

Firecracker Party Mix * (page 32)

Pimento Cheese Spread * (page 87) and saltines

Spinach and Artichoke Dip (page 110) and toasted
  baguette slices

Green Olive Tapenade (page 84)

Gougères * (page 324)

Spanish Tortilla * (page 148) and Aioli (page 16)

Sausage-and-Cheddar Stuffed Mushrooms * (page 216)

Easy Chocolate Truffles (page 366)

Financiers * (page 360)

Champagne Cocktails (page 391)

Wine

Dinner on the Couch

Nibbles for 2

Warm Spiced Almonds (page 33)

Buttered Popcorn (page 30)

Lemon-Pepper Chicken Wings (page 72)

Buckeye Candies * (page 369)

dressing up a small plate

In many cases, the difference between an everyday side dish and something more special—a small plate—is the addition of a finishing touch. A drizzle of sauce, a topping of relish or crisp pickles, or a sprinkling of a fragrant, crunchy spice blend is a great way to introduce a new flavor and add visual and textural interest. We use the following recipes to elevate dishes throughout this book, but you don't have to stick to our suggestions; try pairing any of them with a plain vegetable or protein to create your own improvised small plate.

Sauces and Relishes

pineapple salsa

Makes about 2 cups
Active Time 15 minutes
Total Time 15 minutes

Do not use canned pineapple in this recipe. For a spicier salsa, reserve and add the jalapeño seeds.

- 2 cups (12 ounces) 1-inch pineapple pieces
- 3 jalapeño chiles, stemmed, seeded, and cut into ½-inch pieces
- 1 cup fresh cilantro leaves
- ¼ cup coarsely chopped red onion
- 2 garlic cloves, smashed and peeled
- 1 tablespoon fresh lime juice
- 1 tablespoon extra-virgin olive oil
- ½ teaspoon table salt
- ½ teaspoon pepper

Pulse pineapple, jalapeños, cilantro, onion, and garlic in food processor until coarsely chopped, about 6 pulses, scraping down sides of bowl as needed. Transfer to serving bowl. Stir in lime juice, oil, salt, and pepper. Serve.

Variations

Pineapple-Cucumber Salsa

Decrease pineapple to 1½ cups. Substitute ½ cup fresh mint leaves for cilantro. Add 1 cup (6 ounces) ¼-inch English cucumber pieces to bowl with lime juice.

Pineapple-Mango Salsa

Decrease pineapple to 1½ cups. Substitute ¼ cup chopped fresh chives for cilantro. Add 1½ cups (9 ounces) 1-inch mango pieces to processor with pineapple.

Pineapple–Roasted Red Pepper Salsa

Add ¼ cup rinsed and patted dry jarred roasted red peppers to processor with pineapple.

Pineapple-Watermelon Salsa

Decrease pineapple to 1½ cups. Substitute ½ habanero chile for jalapeños and ½ cup fresh basil leaves for cilantro. Add 1 cup (8 ounces) ¼-inch watermelon pieces to salsa with lime juice.

spicy peanut dipping sauce

Makes about 1 cup
Active Time 15 minutes
Total Time 15 minutes

½ cup creamy or chunky peanut butter

¼ cup hot water

3 tablespoons lime juice (2 limes)

2 scallions, sliced thin

2 tablespoons ketchup

1 tablespoon soy sauce

1 tablespoon packed dark brown sugar

1 tablespoon minced fresh cilantro

1½ teaspoons hot sauce

1 garlic clove, minced

Whisk peanut butter and hot water together in medium bowl. Stir in lime juice, scallions, ketchup, soy sauce, sugar, cilantro, hot sauce, and garlic. Serve.

romesco sauce

Makes about ¾ cup
Active Time 10 minutes
Total Time 10 minutes

⅔ cup jarred roasted red peppers, patted dry

¼ cup slivered almonds, toasted

¼ cup fresh parsley leaves

3 tablespoons extra-virgin olive oil

1 tablespoon sherry vinegar

1 garlic clove, minced

¼ teaspoon table salt

Process all ingredients in food processor until smooth, about 1 minute, scraping down sides of bowl as needed. Season with salt and pepper to taste. (Sauce can be refrigerated for up to 2 days.)

red wine–miso sauce

Makes about ⅓ cup
Active Time 35 minutes
Total Time 35 minutes

1 cup dry red wine

1 cup vegetable broth

2 teaspoons sugar

½ teaspoon soy sauce

1 tablespoon unsalted butter

5 teaspoons miso

Bring wine, broth, sugar, and soy sauce to simmer in 10-inch skillet over medium heat and cook until reduced to ⅓ cup, 20 to 25 minutes. Off heat, whisk in butter and miso until smooth.

aioli

Makes about ¾ cup
Active Time 15 minutes
Total Time 15 minutes

The egg yolks in this recipe are not cooked. If you prefer, ¼ cup Egg Beaters may be substituted.

2 large egg yolks

2 garlic cloves, peeled and smashed

4 teaspoons lemon juice

1 tablespoon water, plus extra as needed

¼ teaspoon Dijon mustard

¼ teaspoon table salt

⅛ teaspoon sugar

¾ cup vegetable oil

Process egg yolks, garlic, lemon juice, water, mustard, salt, and sugar in blender until combined, about 10 seconds, scraping down sides of blender jar as needed. With blender running, slowly add oil and process until emulsified, about 2 minutes. Adjust consistency with extra water as needed. Season with salt and pepper to taste. (Aioli can be refrigerated for up to 3 days.)

Variations

Smoky Aioli

Add 1½ teaspoons smoked paprika to blender with egg yolks.

Herbed Aioli

Add 2 tablespoons chopped fresh basil, 1 tablespoon chopped fresh parsley, and 1 tablespoon minced fresh chives to aioli and pulse until combined but not smooth, about 10 pulses.

browned butter–lemon vinaigrette

Makes about 6 tablespoons
Active Time 10 minutes
Total Time 10 minutes

4 tablespoons unsalted butter

2 tablespoons lemon juice

1 teaspoon Dijon mustard

1 teaspoon maple syrup

¼ teaspoon table salt

⅛ teaspoon pepper

Melt butter in 10-inch skillet over medium heat. Cook, swirling constantly, until butter is dark golden brown and has nutty aroma, 3 to 5 minutes. Off heat, whisk in lemon juice, mustard, maple syrup, salt, and pepper.

maple-chipotle mayonnaise

Makes about ⅔ cup
Active Time 5 minutes
Total Time 5 minutes

For the fullest maple flavor, use maple syrup labeled "Grade A, Dark Amber."

- ½ cup mayonnaise
- 1 tablespoon maple syrup
- 1 tablespoon minced canned chipotle chile in adobo sauce
- ½ teaspoon Dijon mustard

Combine all ingredients in small bowl.

Variations

Basil Mayonnaise

Omit maple syrup, chipotle, and mustard. Add mayonnaise, ½ cup fresh basil leaves, 1 tablespoon water, and 1 teaspoon lemon juice to blender and process until smooth, about 10 seconds, scraping down sides of blender jar as needed. Transfer to bowl and season with salt and pepper to taste.

Red Pepper Mayonnaise

Omit maple syrup, chipotle, and mustard. Combine 1½ teaspoons lemon juice and 1 minced garlic clove in small bowl and let stand for 15 minutes. Add mayonnaise, ¾ cup rinsed jarred roasted red peppers, 2 teaspoons tomato paste, and lemon juice mixture to food processor and process until smooth, about 15 seconds, scraping down sides of bowl as needed. Season with salt to taste. Refrigerate until thickened, about 2 hours.

creamy blue cheese dip

Makes about 2½ cups
Active Time 10 minutes
Total Time 10 minutes, plus 30 minutes chilling

- 6 ounces blue cheese, crumbled (1½ cups)
- ½ cup buttermilk, plus extra as needed
- 1 garlic clove, minced
- ⅓ cup sour cream
- 6 tablespoons mayonnaise
- 2 tablespoons white wine vinegar
- ½ teaspoon sugar
- ½ teaspoon table salt
- ½ teaspoon pepper

Using fork, mash blue cheese, buttermilk, and garlic together in serving bowl until mixture resembles cottage cheese. Stir in sour cream, mayonnaise, vinegar, sugar, salt, and pepper. Add extra buttermilk as needed to adjust dip consistency. Cover and refrigerate until flavors meld, at least 30 minutes or up to 1 day. Season with salt and pepper to taste before serving.

yogurt-tahini sauce

Makes about 1¼ cups
Active Time 10 minutes
Total Time 10 minutes

- 1 cup plain yogurt
- 2 tablespoons lemon juice
- 2 tablespoons tahini
- 1 garlic clove, minced
- ¼ teaspoon table salt

Whisk all ingredients together in bowl. (Sauce can be refrigerated for up to 2 days.)

cilantro-mint chutney

Makes about 1 cup
Active Time 10 minutes
Total Time 10 minutes

  2 cups fresh cilantro leaves
  1 cup fresh mint leaves
⅓ cup plain yogurt
¼ cup finely chopped onion
  1 tablespoon lime juice
1½ teaspoons sugar
½ teaspoon ground cumin
¼ teaspoon table salt

Process all ingredients in food processor until smooth, about 20 seconds, scraping down sides of bowl as needed. (Chutney can be refrigerated for up to 2 days.)

scallion dipping sauce

Makes about ¾ cup
Active Time 10 minutes
Total Time 10 minutes

For a milder dipping sauce, omit the chili oil.

¼ cup soy sauce
  2 tablespoons rice vinegar
  2 tablespoons mirin
  2 tablespoons water
  1 teaspoon chili oil (optional)
½ teaspoon toasted sesame oil
  1 scallion, minced

Combine all ingredients in bowl. (Sauce can be refrigerated for up to 1 day; let come to room temperature before serving.)

soy-vinegar dipping sauce

Makes about ¼ cup
Active Time 5 minutes
Total Time 5 minutes

  2 tablespoons soy sauce
  1 tablespoon water
  2 teaspoons distilled white vinegar
  1 teaspoon sugar

Whisk all ingredients in bowl until sugar is dissolved.

sichuan chili oil

Makes about 1½ cups
Active Time 40 minutes
Total Time 40 minutes, plus 12½ hours cooling and sitting

We prefer a Sichuan chili powder here, but Korean red pepper flakes (gochugaru) are a good alternative.

½ cup Asian chili powder

2 tablespoons sesame seeds

2 tablespoons Sichuan peppercorns, coarsely ground, divided

½ teaspoon table salt

1 cup vegetable oil

1 (1-inch) piece ginger, unpeeled, sliced into ¼-inch rounds and smashed

3 star anise pods

5 cardamom pods, crushed

2 bay leaves

1 Combine chili powder, sesame seeds, half of ground peppercorns, and salt in bowl. Combine oil, ginger, star anise, cardamom, bay leaves, and remaining peppercorns in small saucepan and cook over low heat, stirring occasionally, until spices have darkened and mixture is very fragrant, 25 to 30 minutes.

2 Strain mixture through fine-mesh strainer into bowl with chili powder mixture (mixture may bubble slightly); discard solids in strainer. Stir well to combine. Let sit at room temperature until flavors meld, about 12 hours. (Chili oil can be stored at room temperature for up to 1 week or refrigerated for up to 3 months.)

Pickled Vegetables

quick pickled red onion

Makes about 1 cup
Active Time 10 minutes
Total Time 10 minutes, plus 1 hour cooling

Look for a firm, dry onion with thin, shiny skin and a deep purple color.

1 cup red wine vinegar

⅓ cup sugar

¼ teaspoon table salt

1 red onion, halved through root end and sliced thin

Bring vinegar, sugar, and salt to simmer in small saucepan over medium-high heat, stirring occasionally, until sugar has dissolved. Off heat, stir in onion, cover, and let cool to room temperature, about 1 hour. (Pickled onion can be refrigerated in airtight container for up to 1 week.)

Variation

Quick Pickled Red Onion and Jalapeños

Add 2 jalapeño chiles, sliced crosswise into ¼-inch-thick rings, to saucepan with vinegar.

quick pickled cucumber and bean sprouts

Makes about 2 cups
Active Time 10 minutes
Total Time 10 minutes, plus 1 hour sitting

Be sure to drain the vegetables after 1 hour or their texture will begin to soften rapidly.

- 1 cup unseasoned rice vinegar
- 2 tablespoons sugar
- 1½ teaspoons table salt
- 4 ounces (2 cups) bean sprouts
- 1 cucumber, peeled, quartered lengthwise, seeded, and sliced thin on bias

Whisk vinegar, sugar, and salt in medium bowl until sugar and salt have dissolved. Add bean sprouts and cucumber and toss to combine. Gently press on vegetables to submerge. Cover and let sit at room temperature for 1 hour; drain. Serve. (Pickles can be refrigerated for up to 1 day.)

Variation

Quick Pickled Daikon Radish and Carrot

Substitute ¼ cup lime juice for rice vinegar; 8 ounces daikon radish, peeled and cut into 2-inch matchsticks for bean sprouts; and 1 carrot, peeled and cut into 2-inch matchsticks, for cucumber. Reduce sugar to 1½ teaspoons and salt to ¼ teaspoon. Add ½ teaspoon grated lime zest and 1½ teaspoons fish sauce to lime juice mixture with other ingredients.

Finishing Spice Blends

pistachio dukkah

Makes about ⅓ cup
Active Time 15 minutes
Total Time 15 minutes

- 1½ tablespoons sesame seeds, toasted
- 1½ teaspoons coriander seeds, toasted
- ¾ teaspoon cumin seeds, toasted
- ½ teaspoon fennel seeds, toasted
- 2 tablespoons shelled pistachios, toasted and chopped fine
- ½ teaspoon table salt
- ½ teaspoon pepper

Process sesame seeds in spice grinder or mortar and pestle until coarsely ground; transfer to bowl. Process coriander seeds, cumin seeds, and fennel seeds in now-empty grinder until finely ground. Transfer to bowl with sesame seeds. Stir pistachios, salt, and pepper into sesame mixture until combined. (Dukkah can be refrigerated for up to 1 month.)

Variation

Hazelnut-Nigella Dukkah

Omit pistachios, cumin, and pepper. Reduce sesame seeds to 1 tablespoon and coriander seeds to 1 teaspoon. Increase fennel seeds to 1 teaspoon. Add 1½ tablespoons toasted sunflower seeds and 1½ teaspoons nigella seeds to spice grinder with sesame seeds. Transfer to small bowl and stir in 3 tablespoons toasted finely chopped hazelnuts and 1½ teaspoon paprika.

everything bagel seasoning

Makes 5 teaspoons
Active Time 5 minutes
Total Time 5 minutes

1 teaspoon sesame seeds

1 teaspoon poppy seeds

1 teaspoon dried minced garlic

1 teaspoon dried onion flakes

1 teaspoon kosher salt

Combine all ingredients in bowl. (Seasoning can be stored in airtight container for up to 3 months.)

za'atar

Makes about ⅓ cup
Active Time 10 minutes
Total Time 10 minutes

2 tablespoons dried thyme

1 tablespoon dried oregano

1½ tablespoons ground sumac

1 tablespoon sesame seeds, toasted

¼ teaspoon table salt

Grind thyme and oregano using spice grinder or mortar and pestle until finely ground and powdery. Transfer to bowl and stir in sumac, sesame seeds, and salt. (Za'atar can be stored in airtight container at room temperature for up to 1 year.)

shichimi togarashi

Makes about ½ cup
Active Time 10 minutes
Total Time 10 minutes

1½ teaspoons grated orange zest

4 teaspoons sesame seeds, toasted

1 tablespoon paprika

2 teaspoons pepper

½ teaspoon garlic powder

½ teaspoon ground ginger

¼ teaspoon cayenne pepper

Microwave orange zest in small bowl, stirring occasionally, until dry and no longer clumping together, about 2 minutes. Stir in sesame seeds, paprika, pepper, garlic powder, ginger, and cayenne. (Shichimi togarashi can be stored in airtight container for up to 1 week.)

bar snacks and finger foods

blistered shishito peppers

2 tablespoons vegetable oil

8 ounces shishito peppers

Flake sea salt or kosher salt

WHY THIS RECIPE WORKS Fried blistered little chile peppers that you pick up by the stems and pop into your mouth whole are a bar snack that's super easy to make at home. Ready in just a few minutes, they require no advance prep. Bright-tasting, citrusy, and mild, these green chiles are also thin-skinned, crisp-textured, and crave-worthy. Restaurants often deep-fry them, but we found that cooking shishitos in a small amount of oil works equally well and is much less messy. The larger granules of flake sea salt or kosher salt sprinkled on top add a wonderful crunch, but you can use regular table salt instead, if you prefer. Only one shishito pepper out of 10 is spicy, so even guests who don't like a lot of heat can enjoy them.

Head Start

Blister shishitos after guests arrive so peppers can be served right away and eaten hot.

Finish Line

Serve peppers on a plate large enough so that they won't sit too close together and get oversteamed.

Perfect Pair

These peppers pair well with Japanese bar foods such as Karaage (page 59) or Chilled Marinated Tofu (page 41).

Heat oil in 12-inch skillet over medium-high heat until just smoking. Add peppers and cook, without stirring, until skins are blistered, 3 to 5 minutes. Using tongs, flip peppers; continue to cook until blistered on second side, 3 to 5 minutes longer. Transfer to serving plate, season with flake sea salt or kosher salt to taste, and serve immediately.

Variations

Shishito Peppers with Mint, Poppy Seeds, and Orange
Combine 1 teaspoon dried mint, 1 teaspoon poppy seeds, ½ teaspoon flake sea salt or kosher salt, and ¼ teaspoon grated orange zest in small bowl. Sprinkle over peppers on serving plate. Serve with orange wedges.

Smoky Shishito Peppers with Espelette and Lime
If you can't find Basque Espelette chile powder (also referred to as Piment d'Espelette), you can substitute 1 teaspoon Aleppo pepper or ¼ teaspoon paprika plus ¼ teaspoon red pepper flakes.

Combine 1 teaspoon ground Basque Espelette chile powder, 1 teaspoon smoked paprika, ½ teaspoon flake sea salt or kosher salt, and ¼ teaspoon grated lime zest in small bowl. Sprinkle over peppers on serving plate. Serve with lime wedges.

marinated green and black olives

1 cup brine-cured green olives with pits

1 cup brine-cured black olives with pits

¾ cup extra-virgin olive oil

1 shallot, minced

2 teaspoons grated lemon zest

2 teaspoons minced fresh thyme

2 teaspoons minced fresh oregano

1 garlic clove, minced

½ teaspoon red pepper flakes

½ teaspoon table salt

WHY THIS RECIPE WORKS Why make your own marinated olives when you can buy a wide variety of prepared olive products at the supermarket? Because with just a little effort, you can put together a snack with way more flavor and freshness than anything store-bought. The most important step is to start with good olives and good olive oil. We use olives with pits (pitted olives tend to have less flavor), packed in brine, not oil. To give the dish more variety, we like a combination of green and black olives. Along with the usual aromatics—garlic, thyme, and red pepper flakes—we use shallot, fresh oregano, and grated lemon zest for a bright citrus note.

Pat olives dry with paper towels. Toss with oil, shallot, lemon zest, thyme, oregano, garlic, pepper flakes, and salt in bowl. Cover and refrigerate for at least 4 hours before serving.

Variations

Marinated Olives with Baby Mozzarella
Reduce amount of black and green olives to ½ cup each. Substitute 1 tablespoon shredded fresh basil for oregano. Add 8 ounces fresh baby mozzarella balls (bocconcini), cut into ½-inch pieces (2 cups), to olive mixture.

Marinated Green Olives with Feta
Omit black olives and fresh thyme. Substitute orange zest for lemon zest. Add 8 ounces feta cheese, cut into ½-inch cubes (2 cups), to olive mixture.

Head Start

Refrigerate marinated olives for up to 4 days. Let olives sit at room temperature for at least 30 minutes before serving or oil will look cloudy and congealed.

Finish Line

Next to olives, place toothpicks for guests to pick up olives with and a small empty bowl to discard pits.

Perfect Pair

Serve these olives on a cheese or charcuterie board or pair with Turkish Stuffed Apricots with Rose Water and Pistachios (page 370) or Moroccan-Style Carrot Salad (page 159).

Serves 12 to 16 (makes about 48 cheese straws) | **Active Time** 30 minutes
Total Time 1 hour

southern cheese straws

8 ounces extra-sharp cheddar cheese, shredded (2 cups)

1½ cups (7½ ounces) all-purpose flour

8 tablespoons unsalted butter, cut into 8 pieces and chilled

¾ teaspoon table salt

¾ teaspoon paprika

½ teaspoon baking powder

¼ teaspoon cayenne pepper

3 tablespoons ice water

Head Start

Store in airtight container at room temperature for up to 1 week.

Finish Line

Stand cheese straws in several tall glasses so guests can reach for them when they want a nibble.

Perfect Pair

Serve with Lemonade (page 382), Marinated Green and Black Olives (page 26), Bloody Mary Pickled Asparagus Spears (page 79), or Pork and Ricotta Meatballs (page 278).

WHY THIS RECIPE WORKS These delicate, crumbly, cheesy, buttery crackers from the South are often made at Christmastime but are delicious any time of year. To make a version that mimics their signature straw shape without the aid of a specialized cookie press, we roll out the dough into a square and then cut it into strips before baking. Using a food processor to buzz the grated cheese, chilled butter, flour, and baking powder together results in crackers with a short, extra-tender texture. Cracker-crisp, savory, and lightly peppery, these cheese straws look dainty yet taste anything but. A generous helping of extra-sharp cheddar makes their bold flavor irresistible alongside a glass of sweet tea or a mint julep. Flour the counter and the top of the dough as needed to prevent sticking.

1 Adjust oven rack to middle position and heat oven to 350 degrees. Line rimmed baking sheet with parchment paper. Process cheddar, flour, butter, salt, paprika, baking powder, and cayenne in food processor until mixture resembles wet sand, about 20 seconds. Add ice water and process until dough ball starts to form, about 25 seconds.

2 Turn out dough onto lightly floured counter. Knead briefly until dough fully comes together, 2 to 3 turns. Using your hands, pat dough into rough 4-inch square. Roll dough into 10-inch square, about ¼ inch thick, flouring counter as needed to prevent sticking.

3 Position dough so an edge is parallel to edge of counter. Using rounded side of fork, drag tines across entire surface of dough to make decorative lines.

4 Using pizza cutter or chef's knife, trim away and discard outer ½ inch of dough to make a neat square. Cut dough into 3 equal pieces perpendicular to decorative lines. Working with 1 section of dough at a time, cut into ½-inch-wide strips in direction of lines.

5 Evenly space cheese straws on prepared sheet, about ½ inch apart. Bake until edges of straws are light golden brown, 30 to 35 minutes, rotating sheet halfway through baking. Let straws cool completely on sheet. Serve.

Variation

Parmesan–Black Pepper Cheese Straws
Reduce extra-sharp cheddar to 1½ cups. Add 1 cup grated Parmesan cheese to food processor with flour in step 1. Substitute 1 teaspoon black pepper for cayenne pepper.

crunchy bites

Party mixes, nuts, popcorn, and roasted chickpeas are lip-smacking snacks to offer with small plates and beer, wine, or cocktails. Easy to make, they pack lots of flavor and get a party started.

buttered popcorn

Makes 14 cups
Active Time 15 minutes
Total Time 15 minutes

Heat three test kernels in a saucepan until they pop (that's how you know the oil's hot enough). Adding the rest of the kernels off the burner and letting them sit for 30 seconds ensures all the kernels heat up evenly. That way, they all pop at the same rate.

3 tablespoons vegetable oil

½ cup popcorn kernels

2 tablespoons unsalted butter, melted

¼ teaspoon table salt

1 Heat oil and 3 popcorn kernels in large saucepan over medium-high heat until kernels pop. Remove pan from heat, add remaining kernels, cover, and let sit for 30 seconds.

2 Return saucepan to medium-high heat. Continue to cook with lid slightly ajar until popping slows to about 2 seconds between pops. Transfer popcorn to large bowl. Add melted butter and toss to coat popcorn. Add salt and toss to combine. Serve.

Variations

Parmesan-Pepper Popcorn
Add ½ teaspoon pepper to butter before melting. Add ½ cup grated Parmesan cheese to popcorn when tossing with butter.

Garlic and Herb Popcorn
Add 2 minced garlic cloves and 1 tablespoon minced fresh or 1 teaspoon dried rosemary, thyme, or dill to butter before melting.

Hot and Sweet Popcorn
Add 2 tablespoons sugar, 1 teaspoon ground cinnamon, and ½ teaspoon chili powder to butter before melting.

Cajun-Spiced Popcorn
Add 1 teaspoon red pepper flakes, 1 teaspoon minced fresh thyme, ¾ teaspoon hot sauce, ½ teaspoon garlic powder, ½ teaspoon paprika, and ¼ teaspoon onion powder to butter before melting.

coriander-turmeric roasted chickpeas

Serves 8 to 10 (makes about 1⅔ cups)
Active Time 20 minutes
Total Time 1¼ hours, plus 30 minutes cooling

Use chickpeas as a snack or salad garnish.

2 (15-ounce) cans chickpeas

3 tablespoons extra-virgin olive oil

2 teaspoons paprika

1 teaspoon ground coriander

½ teaspoon ground turmeric

½ teaspoon ground allspice

½ teaspoon ground cumin

½ teaspoon sugar

⅜ teaspoon kosher salt

⅛ teaspoon cayenne pepper

1 Adjust oven rack to middle position and heat oven to 350 degrees. Place chickpeas in colander and let drain for 10 minutes. Line large plate with double layer of paper towels. Spread chickpeas over plate in even layer. Microwave until exteriors of chickpeas are dry and many have split slightly at seams, 8 to 12 minutes.

2 Transfer chickpeas to 13 by 9-inch metal baking pan. Add oil and stir until evenly coated. Using spatula, spread chickpeas into single layer. Transfer to oven and roast for 30 minutes. While chickpeas are roasting, combine paprika, coriander, turmeric, allspice, cumin, sugar, salt, and cayenne in small bowl.

3 Stir chickpeas and crowd toward center of pan, avoiding edges of pan as much as possible. Continue to roast until chickpeas appear dry, slightly shriveled, and deep golden brown, 20 to 40 minutes longer. (To test for doneness, remove a few paler chickpeas and let cool briefly before tasting; if interiors are soft, return to oven for 5 minutes before testing again.)

4 Transfer chickpeas to large bowl. Toss with spice mixture to coat. Season with salt to taste. Let cool completely before serving, about 30 minutes.

Variations

Barbecue-Spiced Roasted Chickpeas
Omit allspice and cumin. Substitute 1 tablespoon smoked paprika for paprika, garlic powder for coriander, and onion powder for turmeric. Increase sugar to 1½ teaspoons.

Smoked Paprika–Spiced Roasted Chickpeas
Omit turmeric, allspice, and sugar. Substitute 1 tablespoon smoked paprika for paprika. Decrease coriander to ½ teaspoon and cumin to ¼ teaspoon.

firecracker party mix

Serves 10 to 12
Active Time 15 minutes
Total Time 1 hour, plus 30 minutes cooling

You can make this mix ahead and store at room temperature for up to a week.

5 cups Corn Chex cereal

2 cups sesame sticks

1 cup wasabi peas

1 cup chow mein noodles

1 cup honey-roasted peanuts

6 tablespoons unsalted butter, melted

2 tablespoons soy sauce

1 teaspoon ground ginger

¾ teaspoon garlic powder

¼ teaspoon cayenne pepper

1 Adjust oven rack to middle position and heat oven to 250 degrees. Combine cereal, sesame sticks, peas, chow mein noodles, and peanuts in large bowl. Whisk melted butter, soy sauce, ginger, garlic powder, and cayenne together in separate bowl, then drizzle over cereal mixture and toss until well combined.

2 Spread mixture on rimmed baking sheet and bake, stirring every 15 minutes, until golden and crisp, about 45 minutes. Let cool to room temperature about 30 minutes before serving.

cinnamon-ginger spiced nuts

Serves 8 to 10
Active Time 10 minutes
Total Time 1 hour, plus 30 minutes cooling

If you can't find superfine sugar, process granulated sugar in a food processor for 1 minute. You can use a mixture of nuts instead of a single type. Nuts can be refrigerated for up to 3 weeks.

⅔ cup superfine sugar

2 teaspoons ground cinnamon

1 teaspoon ground ginger

1 teaspoon ground coriander

1 large egg white

1 tablespoon water

1 teaspoon table salt

1 pound raw whole almonds, cashews, walnuts, and/or shelled pistachios

1 Adjust oven racks to upper-middle and lower-middle positions and heat oven to 275 degrees. Line two rimmed baking sheets with parchment paper. Mix sugar, cinnamon, ginger, and coriander in small bowl.

2 Whisk egg white, water, and salt together in large bowl. Add nuts and toss to coat. Sprinkle spices over nuts, toss to coat, then spread evenly over prepared sheets. Bake until nuts are dry and crisp, about 50 minutes, stirring occasionally. Let nuts cool completely on sheets, about 30 minutes. Break nuts apart and serve.

Variations

Chili-Lime Spiced Nuts
We enjoy a combination of cashews and peanuts here. Substitute 2½ teaspoons chili powder, 1 teaspoon ground cumin, and ½ teaspoon cayenne pepper for cinnamon, ginger, and coriander. Substitute 1 tablespoon lime juice for water and add 1 tablespoon grated lime zest to egg white mixture.

Orange-Cardamom Spiced Nuts
We enjoy a combination of almonds and pistachios here. Substitute 1 teaspoon ground cardamom and ½ teaspoon pepper for cinnamon, ginger, and coriander. Substitute 1 tablespoon orange juice for water and add 1 tablespoon grated orange zest and ¼ teaspoon vanilla extract to egg white mixture.

quick toasted almonds

Serves 6 to 8
Active Time 15 minutes
Total Time 15 minutes

Toasting raw almonds for just 8 minutes in hot oil gives them a round, complex toasted flavor, and they're fresher than store-bought ones. These almonds can be stored at room temperature for up to 5 days.

1 tablespoon extra-virgin olive oil

2 cups skin-on raw whole almonds

1 teaspoon table salt

¼ teaspoon pepper

Heat oil in 12-inch nonstick skillet over medium-high heat until just shimmering. Add almonds, salt, and pepper and reduce heat to medium-low. Cook, stirring often, until fragrant and color deepens slightly, about 8 minutes. Transfer almonds to paper towel–lined plate and let cool before serving.

Variations

Rosemary Almonds
Add ½ teaspoon dried rosemary to skillet with almonds.

Warm-Spiced Almonds
Substitute unsalted butter for olive oil. Add 2 tablespoons sugar, ½ teaspoon ground cinnamon, ⅛ teaspoon ground cloves, and ⅛ teaspoon ground allspice to skillet with almonds.

Smoked Paprika–Spiced Almonds
Add ¾ teaspoon smoked paprika to skillet with almonds.

Five-Spice Almonds
Add 1 teaspoon five-spice powder to skillet with almonds.

Orange-Fennel Almonds
Add 1 teaspoon grated orange zest and ½ teaspoon ground fennel seeds to skillet with almonds.

Perfect Pair
Any of these crunchy snacks can serve as a quick and convenient add-on to a small-plates spread. Use them to add textural contrast to a meal by serving them alongside soft or creamy foods such as cheese, dips, or vegetables, or even sprinkling them over a salad. Use them in conjunction with other supersimple ingredients such as our marinated olives (see page 26), fresh fruit, and crudités to make a meal entirely of Nibbles.

Of all these crunchy bites, only popcorn needs to be made just before serving. We offer different flavors that let you tweak the popcorn to suit the theme of your small plates collection.

caprese skewers

¼ cup extra-virgin olive oil

1 garlic clove, minced to paste

10 ounces grape tomatoes, halved

8 ounces fresh baby mozzarella cheese balls (bocconcini)

1 cup fresh basil leaves

WHY THIS RECIPE WORKS This festive, easy take on caprese salad has just five simple ingredients. We use toothpicks to stand bite-size pieces of fresh mozzarella and basil upright on halved grape tomato pedestals. A quickly prepared garlic-infused oil, made by mincing garlic into a paste and stirring it into fruity extra-virgin olive oil, boosts the flavor of the baby mozzarella balls and tomatoes. Basil leaves, skewered onto our toothpicks whole, complete the caprese flavor profile and add a fresh-from-the-garden touch. You can use larger fresh mozzarella balls here, but they should be cut into ¾- to 1-inch pieces before marinating. You will need 30 sturdy wooden toothpicks for this recipe; avoid using thin, flimsy toothpicks here.

Finish Line

Cover platter with plastic wrap until ready to serve.

Perfect Pair

Serve skewers alongside Quick Giardiniera (page 76), Albóndigas en Salsa de Almendras (page 276), or Fava Bean and Radish Salad (page 178).

1 Whisk oil and garlic together in small bowl. In separate bowl, toss tomatoes and mozzarella with 2 tablespoons garlic oil and season with salt and pepper.

2 Skewer tomatoes, mozzarella, and basil leaves in following order from top to bottom: tomato half, basil leaf (folded if large), mozzarella ball, and tomato half with flat side facing down. Stand skewers upright on serving platter, drizzle with remaining garlic oil, and season with salt and pepper. Serve.

olives all'ascolana

2 tablespoons plus 3 cups extra-virgin olive oil, divided

1 carrot, chopped

1 shallot, chopped

⅛ teaspoon table salt

⅛ teaspoon pepper

4 ounces ground pork

1 ounce prosciutto, chopped

⅛ teaspoon ground nutmeg

¼ cup dry white wine

¼ cup grated Parmesan cheese

1 large egg yolk, plus 2 large eggs, divided

¼ teaspoon grated lemon zest

45 large brine-cured green olives with pits

1½ cups panko bread crumbs

1 cup (5 ounces) all-purpose flour

WHY THIS RECIPE WORKS These crisp-coated, salty fried olives stuffed with a rich meat filling are a regional specialty of Le Marche in Italy. This culinary marvel of taste and texture makes a tantalizing small bite to accompany an Aperol spritz or glass of white wine. To remove the olive pits, we leave the olive flesh in one piece, slicing down one side of the olive and cutting around the pit with a paring knife as if peeling an apple. The process goes quickly once you practice pitting the first few. With these olives, the filling shares the spotlight. Ground pork, prosciutto, sautéed carrot, and shallot build beautiful layers of flavor. Nutmeg provides warm spice and aroma, while wine adds brightness. Egg yolk and Parmesan bring richness and a creamy texture to the filling. Use a Dutch oven that holds 6 quarts or more. We use large, mild-flavored Cerignola olives, but other large, brine-cured green olives will work, too.

1 Heat 2 tablespoons oil in 12-inch skillet over medium heat until shimmering. Add carrot, shallot, salt, and pepper and cook until softened and lightly browned, 3 to 5 minutes. Add pork and cook, breaking up meat with wooden spoon, until browned, about 4 minutes. Stir in prosciutto and nutmeg and cook until fragrant, about 30 seconds. Stir in wine and cook until nearly evaporated, about 1 minute. Process pork mixture in food processor until smooth, about 2 minutes, scraping down sides of bowl as needed. Add Parmesan, egg yolk, and lemon zest and pulse to combine, about 5 pulses. Transfer filling to bowl and let cool slightly.

2 Working with 1 olive at a time, use paring knife to cut lengthwise down one side of pit (do not cut through olive). Continue to cut around pit until released, rotating olive as needed and keeping as much of olive intact as possible. Spoon scant 1 teaspoon filling into each olive (olives should be full but not overflowing), then close sides around filling, gently squeezing to seal.

3   Line rimmed baking sheet with triple layer of paper towels. Process panko in clean food processor to fine crumbs, about 20 seconds; transfer to shallow dish. Spread flour in second shallow dish. Beat eggs in third shallow dish. Working with several olives at a time, dredge in flour, dip in egg, and coat with panko, pressing firmly to adhere. Transfer to large plate and let sit for 5 minutes.

4   Heat remaining 3 cups oil in Dutch oven over medium-high heat to 375 degrees. Add half of olives and cook, stirring occasionally to prevent sticking, until golden brown and crisp, about 2 minutes. Using wire skimmer or slotted spoon, transfer olives to prepared sheet and let drain. Return oil to 375 degrees and repeat with remaining olives. Serve warm.

Head Start

Pit olives 1 day before you need them. Recipe calls for extra olives so you can practice removing pit and keeping flesh intact. Refrigerate filling for up to 2 days.

Finish Line

Let olives cool slightly before serving so they are not too hot to bite into.

Perfect Pair

Serve olives with Lamb Rib Chops with Mint-Rosemary Relish (page 283) or Peach Caprese Salad (page 169).

fried pickles

½ cup cornmeal

4 whole kosher dill pickles, quartered lengthwise, patted dry with paper towels

1 cup (5 ounces) all-purpose flour

1 cup (4 ounces) cornstarch

2 teaspoons baking powder

1 teaspoon table salt

½ teaspoon cayenne pepper

1 (12-ounce) bottle cold beer

3 quarts vegetable oil for frying

Perfect Pair

Serve with Creamy Blue Cheese Dip (page 17). Add Shaved Zucchini Salad with Pepitas (page 155).

WHY THIS RECIPE WORKS A Southern treat that combines deep-fried richness with characteristic pickle tang, these spears are crunchy to bite into with a soft tartness inside, making them a great accompaniment to serve with drinks. Easy to make fresh and enjoy with an array of other small bites such as cheese, cold cuts, and salads, these pickles are perfect for both for kids and adults. Ketchup, barbecue sauce, and ranch dressing make easy, delicious dipping sauces. Use a Dutch oven that holds 6 quarts or more. Use whole kosher dill pickles that you cut into spears yourself, because they're firmer than precut pickles. With the exception of dark stouts and ales, any beer will work in this recipe—even nonalcoholic.

1 Place cornmeal in shallow dish. Dredge pickle spears in cornmeal and transfer to plate. Combine flour, cornstarch, baking powder, salt, and cayenne in large bowl. Slowly whisk in beer until smooth.

2 Heat oil in large Dutch oven over medium-high heat until 350 degrees. Rewhisk batter. Transfer half of pickles to batter. One at a time, remove pickles from batter (allowing excess to drip back into bowl) and fry in hot oil until golden brown, 2 to 3 minutes. Drain pickles on wire rack set in rimmed baking sheet. Bring oil back to 350 degrees and repeat with remaining pickles. Serve.

chilled marinated tofu

14 ounces firm tofu, halved lengthwise, then cut crosswise into ½-inch-thick squares

2 cups boiling water

¼ cup fish sauce

¼ cup mirin

4 teaspoons sugar

¼ ounce wakame

¼ ounce kombu

4 teaspoons rice vinegar

2 sheets (8 by 7½-inch) toasted nori, crumbled

2 scallions, sliced thin on bias

Toasted sesame oil

WHY THIS RECIPE WORKS Marinated raw tofu (hiyayakko or yakko-dofu) is a popular bar snack in Japan. In the best renditions, a flavorful marinade and some choice garnishes amplify the tofu's delicate sweetness. The marinade is typically a soy sauce–enhanced dashi, the Japanese broth prepared from kombu seaweed and bonito (skipjack tuna) flakes. We replace it with a combination of wakame seaweed, fish sauce, mirin, and sugar, which produces a sweet, salty, robust marinade. Garnishes such as crumbled nori, sliced scallions, and toasted sesame oil add crunch and richness. For an accurate measurement of boiling water, bring a kettle of water to a boil and then measure out the desired amount. For a vegetarian dish, you can swap in either Bragg-Liquid Aminos or a vegetarian fish sauce substitute for the fish sauce.

1 Spread tofu over paper towel–lined baking sheet, let drain for 20 minutes, then gently press dry with paper towels and season with salt and pepper.

2 Meanwhile, combine boiling water, fish sauce, mirin, sugar, wakame, and kombu in small bowl. Cover and let sit for 15 minutes. Strain liquid through fine-mesh strainer, discarding solids, then return broth to medium bowl.

3 Add tofu and vinegar; cover; and refrigerate until cool, at least 2 hours. To serve, use slotted spoon to transfer tofu to platter, top with nori and scallions, and drizzle with sesame oil to taste.

Head Start
Refrigerate marinated tofu for up to 2 days.

Finish Line
To add fragrant spice and crunch, sprinkle tofu with Shichimi Togarashi (page 21).

Perfect Pair
Serve tofu as a cool counterpoint to grilled meats such as Keftedes (page 280) or use it to complement the flavor of Pajeon (page 54).

prosciutto-wrapped figs with gorgonzola

2 ounces Gorgonzola cheese

16 fresh figs, stemmed and halved lengthwise

1 tablespoon honey

16 thin slices prosciutto (8 ounces), cut in half lengthwise

WHY THIS RECIPE WORKS We pair sweet, ripe figs with savory, salty prosciutto and bold, pungent blue cheese for a delectable bite. We halve the figs so they are easy to eat, then wrap them in thin slices of the ham. For more flavor and to play off the savory notes of the prosciutto, we add a bit of honey. Briefly microwaving the honey ensures it is easy to drizzle. Place small mounds of creamy, assertive Gorgonzola in the center of each fig before adding the honey. It offers a rich, bold counterpoint to the fig's tender flesh and sweet flavor. To guarantee the prosciutto stays put, stick a toothpick through the center of each bundle.

Mound 1 teaspoon Gorgonzola into center of each fig half. Microwave honey in bowl to loosen, about 10 seconds, then drizzle over cheese. Wrap prosciutto securely around figs, leaving fig ends uncovered. Secure prosciutto with toothpick and serve.

Head Start

Cover prepared figs with plastic wrap and refrigerate for up to 8 hours; let them come to room temperature before serving.

Perfect Pair

Serve figs with Pan-Seared Scallops with Mango-Cucumber Salad (page 294) or Smoked Salmon Deviled Eggs (page 129).

jalapeño poppers

8 ounces cream cheese, softened

2 ounces cheddar cheese, shredded (½ cup)

2 ounces deli ham, minced

2 scallions, minced

1 tablespoon lime juice

1 teaspoon chili powder

½ teaspoon table salt

12 jalapeño chiles, halved and seeded

WHY THIS RECIPE WORKS We streamline this popular bar snack by not coating the jalapeños and baking instead of deep frying them. Cream cheese is the base for our filling, with a hefty dose of shredded cheddar for substance and flavor and minced deli ham for meaty depth. Instead of breading and frying these stuffed chiles, we find that just 20 minutes in the oven softens them and ensures the filling is heated through. To soften cream cheese quickly, microwave it for 20 to 30 seconds. You can use red and green jalapeños interchangeably because chile heat is not determined by color.

Adjust oven rack to middle position and heat oven to 350 degrees. Line rimmed baking sheet with parchment paper. Combine cream cheese, cheddar, ham, scallions, lime juice, chili powder, and salt in bowl. Spoon cream cheese mixture into jalapeño halves and arrange on prepared baking sheet. Bake until cheese is hot, about 20 minutes. Serve warm.

Head Start

Cover and refrigerate filled, unbaked jalapeños for up to 1 day before baking.

Perfect Pair

Serve with Esquites (page 177) or Naan with Fig Jam, Blue Cheese, and Prosciutto (page 335).

pigs in blankets

Pigs

- 1 (9½ by 9-inch) sheet puff pastry, thawed
- 1 large egg, beaten with 1 tablespoon water
- 32 cocktail franks, patted dry
- ¼ cup grated Parmesan cheese
- 2 teaspoons Everything Bagel Seasoning (page 21)
- ½ teaspoon pepper

Mustard Sauce

- ⅓ cup yellow mustard
- 2 tablespoons cider vinegar
- 2 tablespoons packed brown sugar
- 1 tablespoon ketchup
- ½ teaspoon Worcestershire sauce
- ½ teaspoon hot sauce
- ¼ teaspoon pepper

Head Start

Thaw frozen pastry for 1 day in refrigerator or 30 minutes to 1 hour on counter. Refrigerate shaped pigs for up to 1 day before baking.

Perfect Pair

Add Beet-Pickled Eggs (page 132) and Moroccan-Style Carrot Salad with Harissa and Feta (page 159).

WHY THIS RECIPE WORKS For a sophisticated yet simple version of the retro-campy childhood classic, we use puff pastry. It has a flakier texture than the more typical refrigerated crescent roll dough but is equally easy to use. We unroll the puff pastry sheet, slice it into 32 equal strips, and roll a little cocktail frank in each strip. Then we place the strips on a parchment-lined baking sheet, with a little space between them to allow for the inevitable puffing. Next, we brush each li'l piggy with egg wash and sprinkle on grated Parmesan cheese for a savory punch. A sprinkle of Everything Bagel Seasoning adds textural and visual interest. While the pigs bake, we stir together a pantry-friendly mustard dipping sauce. One 10- to 13-ounce package of cocktail franks usually contains 32 franks. This recipe can be easily doubled; bake the pigs in blankets on two separate sheets, one sheet at a time.

1 **For the pigs** Adjust oven rack to middle position and heat oven to 400 degrees. Line rimmed baking sheet with parchment paper. Unfold puff pastry on lightly floured counter and roll into 12 by 9-inch rectangle with short side parallel to edge of counter, flouring top of dough as needed to prevent sticking.

2 Using pizza wheel or chef's knife, trim dough to 12 by 8-inch-rectangle. Cut dough lengthwise into eight 1-inch strips. Cut dough crosswise at three 3-inch intervals. (You should have thirty-two 3 by 1-inch dough strips.)

3 Lightly brush 1 row of dough strips with egg wash. Roll 1 frank in each dough strip and transfer bundle, seam side down, to prepared sheet. Repeat with remaining dough strips and franks, spacing bundles ½ inch apart.

4 Combine Parmesan, bagel seasoning, and pepper in bowl. Working with a few bundles at a time, brush tops with egg wash and sprinkle with Parmesan mixture. Bake until pastry is golden brown, about 23 minutes.

5 **For the mustard sauce** Meanwhile, whisk all ingredients together in bowl.

6 Let pigs cool on sheet for 10 minutes. Serve with mustard sauce.

pakoras

- 1 large russet potato, peeled and shredded (1½ cups/6½ ounces)
- 1 large red onion, halved and sliced thin (1½ cups/5 ounces)
- 1 cup baby spinach, chopped
- 1 serrano chile, stemmed and minced
- 1 teaspoon ground cumin
- 1 teaspoon ground coriander
- 1 teaspoon ajwain
- ½ teaspoon table salt
- ½ teaspoon Kashmiri chile powder
- ¼ teaspoon ground fenugreek
- ¾ cup besan
- 1 teaspoon baking powder
- ½ teaspoon ground turmeric
- ¼ cup water
- 2 quarts vegetable oil for frying

Finish Line

Bite into pakoras carefully, as they retain heat after deep frying.

Perfect Pair

Serve with Orange-Cardamom Spiced Nuts (page 33) and Gajarachi Koshimbir (page 160).

WHY THIS RECIPE WORKS These spiced vegetable fritters are a beloved treat at teatime in India, especially during the rainy season. Mouthwatering served with a hot cup of chai, you can also serve them with cocktails or beer any time you want a slightly spicy lift. Use the large holes of a box grater to shred the potato. For the best texture, we recommend measuring the prepped onion and potato by weight. Besan, along with ajwain and Kashmiri chile powder, can be found in South Asian markets. If ajwain is unavailable, substitute dried thyme. If fenugreek is unavailable, it can be omitted. Besan (also known as gram flour) is made by milling skinned and split brown chickpeas. To substitute standard chickpea flour (made from white chickpeas), add an additional 2 tablespoons of water to the batter. Use a Dutch oven that holds 6 quarts or more. Serve hot with Cilantro-Mint Chutney (page 18).

1 In large bowl, combine potato, onion, spinach, serrano, cumin, coriander, ajwain, salt, chile powder, and fenugreek. Toss vegetables until coated with spices. Using your hands, squeeze mixture until vegetables are softened and release some liquid, about 45 seconds (do not drain).

2 In small bowl, mix together besan, baking powder, and turmeric. Sprinkle over vegetable mixture and stir until besan is no longer visible and mixture forms sticky mass. Add water and stir vigorously until water is well incorporated.

3 Adjust oven rack to middle position and heat oven to 200 degrees. Set wire rack in rimmed baking sheet. Add oil to large Dutch oven until it measures about 1½ inches deep and heat over medium-low heat to 375 degrees.

4 Transfer heaping tablespoonful of batter to oil, using second spoon to ease batter out of spoon. Stir batter briefly and repeat portioning until there are 5 pakoras in oil. Fry, adjusting burner if necessary to maintain oil temperature of 370 to 380 degrees, until pakoras are deep golden brown, 1½ to 2 minutes per side. Using spider skimmer or slotted spoon, transfer pakoras to prepared rack and place in oven. Return oil to 375 degrees and repeat with remaining batter in two additional batches. Serve immediately.

socca with caramelized onions and rosemary

Socca

1½ cups water

1⅓ cups (6 ounces) chickpea flour

¼ cup extra-virgin olive oil, divided

1 teaspoon table salt

¼ teaspoon ground cumin

Topping

2 tablespoons extra-virgin olive oil, plus extra for drizzling

2 cups thinly sliced onions

½ teaspoon table salt

1 teaspoon chopped fresh rosemary

Coarse sea salt

WHY THIS RECIPE WORKS These thin, crisp, nutty-tasting chickpea pancakes will transport you right to the French Riviera, where they are a popular street food or snack at outdoor cafés alongside a glass of chilled rosé. Traditionally, the batter is poured into a large cast-iron skillet and baked in a very hot wood-burning oven to make one large pancake with a blistered top and smoky flavor. It is then cut into wedges for serving. You will "bake" these supereasy smaller versions entirely on the stovetop, using a preheated nonstick skillet and flipping them to get a great crust on both sides. The smaller socca are easier to flip than one large pancake, and the direct heat of the stovetop ensures a crispy exterior on both sides, giving the socca a higher ratio of crunchy crust to tender interior. A topping of golden caramelized onions enhanced with rosemary complements these savory flatbreads. Or try the variation with Swiss chard, pistachios, and dried apricots. Both taste good with that glass of chilled wine.

1 **For the socca** Adjust oven rack to middle position and heat oven to 200 degrees. Set wire rack in rimmed baking sheet and place in oven to preheat. Whisk water, flour, 4 teaspoons oil, salt, and cumin in bowl until no lumps remain. Let batter rest while preparing topping, at least 10 minutes.

2 **For the topping** Heat oil in 10-inch nonstick skillet over medium-high heat until just smoking. Add onions and salt and cook until onions start to brown around edges but still have some texture, 7 to 10 minutes. Add rosemary and cook until fragrant, about 1 minute. Transfer onion mixture to bowl; set aside. Wipe skillet clean with paper towels.

3 Heat 2 teaspoons oil in now-empty skillet over medium-high heat until just smoking. Lift skillet off heat and pour ½ cup batter into far side of skillet; swirl gently in clockwise direction until batter evenly covers bottom of skillet.

4 Return skillet to heat and cook socca, without moving it, until well browned and crisp around bottom edge, 3 to 4 minutes (you can peek at underside of socca by loosening it from side of skillet with heat resistant rubber spatula). Flip socca with rubber spatula and cook until second side is just cooked, about 1 minute. Transfer socca, browned side up, to prepared wire rack in oven. Repeat 3 more times, using 2 teaspoons oil and ½ cup batter per batch.

5 Transfer socca to cutting board and cut each into wedges. Serve, topped with sautéed onions, drizzled with extra oil, and sprinkled with sea salt.

Variation

Socca with Swiss Chard, Apricots, and Pistachios

Omit onion topping. Heat 1 tablespoon oil in 12-inch nonstick skillet over medium heat until shimmering. Add 1 finely chopped onion and cook until softened, about 5 minutes. Stir in 2 minced garlic cloves, ¾ teaspoon ground cumin, ¼ teaspoon salt, and ⅛ teaspoon ground allspice and cook until fragrant, about 30 seconds. Stir in 12 ounces stemmed and chopped Swiss chard and 3 tablespoons finely chopped dried apricots and cook until chard is wilted, 4 to 6 minutes. Off heat, stir in 2 tablespoons finely chopped toasted pistachios and 1 teaspoon white wine vinegar, and season with salt and pepper to taste. Top each cooked socca with ⅓ cup chard mixture, slice, and serve.

Head Start

Make topping up to 1 day ahead and bring to room temperature before using. Make batter up to 2 hours ahead (whisk to recombine before cooking).

Finish Line

If serving more than 6 to 8 people, cut socca into small squares.

Perfect Pair

Serve with Marinated Manchego (page 127), Carciofi alla Giudia (page 233), or Pressure-Cooker Winter Squash with Halloumi and Brussels Sprouts (page 252).

grilled polenta with charred scallion and gorgonzola topping

2 cups water

1 tablespoon chopped fresh rosemary

½ teaspoon table salt

1 cup instant polenta

3 tablespoons plus 1 teaspoon extra-virgin olive oil

4 scallions, trimmed

4 ounces gorgonzola cheese, softened

1 tablespoon heavy cream

1 tablespoon honey

WHY THIS RECIPE WORKS When you're grilling meat and a vegetable, it's nice to add a side too. For this great alternative to crostini, we make the polenta ahead of time and cut it into triangles. Then we grill it with scallions, building smokiness in both base and topping. Gorgonzola add welcome funkiness. Using a low liquid-to-cornmeal ratio when simmering the polenta ensures that the wedges will be sturdy enough to hold together during grilling. Extra-virgin olive oil contributes richness and keeps the polenta from being sticky. After chilling in a baking pan, the cooked polenta is firm enough to slice; 5 minutes over a hot fire crisps the outside while the insides stay soft. Be sure that the Gorgonzola is at room temperature so that it blends smoothly.

1 Grease 8 x 8-inch square baking pan, line with parchment paper, and grease parchment. Bring water to boil in medium saucepan over medium-high heat. Stir in rosemary and salt. Slowly pour polenta into water in steady stream while whisking constantly and return to boil. Reduce heat to medium-low and continue cooking until grains of cornmeal are tender, about 30 minutes, stirring every few minutes. (Polenta should be very thick.) Off heat, stir in 3 tablespoons olive oil and transfer polenta into prepared pan, smooth top using a rubber spatula and let cool completely, about 30 minutes. Wrap tightly in plastic wrap and refrigerate until polenta is very firm, 2 hours.

2 Remove polenta from baking pan and flip onto cutting board; discard parchment. Slice into 4 equal squares and then cut each square into 4 triangles; refrigerate until ready to grill. Toss scallions with remaining teaspoon oil.

3A **For a charcoal grill** Open bottom vent completely. Light large chimney starter filled with charcoal briquettes (6 quarts). When top coals are partially covered with ash, pour evenly over half of grill. Set cooking grate in place, cover, and open lid vent completely. Heat grill until hot, about 5 minutes.

3B **For a gas grill** Turn all burners to high, cover, and heat grill until hot, about 15 minutes.

4 Clean and oil cooking grate, then repeatedly wipe grate with well-oiled paper towels until grate is black and glossy, 5 to 10 times. Grill polenta triangles and scallions (covered if using gas) until polenta and scallions are lightly charred on both sides, 5 to 7 minutes, turning as needed. As polenta and scallions finish cooking, transfer polenta to serving platter and scallions to cutting board. Chop scallions and combine with gorgonzola and cream in small bowl.

5 Top each polenta wedge with heaping teaspoon of gorgonzola mixture. Drizzle with honey and serve.

Head Start

Cooked polenta can be refrigerated, wrapped, for up to 3 days.

Perfect Pair

Serve with Peruvian Ceviche with Radishes and Orange (page 270) or Caponata (page 104).

Serves 6 to 8 (makes two 10-inch pancakes) | **Active Time** 50 minutes
Total Time 50 minutes

pajeon

Dipping Sauce

- 2 tablespoons soy sauce
- 1 tablespoon water
- 2 teaspoons unseasoned rice vinegar
- 1 teaspoon toasted sesame oil
- ½–1 teaspoon gochugaru
- ½ teaspoon sugar

Pancakes

- 10 scallions
- 1 cup (5 ounces) all-purpose flour
- ¼ cup (1 ounce) potato starch
- 1 teaspoon sugar
- 1 teaspoon baking powder
- ½ teaspoon pepper
- ¼ teaspoon baking soda
- ¼ teaspoon table salt
- 1 cup ice water
- 2 garlic cloves, minced
- 6 tablespoons vegetable oil, divided

WHY THIS RECIPE WORKS Korea's renowned scallion pancake is an ideal anytime treat that you'll be tempted to eat right out of the pan alongside its tart, sweet-spicy dipping sauce. The filling-to-batter ratio is high in these crisp-chewy pancakes, and the scallions are typically cut into lengths, so the effect resembles a nest of verdant stalks bound together by the viscous batter. As it sizzles in the skillet, the pancake browns and the interior sets up soft and dense. Adding potato starch to the all-purpose flour equips the batter with more starch for crisping up; the chemical makeup of potato starch also helps keep the starch molecules separate after cooling so that the crust stays crispy. Since starches absorb cold water more slowly than they do room-temperature water, using ice water in the batter minimizes hydration, helping the pancakes crisp more easily during frying. Baking soda raises the batter's pH and boosts browning; baking powder opens up the crumb so that it's not gummy. Pressing the pancakes into the skillet after flipping them also encourages browning. Purchase the coarse variety of gochugaru (Korean red pepper flakes), which is sometimes labeled "coarse powder." Use a full teaspoon if you prefer a spicier dipping sauce. You can substitute cornstarch for potato starch.

1 **For the dipping sauce** Whisk all ingredients together in small bowl; set aside.

2 **For the pancakes** Line 2 large plates with double layer of paper towels and set aside. Separate dark-green parts of scallions from white and light-green parts. Halve white and light-green parts lengthwise. Cut all scallion parts into 2-inch lengths and set aside. Whisk flour, potato starch, sugar, baking powder, pepper, baking soda, and salt together in medium bowl. Add ice water and garlic and whisk until smooth. Using rubber spatula, fold in scallions until mixture is evenly combined.

3 Heat 2 tablespoons vegetable oil in 10-inch nonstick skillet over medium-high heat until just smoking. Stir batter to recombine. Run blade of spatula through center of batter to halve, then scrape half of batter into center of skillet. Spread into round of even thickness, covering bottom of skillet, using spatula or tongs to move scallions

as necessary so they are evenly distributed in single layer. Shake skillet to distribute oil beneath pancake and cook, adjusting heat as needed to maintain gentle sizzle (reduce heat if oil begins to smoke), until bubbles at center of pancake burst and leave holes in surface and underside is golden brown, 3 to 5 minutes. Flip pancake and press firmly into skillet with back of spatula to flatten. Add 1 tablespoon vegetable oil to edges of skillet and continue to cook, pressing pancake occasionally to flatten, until second side is spotty golden brown, 2 to 4 minutes. Transfer to prepared plate.

4 Repeat with remaining 3 tablespoons vegetable oil and remaining batter. Let second pancake drain on second prepared plate for 2 minutes. Cut each pancake into 6 wedges and transfer to platter. Serve, passing sauce separately.

Head Start

Make dipping sauce up to 1 day ahead; refrigerate until 30 minutes before serving.

Finish Line

To serve more than 6 guests, cut pancakes into narrower wedges.

Perfect Pair

Accompany pancakes with bites such as Marinated Eggplant with Capers and Mint (page 209) or Crab Croquettes (page 272).

Serves 10 to 12 (makes 32 squares) | **Active Time** 20 minutes
Total Time 1 hour, plus 20 minutes cooling

spinach squares

1 cup (5 ounces) plus
  2 tablespoons all-purpose
  flour

1 teaspoon baking powder

¾ teaspoon table salt

½ teaspoon pepper

¼ teaspoon cayenne pepper

1 cup chicken broth

3 large eggs

20 ounces frozen chopped
  spinach, thawed and
  squeezed dry

12 ounces Gruyère cheese,
  shredded (3 cups)

1 onion, chopped fine

2 garlic cloves, minced

1 ounce Parmesan cheese,
  grated (½ cup)

WHY THIS RECIPE WORKS A simple stir-and-bake technique, loads of cheese flavor, and finger-food ease have made this spinach hors d'oeuvre a harried host or hostess's helper for decades. Cheddar is often used in the South, where this appetizer is popular, but we prefer a combination of nutty Gruyère and Parmesan. We also exchange the milk traditionally used in the dough for savory chicken broth. Removing extra moisture from the spinach prevents our squares from turning soggy. Increasing the oven temperature, cooking the squares on the upper-middle rack, and sprinkling more Parmesan over the squares gives us a browned, crispy top. Thaw spinach in the microwave or overnight in the refrigerator. To squeeze the spinach dry, place it in a clean dish towel, gather the edges, and wring it out.

1 Adjust oven rack to upper-middle position and heat oven to 375 degrees. Spray 13 by 9-inch baking dish with vegetable oil spray. Whisk flour, baking powder, salt, pepper, and cayenne together in large bowl. Add broth and eggs and whisk until smooth. Stir in spinach, Gruyère, onion, and garlic until combined.

2 Transfer mixture to prepared baking dish and sprinkle with Parmesan. Bake until browned on top and bubbling around edges, 40 to 45 minutes. Let cool in pan for 20 minutes. Cut into 32 equal-size squares. Serve warm.

Head Start

Bake and cool squares, then refrigerate for up to 1 day. Reheat refrigerated squares, covered in foil, in 375-degree oven for 25 minutes.

Perfect Pair

Add refreshing accompaniments such as Horiatiki Salata (page 182) or Apple-Fennel Rémoulade (page 162).

karaage

3 tablespoons soy sauce

2 tablespoons sake

1 tablespoon grated fresh ginger

2 garlic cloves, minced

¾ teaspoon sugar

⅛ teaspoon table salt

1½ pounds boneless, skinless chicken thighs, trimmed and cut crosswise into 1- to 1½-inch-wide strips

1¼ cups (5 ounces) cornstarch

1 quart vegetable oil for frying

Lemon wedges

Head Start

Cut chicken thighs into strips up to 1 day ahead. Refrigerate until time to marinate.

Finish Line

Aioli (page 16) and Creamy Blue Cheese Dip (page 17) are great dipping sauces.

Perfect Pair

Try Cinnamon-Ginger Spiced Nuts (page 32) or Citrus and Radicchio Salad with Dates and Smoked Almonds (page 166) alongside the karaage.

WHY THIS RECIPE WORKS This Japanese bar snack is a dream for fried chicken lovers: juicy, deeply seasoned strips of boneless, skinless chicken thighs encased in a supercrispy crust. Minimal oil and fast frying make it a cinch to cook. Briefly marinating the meat in a mixture of soy sauce, sake, ginger, garlic, sugar, and salt imbues the chicken with savory, aromatic flavor. Dredging the chicken in cornstarch—instead of the traditional potato starch—makes for a less-sticky coating. Shaking off excess starch and letting the dredged pieces rest while the oil heats gives the starch time to hydrate. Dabbing any dry patches with reserved marinade prevents dustiness. We recommend using a rasp–style grater to grate the ginger. Use a Dutch oven that holds 6 quarts or more. Do not substitute chicken breasts for thighs; they will dry out during frying. There's no need to check the chicken's temperature: It will be cooked through by the time it is golden brown and crispy.

1 Combine soy sauce, sake, ginger, garlic, sugar, and salt in medium bowl. Add chicken and toss to combine. Let sit at room temperature for 30 minutes. While chicken is marinating, line rimmed baking sheet with parchment paper. Set wire rack in second rimmed baking sheet and line rack with triple layer of paper towels. Place cornstarch in wide bowl.

2 Lift chicken from marinade, 1 piece at a time, allowing excess marinade to drip back into bowl but leaving any garlic or ginger bits on chicken. Coat chicken with cornstarch, shake off excess, and place on parchment-lined sheet. Reserve marinade.

3 Heat oil in large Dutch oven over medium-high heat to 325 degrees. While oil heats, check chicken pieces for white patches of dry corn-starch. Dip back of spoon in reserved marinade and gently press onto dry spots to lightly moisten.

4 Using tongs, add half of chicken, one piece at a time, to oil in single layer. Cook, adjusting burner if necessary to maintain oil temperature between 300 and 325 degrees, until chicken is golden brown and crispy, 4 to 5 minutes. Using spider skimmer or slotted spoon, transfer chicken to paper towel–lined rack. Return oil to 325 degrees and repeat with remaining chicken. Serve with lemon wedges.

oven-baked buffalo wings

3 pounds chicken wings, halved at joint and wingtips removed, trimmed

1 tablespoon baking powder

½ teaspoon table salt

⅔ cup Frank's RedHot Original Cayenne Pepper Sauce

1 tablespoon unsalted butter, melted

1 tablespoon molasses

WHY THIS RECIPE WORKS For this barroom classic, we set out to ditch the deep fryer but still turn out wings that wouldn't disappoint. Baking them means that we can use the stovetop to prepare other small plates and have everything ready at the same time. Baking powder helps to dry out the skin on our wings so it becomes crisp when roasted in a superhot oven; baking them on a wire rack lets the rendered fat drip away. A quick stint under the broiler crisps the skin even further and ensures a flavorful char. A spoonful of molasses adds depth and richness to these oven-baked yet still finger-licking-good wings that are wonderful with Creamy Blue Cheese Dip (page 17). The mild flavor of Frank's Red-Hot Original Cayenne Pepper Sauce is crucial to the flavor of this dish; we don't suggest substituting another hot sauce here.

Perfect Pair

Maple-Chipotle Mayonnaise (page 17) is another great dipping sauce. Add freshness with Horiatiki Salata (page 182) or Fennel, Orange, and Olive Salad (page 165) and Marinated Cauliflower and Chickpeas with Saffron (page 209).

1 Adjust oven rack to middle position and heat oven to 475 degrees. Line rimmed baking sheet with aluminum foil and top with wire rack. Pat wings dry with paper towels, then toss with baking powder and salt in bowl. Arrange wings in single layer on wire rack. Roast wings until golden on both sides, about 40 minutes, flipping wings over and rotating sheet halfway through roasting.

2 Meanwhile, whisk hot sauce, butter, and molasses together in large bowl.

3 Remove wings from oven. Adjust oven rack 6 inches from broiler element and heat broiler. Broil wings until golden brown on both sides, 6 to 8 minutes, flipping wings over halfway through broiling. Add wings to sauce and toss to coat. Serve.

easy egg rolls

8 ounces ground pork

6 scallions, white and green parts separated and sliced thin

3 garlic cloves, minced

2 teaspoons grated fresh ginger

3 cups (7 ounces) coleslaw mix

4 ounces shiitake mushrooms, stemmed and chopped

3 tablespoons soy sauce

1 tablespoon sugar

1 tablespoon distilled white vinegar

2 teaspoons toasted sesame oil

8 egg roll wrappers

2 cups vegetable oil

WHY THIS RECIPE WORKS Egg rolls are the perfect bar snack, easy to pick up and crunch as you sip your drink. For egg rolls quick enough to make at home, we use bagged coleslaw mix and ground pork, which makes an easy, delicious substitute for the minced fresh pork traditional recipes call for. A simple mix of flavorful ingredients—garlic, ginger, soy sauce, and sugar—makes a tasty sauce to flavor the filling. Shallow-frying the rolls in a skillet in just ½ inch of oil rather than deep frying makes cooking easier and cleanup faster while still ensuring crispy, delicious egg rolls. This recipe can be easily doubled: Extend the cooking time of the pork mixture to about 5 minutes in step 1 and fry the egg rolls in two batches.

1 Cook pork in 12-inch nonstick skillet over medium-high heat until no longer pink, about 5 minutes, breaking up meat with wooden spoon. Add scallion whites, garlic, and ginger and cook until fragrant, about 1 minute. Add coleslaw mix, mushrooms, soy sauce, sugar, and vinegar and cook until cabbage is just softened, about 3 minutes.

2 Off heat, stir in sesame oil and scallion greens. Transfer pork mixture to large plate, spread into even layer, and refrigerate until cool enough to handle, about 5 minutes. Wipe skillet clean with paper towels.

3 Fill small bowl with water. Working with one egg roll wrapper at a time, orient wrappers on counter so one corner points toward edge of counter. Place lightly packed ⅓ cup filling on lower half of wrapper and mold it with your fingers into neat cylindrical shape. Using your fingertips, moisten entire border of wrapper with thin film of water.

4 Fold bottom corner of wrapper up and over filling and press it down on other side of filling. Fold both side corners of wrapper in over filling and press gently to seal. Roll filling up over itself until wrapper is fully sealed. Leave egg roll seam side down on counter and cover with damp paper towel while filling and shaping remaining egg rolls.

5 Line large plate with triple layer of paper towels. Heat vegetable oil in now-empty skillet over medium heat to 325 degrees. Using tongs, place all egg rolls in skillet, seam side down, and cook until golden brown, 2 to 4 minutes per side. Transfer to prepared plate and let cool slightly, about 5 minutes. Serve.

Head Start

Transfer shaped egg rolls to parchment paper–lined plate, wrap tightly in plastic wrap, and refrigerate for up to 1 day. Alternatively, freeze egg rolls on plate, transfer to zipper-lock bag, and freeze for up to 1 month. Do not thaw before cooking; increase cooking time by about 1 minute per side.

Finish Line

Serve egg rolls hot with duck sauce, Chinese hot mustard, or Soy-Vinegar Dipping Sauce (page 18).

Perfect Pair

Serve with Stir-Fried En Choy with Garlic (page 220), Tempeh with Sambal Sauce (page 291), or Cantaloupe Salad with Olives and Red Onion (page 172).

spinach and edamame brown rice cakes

Soy Dipping Sauce

¼ cup soy sauce

2 tablespoons unseasoned rice vinegar

2 tablespoons mirin

2 tablespoons water

1 scallion, sliced thin

½ teaspoon toasted sesame oil

Rice Cakes

1¾ cups water

1 cup short-grain brown rice

1 cup baby spinach

¾ cup frozen shelled edamame, thawed and patted dry

2 (8 by 7½-inch) sheets nori, crumbled

2 scallions, sliced thin

¼ cup white sesame seeds, toasted, divided

2 teaspoons grated fresh ginger

½ teaspoon table salt

2 teaspoons toasted sesame oil

WHY THIS RECIPE WORKS For bite-size morsels with craveable complexity, we took inspiration from onigiri, a Japanese bento box staple of white rice that's usually shaped into triangular bundles and stuffed with bits of fish, pickled plums, sea vegetables, or other ingredients. Our recipe departs from the traditional preparation by starting with short-grain brown rice, which we pulse in the food processor along with spinach and edamame. This processing step releases starch from the rice, which makes the mixture easy to shape and also enables us to combine a good amount of spinach mixture with the rice. We scoop out portions of the rice mixture and, with lightly moistened hands, press each into a petite disk. We roll the edges in toasted sesame seeds, which add a crunchy, nutty contrast to the rice. A simple soy dipping sauce makes a tasty accompaniment to this fresh bite.

1 **For the soy dipping sauce** Combine all ingredients in small bowl; set aside.

2 **For the rice cakes** Bring water and rice to simmer in large saucepan over high heat. Reduce heat to low, cover, and simmer gently until rice is tender and water is absorbed, 40 to 45 minutes. Off heat, lay clean dish towel underneath lid, and let sit for 10 minutes. Fluff rice with fork and cover.

3 Pulse spinach, edamame, nori, scallions, 2 tablespoons sesame seeds, ginger, salt, and sesame oil in food processor until mixture is finely ground (it should not be smooth), about 10 pulses. Add rice and pulse until rice is coarsely chopped and mixture is well combined, about 8 pulses.

4 Divide rice mixture into 24 portions (about 1½ tablespoons each) and arrange on parchment-lined baking sheet. Using lightly moistened hands, roll each into ball, then press into disk about 1½ inches wide and ¾ inch thick. Spread remaining 2 tablespoons sesame seeds onto plate. Gently roll sides of disks in sesame seeds, pressing lightly to adhere, and transfer to serving platter. Serve with soy dipping sauce.

Head Start

Refrigerate rice cakes, covered, for up to 1 day before you plan to serve them; let come to room temperature before serving.

Perfect Pair

For a filling small plates spread, serve with Soy-Marinated Eggs (page 131) and Crab and Mizuna Salad (page 202).

green chile cheeseburger sliders

5 tablespoons vegetable oil, divided

1 onion, chopped fine

3 (4-ounce) cans chopped green chiles, drained

1 garlic clove, minced

¼ cup mayonnaise

1 tablespoon lime juice

¾ teaspoon table salt, divided

1 pound 85 percent lean ground beef

¼ teaspoon pepper

4 ounces pepper Jack cheese, shredded (1 cup)

12 soft white dinner rolls or slider hamburger buns, sliced and toasted

WHY THIS RECIPE WORKS For these sliders, we wanted all the great char and juicy meat of a full-size burger stuffed into a diminutive package. To create a flavorful crust on a small burger while retaining a moist interior, you need a real blast of heat that can sear the outside quickly, so we use a cast-iron skillet. To take the flavor to the next level, we add a double dose of green chiles, both in the meat and on top of the burgers. We sauté onion, garlic, and canned green chiles, then puree part of that mixture and add it to the ground beef. Refrigerating the patties for 30 minutes ensures that the thin, delicate disks are easy to handle. For the topping, we reserve ½ cup of the unpureed sautéed green chile mixture and combine it with mayonnaise, lime juice, and salt for a spread that adds moisture and extra flavor to the sliders. Using shredded pepper Jack helps ensure that the cheese melts evenly on the burgers. Form the patties ½ inch wider than the buns; after the patties shrink during cooking, they will be the perfect size. When flipping these thin, moist patties, it's helpful to use two spatulas.

1 Heat 12-inch cast-iron skillet over medium heat for 3 minutes. Add 2 tablespoons oil and heat until shimmering. Add onion and cook until softened, about 5 minutes. Stir in chiles and garlic and cook until fragrant, about 1 minute. Transfer mixture to food processor and process to smooth paste, about 1 minute, scraping down sides of bowl as needed. Combine ½ cup processed chile paste, mayonnaise, lime juice, and ¼ teaspoon salt in bowl; set aside for serving.

2 Add remaining chile paste, beef, ½ teaspoon salt, and ¼ teaspoon pepper to large bowl and knead with your hands until uniformly combined. Divide meat mixture into 12 lightly packed balls, then flatten into ¼-inch-thick patties. Transfer patties to platter and refrigerate until chilled, about 30 minutes.

3 Wipe now-empty skillet clean with paper towels and heat over medium heat for 5 minutes. Add 1 tablespoon oil and heat until just smoking. Place 4 burgers in skillet and cook, without moving, until well browned on first side, about 2 minutes. Flip burgers and top with 1 heaping tablespoon pepper Jack. Cover and continue to cook until well browned on second side and cheese is melted, about 2 minutes.

4 Repeat in two batches with remaining 2 tablespoons oil, burgers, and pepper Jack. Serve burgers in buns, topped with chile sauce.

Head Start

Make and refrigerate patties and sauce for up to 1 day before cooking.

Perfect Pair

Serve sliders with Fried Green Tomatoes (page 215) or Spiralized Sweet Potatoes with Crispy Shallots, Pistachios, and Urfa (page 250).

classic pub plant-based sliders

Burger Sauce

- 2 tablespoons plant-based or egg-based mayonnaise
- 1 tablespoon ketchup
- 1 teaspoon sweet pickle relish
- ½ teaspoon sugar
- ½ teaspoon distilled white vinegar
- ½ teaspoon pepper

Sliders

- 12 ounces plant-based ground meat
- ¼ teaspoon table salt
- ¼ teaspoon pepper
- 8 slider hamburger buns
- 4 slices plant-based or dairy cheese (4 ounces)
- 4 teaspoons vegetable oil, divided
- ¼ cup finely chopped onion, divided
- ¼ cup water, divided

WHY THIS RECIPE WORKS Sliders feature all the hearty goodness of a full-size burger concentrated in a few bites, perfect for a small plates spread. The juicy patty with a charred exterior is embedded with chopped onion, covered in melted cheese, and sandwiched in a soft steamed bun. These sliders feature plant-based meat, suitable for vegans and vegetarians. The meat cooks through in minutes (quicker than ground beef), so we press the patties into uniform 3-inch disks to ensure that they all cook at the same rate. The patties are also more delicate than those made from beef, so chilling them briefly before cooking makes them easier to handle. Pressing chopped onion into the patties with a spatula helps it adhere. After flipping the patties, we top them with cheese and the bun tops, add some water to the pan, and cover it to soften the onion and melt the cheese to perfection. You can use any pie plate or baking dish to press the patties, but we prefer glass so that you can see the size of the patty as you're pressing.

1 **For the burger sauce** Whisk all ingredients together in bowl.

2 **For the sliders** Cut sides of 1-quart zipper-lock bag, leaving bottom seam intact. Using your moistened hands, pinch off and roll ground meat into 8 balls (1½ ounces each). Enclose 1 ball in split bag. Using clear pie plate or baking dish, press ball into even 3-inch-wide patty. Remove patty from bag and transfer to baking sheet. Repeat with remaining balls. Sprinkle patties with salt and pepper. Transfer patties to refrigerator and chill for 15 minutes.

3 Divide sauce evenly among bun bottoms. Arrange bun bottoms on serving platter. Stack cheese and cut into quarters (you will have 16 pieces).

4 Heat 2 teaspoons oil in 12-inch nonstick skillet over medium-high heat until just smoking. Using spatula, transfer 4 patties to skillet. Sprinkle 2 tablespoons onion evenly over tops of patties and press firmly into patties with back of spatula. Cook patties until well browned on first side, about 1 minute. Flip patties and top each with 2 pieces cheese; add bun tops. Add 2 tablespoons water to skillet (do not wet buns), cover, and continue to cook until cheese is melted, about 90 seconds.

5 Transfer sliders to prepared bun bottoms, tent with aluminum foil, and set aside while cooking remaining patties. Wipe skillet clean with paper towels. Repeat with remaining 2 teaspoons oil, remaining 4 patties, remaining 2 tablespoons onion, remaining buns, and remaining 2 tablespoons water. Serve.

Head Start

Shape and refrigerate patties for up to 1 day before cooking. Refrigerate sauce for up to 4 days.

Perfect Pair

While sliders cook, offer your guests Easy Mushroom Pâté (page 120), Smoked Paprika–Spiced Almonds (page 33), or Quick Fennel Pickles (page 76).

air-fryer apps

Pull out your air fryer when you want to make small bites for small groups. You'll avoid overheating the kitchen and your stove and oven will be available if you want to cook other dishes. Our air-fried appetizers, from fries to wings, are both easy to make and to devour.

Got more people to feed? All of these recipes can be doubled. Simply double all ingredients and cook in batches.

whole-wheat pita chips with salt and pepper

Serves 2 to 4 (makes 16 chips)
Active Time 10 minutes
Total Time 15 minutes, plus 30 minutes cooling

We use whole wheat pita bread, but traditional pita also works well here.

1 (8-inch) 100-percent whole-wheat pita
Olive oil spray
⅛ teaspoon table salt
⅛ teaspoon pepper

1 Using kitchen shears, cut around perimeter of pita and separate into 2 thin rounds. Lightly spray both sides of each cut round with oil spray and sprinkle with salt and pepper. Cut each round into 8 wedges.

2 Arrange wedges into two even layers in air-fryer basket. Place basket into air fryer and set temperature to 300 degrees. Cook until wedges are light golden brown on edges, 3 to 5 minutes. Using tongs, toss wedges gently to redistribute and continue to cook until golden brown and crisp, 3 to 5 minutes. Let cool completely, about 30 minutes, before serving. (Chips can be stored in airtight container for up to 3 days.)

Variations

Buttermilk-Ranch Whole-Wheat Pita Chips
Omit salt and pepper. Sprinkle each oiled pita round with ½ teaspoon buttermilk-ranch seasoning powder before cutting into wedges.

Ras el Hanout Whole-Wheat Pita Chips
Omit pepper. Sprinkle each oiled pita round with ¼ teaspoon ras el hanout before cutting into wedges.

parmesan, rosemary, and black pepper french fries

Serves 2 to 4
Active Time 30 minutes
Total Time 1 hour

Frequently tossing fries ensures the most even cooking and the best browning. Tossing fries in a bowl, rather than in the air-fryer basket, yields the best results and the fewest broken fries. Do not clean out tossing bowl while you are cooking; the residual oil helps the crisping process.

1½ pounds russet potatoes, unpeeled
 2 tablespoons vegetable oil, divided
1½ ounces Parmesan cheese, grated (¾ cup), divided
 4 teaspoons minced fresh rosemary, divided
 ¼ teaspoon table salt
 ¼ teaspoon pepper

1 Cut potatoes lengthwise into ½-inch-thick planks. Stack 3 or 4 planks and cut into ½-inch-thick sticks; repeat with remaining planks.

2 Submerge potatoes in large bowl of water and rinse to remove excess starch. Drain potatoes and repeat process as needed until water remains clear. Cover potatoes with hot tap water and let sit for 10 minutes. Drain potatoes, transfer to paper towel–lined rimmed baking sheet, and thoroughly pat dry.

3 Toss potatoes with 1 tablespoon oil in clean, dry bowl, then transfer to air-fryer basket. Place basket in air fryer, set temperature to 350 degrees, and cook for 8 minutes. Transfer potatoes to now-empty bowl and toss gently to redistribute. Return potatoes to air fryer and cook until softened and fries have turned from white to blond (they may be spotty brown at tips), 5 to 10 minutes.

4 Transfer fries to now-empty bowl and toss with ¼ cup Parmesan, 1 tablespoon rosemary, remaining 1 tablespoon oil, salt, and pepper. Return to air fryer, increase temperature to 400 degrees, and cook until golden brown and crispy, 15 to 20 minutes, tossing gently in bowl to redistribute every 5 minutes.

5 Transfer fries to bowl and toss with ¼ cup Parmesan and remaining 1 teaspoon rosemary. Season with salt and pepper to taste. Transfer to large plate and sprinkle with remaining ¼ cup Parmesan. Serve immediately.

asparagus fries with yogurt sauce

Serves 2 to 4
Active Time 20 minutes
Total Time 30 minutes

We arrange a layer of coated asparagus pieces in one direction, then add a layer perpendicular to the first, alternating until all asparagus is used. This allows for maximum air circulation. Look for asparagus that is approximately ½ inch wide at the base.

 ½ cup plain yogurt
 1 tablespoon whole-grain mustard
 ¾ cup panko bread crumbs
 2 tablespoons extra-virgin olive oil
 1 ounce Parmesan cheese, grated (½ cup)
 1 large egg
 1 tablespoon all-purpose flour
 ½ teaspoon herbes de Provence
 ½ teaspoon table salt
 ¼ teaspoon pepper
 1 pound asparagus, trimmed and halved crosswise
    Lemon wedges

1 Whisk yogurt and mustard together in small bowl; set aside. Toss panko with oil in shallow dish until evenly coated. Microwave, stirring frequently, until light golden brown, 1 to 3 minutes. Let cool slightly, then stir in Parmesan. Whisk egg, flour, herbes de Provence, salt, and pepper together in second shallow dish. Working with several asparagus pieces at a time, dredge in egg mixture, letting excess drip off, then coat with panko mixture, pressing gently to adhere; transfer to large plate.

2 Lightly spray base of air-fryer basket with vegetable oil spray. Arrange half of asparagus pieces parallel to each other in prepared basket, spaced evenly apart. Arrange remaining asparagus pieces on top, perpendicular to first layer. Place basket into air fryer and set temperature to 400 degrees. Cook until asparagus is tender and crisp, 10 to 12 minutes, shaking basket gently to loosen pieces halfway through cooking. Serve with yogurt sauce and lemon wedges.

ricotta tartlets with tomato-basil topping

Serves 8 to 10 (makes 12 tartlets)
Active Time 15 minutes
Total Time 20 minutes

Do not thaw the phyllo cups before baking.

4 ounces (½ cup) whole-milk ricotta

1 tablespoon extra-virgin olive oil, divided, plus extra for drizzling

1 teaspoon grated lemon zest

⅛ teaspoon table salt

⅛ teaspoon pepper

12 frozen mini phyllo cups

1 large tomato, cored, seeded, and chopped

1 small shallot, minced

1 tablespoon shredded fresh basil

1 Whisk ricotta, 2 teaspoons oil, lemon zest, salt, and pepper together in bowl. Divide ricotta mixture evenly among phyllo cups, then transfer phyllo cups to air-fryer basket. Place basket into air fryer and set temperature to 300 degrees. Cook until ricotta is heated through and spotty brown, 5 to 7 minutes. Transfer to serving platter.

2 Combine tomato, shallot, basil, and remaining 1 teaspoon oil in bowl and season with salt and pepper to taste. Top tartlets with tomato mixture and drizzle with extra oil. Serve.

lemon-pepper chicken wings

Serves 2 to 4
Active Time 10 minutes
Total Time 30 minutes

In the intense, evenly circulating heat, the fat renders as the skin crisps, then conveniently accumulates at the bottom of the air fryer without smoking up your kitchen. If you buy chicken wings that are already split, with the tips removed, you need only 1 pound. This recipe can be easily doubled; simply cook the wings in batches.

1¼ pounds chicken wings, halved at joints, wingtips discarded

⅛ teaspoon table salt

¼ teaspoon pepper

1 tablespoon grated lemon zest, plus lemon wedges for serving

1 tablespoon minced fresh parsley, dill, and/or tarragon

1 Pat wings dry with paper towels and sprinkle with salt and pepper. Arrange wings in even layer in air-fryer basket. Place basket into air fryer and set temperature to 400 degrees. Cook until wings are golden brown and crisp, 18 to 24 minutes, flipping wings halfway through cooking.

2 Combine lemon zest and parsley in large bowl. Add wings and toss until evenly coated. Serve with lemon wedges.

Variations

Parmesan-Garlic Chicken Wings
Add 1 tablespoon grated Parmesan cheese and 1 minced garlic clove to lemon zest–parsley mixture.

Cilantro-Lime Chicken Wings
Substitute lime zest and wedges for lemon and cilantro for parsley. Add 1 tablespoon minced jalapeño chile to lime zest–cilantro mixture.

Perfect Pair

Since an air fryer does not give off heat, unlike a stove or oven, and it leaves those pieces of equipment free for other cooking, it is great to use for cooking on a hot summer day. Use it to make a batch of asparagus or potato fries to serve with chicken wings or other proteins, when you are cooking just for family or a small group of guests.

pickles, dips, and spreads

quick pickles

Homemade quick pickles are snappy, tangy, and surprisingly easy to make—great for making well in advance and keeping on hand for midday snacking or rounding out a simple mix-and-match spread.

quick carrot pickles

Serves 16 (makes 1 quart)
Active Time 20 minutes
Total Time 20 minutes, plus 3 hours chilling

Be sure to use seasoned rice vinegar here. Pickles can be refrigerated for up to 1 month; note that vegetables will soften over time.

- 1 pound carrots, peeled and cut into 4- by ½-inch sticks
- 5 sprigs fresh tarragon
- 1¼ cups seasoned rice vinegar
- ¼ cup water
- 2 garlic cloves, peeled and halved
- ¼ teaspoon black peppercorns
- ¼ teaspoon yellow mustard seeds

Place carrots and tarragon in 1-quart glass jar with tight-fitting lid. Combine vinegar, water, garlic, peppercorns, and mustard seeds in small saucepan and bring to boil. Pour brine into jar, making sure all vegetables are submerged. Let cool completely. Cover with lid and refrigerate for at least 3 hours before serving.

Variations

Quick Fennel Pickles
Substitute 1 fennel bulb, stalks discarded, bulb halved, cored, and cut crosswise into ¼-inch-thick slices, for carrots. Omit tarragon. Add two 1-inch strips orange zest and ½ teaspoon fennel seeds to saucepan with vinegar.

Quick Giardiniera
Substitute 6 ounces cauliflower, cut into 1-inch florets; 1 celery rib, sliced ¼ inch thick; and 1 carrot, sliced ¼ inch thick, for carrots. Omit tarragon. Add ½ teaspoon red pepper flakes to saucepan with vinegar.

quick pickled chard stems

Serves 4 (makes about 1 cup)
Active Time 20 minutes
Total Time 20 minutes, plus 5 hours cooling and chilling

Depending on the size of your container, you may have extra pickling brine. Pickles can be refrigerated for up to 1 month; note that chard will soften over time.

Stems from 12 ounces Swiss chard, ends trimmed and discarded, stems sliced on bias ¼ inch thick (about 1½ cups)

⅓ cup red wine vinegar

⅓ cup water

⅓ cup sugar

4 sprigs fresh thyme

4 garlic cloves, smashed and peeled

2 bay leaves

2 teaspoons kosher salt

1 teaspoon black peppercorns

½ teaspoon red pepper flakes

1 Combine all ingredients in small saucepan and bring to boil over medium-high heat, stirring to dissolve sugar. Reduce heat to medium and simmer until chard stems are just softened, about 3 minutes. Remove from heat and let cool completely, about 1 hour.

2 Transfer to airtight container and refrigerate for at least 4 hours before serving.

pink pickled turnips

Serves 16 (makes 1 quart)
Active Time 20 minutes
Total Time 45 minutes, plus 2 days pickling

The two-day refrigeration period is necessary to allow the brine to fully penetrate and pickle the vegetables. Pickles can be refrigerated for up to 1 month; note that vegetables will soften over time.

1¼ cups white wine vinegar

1¼ cups water

2½ tablespoons sugar

1½ tablespoons kosher salt

3 garlic cloves, smashed and peeled

¾ teaspoon whole allspice berries

¾ teaspoon black peppercorns

1 pound turnips, peeled and cut into 2 by ½-inch sticks

1 small beet, trimmed, peeled, and cut into 1-inch pieces

1 Bring vinegar, water, sugar, salt, garlic, allspice, and peppercorns to boil in medium saucepan over medium-high heat. Cover, remove from heat, and let steep for 10 minutes. Strain brine through fine-mesh strainer, then return to saucepan.

2 Pack turnips vertically into clean 1-quart jar with beet pieces evenly distributed throughout.

3 Return brine to brief boil. Using funnel and ladle, pour hot brine over vegetables to cover. Let jar cool completely, cover with lid, and refrigerate for at least 2 days before serving.

Perfect Pair

Quick pickles are versatile accompaniments to just about anything you can think of. Pair them with savory proteins to provide acidic counterbalance, or create a light grazing platter for one or two by pairing them with other finger foods such as Southern Cheese Straws (page 28) or roasted chickpeas (page 31). To create a simple charcuterie or cheese board, serve pickles with cured meats; dried fruit; spiced nuts (see pages 32–33); cheese, such as Marinated Manchego (page 127) or Baked Brie with Honeyed Apricots (page 140); and pâté (see pages 116–120).

bloody mary pickled asparagus spears

2½ cups cider vinegar

2½ cups water

1½ cups tomato juice

8 garlic cloves, minced

3 tablespoons lemon juice, plus two ¼-inch-thick round lemon slices (2 lemons)

2 tablespoons Worcestershire sauce

1 tablespoon kosher salt

1 tablespoon prepared horseradish

2 teaspoons celery seeds

1½ teaspoons red pepper flakes

1 teaspoon pepper

2 pounds thick asparagus, trimmed to measure 6 inches long

WHY THIS RECIPE WORKS With just a little planning ahead (the asparagus takes five days to reach pickled perfection), you can enjoy all the kick of the feisty brunch cocktail, minus the vodka, in these flavorful, crisp spears. Apple cider vinegar gives the brine a bright, slightly fruity background upon which we build layer upon layer of flavor using a handful of key Bloody Mary ingredients: tomato juice for sweetness and tomato flavor, Worcestershire sauce for depth, horseradish and garlic for earthy pungency, celery seeds for a heady aroma, black pepper for spice, and red pepper flakes for heat. Briefly cooking the asparagus spears in hot brine jump-starts the pickling process. To keep the tips of the spears submerged in brine while adding a burst of citrus fragrance, we press a slice of lemon over the asparagus tips. Avoid using thin asparagus spears for this recipe, as they turn too floppy.

1 Bring vinegar, water, tomato juice, garlic, lemon juice, Worcestershire, salt, horseradish, celery seeds, pepper flakes, and pepper to boil in Dutch oven over medium-high heat. Carefully add asparagus to vinegar mixture with tips facing same direction. Briefly return to boil, then immediately remove from heat.

2 Using tongs, carefully pack asparagus into 2 clean 1-quart jars, tips facing up. Using funnel and ladle, pour hot brine over asparagus to cover. Gently press 1 lemon slice into each jar until just submerged.

3 Let jars cool completely, cover with lids, and refrigerate for at least 5 days before serving.

Head Start

Refrigerate pickled asparagus for up to 1 month

Perfect Pair

Serve with pâté (pages 116–120) and a cheese log (pages 134–136), or with Crab Croquettes (page 272) or Gochujang and Cheddar Pinwheels (page 320).

cajun pickled okra

1½ cups white wine vinegar

1 cup water

2 tablespoons sugar

2 tablespoons kosher salt

1 teaspoon smoked paprika

1 teaspoon dried oregano

½ teaspoon cayenne pepper

6 garlic cloves, minced

14 ounces small fresh okra
    (3 inches or smaller), trimmed

Head Start

Refrigerate pickled okra for up to
3 weeks.

Perfect Pair

Serve with fried chicken, Oven-
Baked Buffalo Wings (page 61),
or Pretzel-Crusted Chicken
Fingers with Honey Mustard (page
300); or use to garnish Berbere-
Spiced Bloody Marys (page 388)
along with Bloody Mary Pickled
Asparagus Spears (page 79).

WHY THIS RECIPE WORKS Pickling okra transforms this oft-maligned vegetable into something even okra skeptics can get behind: crunchy, tangy pods without a trace of sliminess. The salt in the pickling liquid pulls moisture from the pods, creating a sticky exterior to which spices and aromatics (such as the paprika, oregano, cayenne, and garlic in this Cajun-spiced version) can cling, so every bite is full of satisfying flavor. Adding the garlic to the jars raw (rather than first steeping it in the hot brine) gives the pickles the sharp, peppery backbone needed to make them the ultimate Cajun treat. This pickle needs one week for the brine to fully penetrate the okra and for the flavors to develop; it will continue to get more crisp as it sits in the refrigerator.

1 Bring vinegar, water, sugar, salt, paprika, oregano, and cayenne to boil in medium saucepan over medium-high heat; cover and remove from heat.

2 Portion garlic into 2 clean 1-pint jars. Tightly pack okra vertically into jars, alternating them upside down and right side up for best fit.

3 Briefly return brine to boil. Using funnel and ladle, pour hot brine over vegetables to cover, leaving ½ inch headspace. Slide wooden skewer along inside of jar, pressing slightly on vegetables, to remove air bubbles, then add extra brine as needed.

4 Let jars cool completely, cover with lids, and refrigerate for at least 1 week before serving.

stuffed pickled cherry peppers

20 pickled sweet cherry peppers (14 ounces)

2 ounces provolone cheese, cut into ½-inch cubes

2 ounces thinly sliced prosciutto

2 sprigs fresh basil

2 cups extra-virgin olive oil

WHY THIS RECIPE WORKS A popular Italian deli item, pickled cherry peppers stuffed with prosciutto and provolone (sometimes known as cherry pepper shooters or poppers) are a great party (or anytime) snack—and they're even more convenient when you start with store-bought pickled peppers. Because sweet, tangy pickled cherry peppers have so much character on their own, we keep the stuffing simple, adding just cheese and prosciutto for salty, savory richness. Placing a couple sprigs of fresh basil in the jars with the peppers before covering them with olive oil subtly infuses the oil and peppers with sweet herbal notes. A brief hands-off rest allows the flavors to meld.

1 Remove stem and core of peppers with paring knife. Rinse peppers well and pat dry with paper towels.

2 Wrap cheese cubes in prosciutto and gently stuff into peppers. Divide basil between two 1-pint jars, then pack tightly with stuffed peppers. Pour oil over peppers to cover. Cover jars and refrigerate for at least 1 hour before serving.

Head Start

Refrigerate stuffed peppers, covered in oil, for up to 4 days; note that after 4 days any remaining stuffed peppers must be discarded.

Perfect Pair

Serve with Spanish Tortilla (page 148) or Crispy Lentil and Herb Salad (page 198).

green olive tapenade

2 cups pitted Castelvetrano olives, divided

5 tablespoons extra-virgin olive oil, plus extra for drizzling

2 tablespoons capers, rinsed

2 tablespoons coarsely chopped fresh parsley

3 anchovy fillets

2 garlic cloves, chopped

2 teaspoons grated lemon zest plus 2 teaspoons juice

1 teaspoon minced fresh thyme

¼ teaspoon red pepper flakes

WHY THIS RECIPE WORKS This Mediterranean spread is piquant, rich, savory, and spreadable, a popular choice for scooping up with crackers and also as an accompaniment to meat, fish, and vegetables. For an eye-catching green version, we use buttery Castelvetrano olives. For ease, we process the olives and other ingredients in a food processor rather than a traditional mortar and pestle, adding the olives in two stages to achieve an appealingly varied texture. The resulting mix is pungent, zesty, and slightly briny, with clear olive notes and discernible olive pieces. Swapping Kalamata and salt-cured black olives for the Castelvetrano olives results in an earthy, balanced black olive tapenade. If you cannot find Castelvetrano olives, you can substitute rinsed, unstuffed Manzanilla olives and omit the lemon juice.

Pulse 1¾ cups olives, oil, capers, parsley, anchovies, garlic, lemon zest and juice, thyme, and pepper flakes in food processor until olives are finely minced and mixture begins to look like chunky paste, 10 to 12 pulses, scraping down sides of bowl as needed. Add remaining ¼ cup olives and pulse until coarsely chopped, about 6 pulses. Transfer to serving bowl. Serve, drizzled with extra olive oil.

Head Start

Refrigerate tapenade, with plastic wrap pressed against surface, for up to 3 days.

Finish Line

Sprinkle tapenade with pine nuts and/or fresh thyme before serving.

Perfect Pair

Serve with Baked Brie with Honeyed Apricots (page 140), Fingerling Potato Salad (page 186), or Gambas al Ajillo (page 263).

Variation

Black Olive Tapenade
Substitute 1½ cups pitted Kalamata olives and ½ cup pitted salt-cured black olives for Castelvetrano olives, reduce oil to ¼ cup, increase capers to 3 tablespoons, reduce anchovies to 2, and reduce garlic to ½ clove. Process ⅓ cup pine nuts in food processor to mostly smooth paste, scraping bowl as needed. Add olives, oil, capers, anchovies, garlic, and 2 teaspoons Dijon mustard to processor with pine nut paste and pulse until finely chopped, about 15 pulses. Serve.

pimento cheese spread

½ cup jarred pimentos, drained and patted dry

6 tablespoons mayonnaise

2 garlic cloves, minced

1½ teaspoons Worcestershire sauce

1 teaspoon hot sauce, plus extra for seasoning

1 pound extra-sharp cheddar cheese, shredded (4 cups)

WHY THIS RECIPE WORKS Although pimento cheese spread is sacred for most Southerners (it's even known by some as the pâté of the South), this iconic snack was actually created in the North, as were fried green tomatoes (see page 215 for our recipe). The recipe emerged around the turn of the 20th century and showed off the benefits of a new invention: canning. Whatever its origins, this rosy-tinted cheese spread made with canned pimentos was quickly adopted by Southern cooks and has since become a party food fixture there. Some recipes call for a combination of extra-sharp cheddar cheese and a milder cheddar or Monterey Jack, but we prefer the bolder flavor of the spread made with all extra-sharp cheddar. Worcestershire sauce, garlic, and a few dashes of hot sauce add a kick. Don't substitute preshredded cheese here; it includes added starches (meant to prevent the shreds from sticking together) that will result in a dry spread.

Process pimentos, mayonnaise, garlic, Worcestershire, and hot sauce in food processor until smooth, about 20 seconds. Add cheddar and pulse until uniformly blended, with fine bits of cheese throughout, about 20 pulses. Season with salt, pepper, and extra hot sauce to taste, and serve.

Head Start

Refrigerate cheese spread for up to 2 weeks; let spread come to room temperature before serving.

Finish Line

Serve cheese spread in Mason jars for a fun and rustic presentation.

Perfect Pair

Serve spread with stuffed tomatoes (page 240), Fried Pickles (page 38), or Texas Caviar (page 196).

whipped feta dip

1½ teaspoons lemon juice

¼ teaspoon minced garlic

8 ounces cow's-milk
   feta cheese

3 tablespoons milk

2 tablespoons plus 2 teaspoons
   extra-virgin olive oil, divided

2 teaspoons minced
   fresh oregano

WHY THIS RECIPE WORKS You can never go wrong serving a cheesy dip with crackers and crudités—and that goes double for this salty, unbelievably light whipped feta dip. To ensure that the dip is loose enough for easy scooping, we process the feta (rinsed briefly to guard against an overly salty dip) with a few tablespoons of milk and extra-virgin olive oil. Using cow's-milk feta, rather than a true Greek feta made with sheep's or goat's milk or a combination, produces a firmer dip that holds up well at room temperature. A little garlic and lemon juice, along with fresh oregano, contribute fresh tang and savory herbal notes. Do not substitute sheep's-milk feta for the cow's-milk feta in this recipe. Avoid serving this dip with salted chips, as the feta is already quite salty.

1 Combine lemon juice and garlic in small bowl and set aside. Break feta into rough ½-inch pieces and place in medium bowl. Add water to cover, then swish briefly to rinse. Transfer to fine-mesh strainer and drain well.

2 Transfer feta to food processor. Add milk and reserved lemon juice mixture and process until feta mixture resembles ricotta cheese, about 15 seconds. With processor running, slowly drizzle in 2 tablespoons oil. Continue to process until mixture has Greek yogurt–like consistency (some small lumps will remain), 1½ to 2 minutes, stopping once to scrape down bottom and sides of bowl. Add oregano and pulse to combine. Transfer dip to bowl. Drizzle with remaining 2 teaspoons oil and serve.

Head Start

Refrigerate dip for up to 3 days; let sit at room temperature for 30 minutes before serving.

Finish Line

For attractive presentation, serve dip in wide, shallow bowl (or several smaller bowls) and finish with drizzles of olive oil and/or sprinkles of chopped nuts, sumac, or Aleppo pepper.

Perfect Pair

Serve with Fennel, Orange, and Olive Salad (page 165) or Pan-Seared Shrimp with Pistachios, Cumin, and Parsley (page 264).

Variations

Whipped Feta Dip with Dill and Parsley
Substitute 1 tablespoon minced fresh dill (or mint, if desired) and 1 tablespoon minced fresh parsley for oregano.

Whipped Feta and Roasted Red Pepper Dip
Substitute red wine vinegar for lemon juice. Reduce milk to 2 tablespoons. Add ¼ cup jarred roasted red peppers, chopped; ½ teaspoon smoked paprika; and pinch cayenne pepper with milk. Omit oregano.

homemade labneh

2 cups plain yogurt

2 tablespoons dukkah

Extra-virgin olive oil

WHY THIS RECIPE WORKS Lusciously creamy labneh can be scooped up and eaten like a dip, but this Middle Eastern ingredient, also known as yogurt cheese, can just as easily be layered with additional flavors and textures to create a snackable small plate. We like to top it with a Middle Eastern spice blend, dukkah, as the thickened yogurt's tang is a nice foil to the blend's toasty flavors. To end up with about 1 cup of yogurt cheese, we start with 2 cups of traditional yogurt, draining off the whey in a cheesecloth-lined strainer. Both regular and low-fat yogurt will work well here; do not use nonfat yogurt. Avoid yogurts containing modified food starch, gelatin, or gums, since they prevent the yogurt from draining. We prefer to use our Pistachio Dukkah or Hazelnut-Nigella Dukkah (page 20) here, but you can use store-bought dukkah too.

1 Line colander or fine-mesh strainer with triple layer of cheesecloth and place over large bowl or measuring cup. Place yogurt in colander, cover with plastic wrap (plastic should not touch yogurt), and refrigerate until 1 cup whey has drained from yogurt, at least 8 hours or up to 12 hours. (If more than 1 cup whey drains from yogurt, stir extra back into yogurt.)

2 Spread drained yogurt attractively over serving plate. Sprinkle with dukkah and drizzle with oil to taste. Serve.

Head Start

Refrigerate labneh in airtight container for up to 1 week.

Finish Line

To create more surface area for drizzling with olive oil and sprinkling with spice, serve labneh in wide, shallow bowl. For a flavor twist, try substituting sumac, Za'atar (page 21), or another finishing spice blend for dukkah.

Perfect Pair

Serve with Marinated Cauliflower and Chickpeas with Saffron (page 209) or Lamb Fatayer (page 340). Or serve as mildly sweet dessert by omitting spice blend, drizzling labneh with honey, and serving with fresh fruit.

chunky guacamole

3 ripe avocados, divided

¼ cup minced fresh cilantro

1 jalapeño chile, stemmed, seeded, and minced

2 tablespoons finely chopped red onion

2 tablespoons lime juice

2 garlic cloves, minced

¾ teaspoon table salt

½ teaspoon ground cumin

WHY THIS RECIPE WORKS Traditional Mexican guacamole is usually quite simple, often consisting of little more than roughly mashed avocados mixed with lime juice and a sprinkle of salt. Enamored with the way this simplicity highlights the dense, buttery texture and distinct flavor of the avocado, we follow suit in this chunky guacamole, lightly mashing one avocado with a few flavorful ingredients before gently mixing in additional diced avocado. Just 2 tablespoons of chopped onion and two minced garlic cloves provide a nice bite, a small amount of cumin contributes a warm background note, and cilantro and minced jalapeño give the guacamole a bright boost. Very ripe avocados are key in this recipe; a ripe avocado should yield slightly to a gentle squeeze. If in doubt of ripeness, try to remove the avocado's small stem; it should flick off easily and reveal green underneath. Use small, dark, pebbly-skinned Hass avocados here. To minimize discoloration, prepare the minced ingredients first so they are ready to mix in as soon as the avocados are cut.

Head Start

Refrigerate guacamole, with plastic wrap pressed tightly against surface, for up to 1 day.

Perfect Pair

Serve guacamole with Watermelon Salad with Cotija and Serrano Chiles (page 172), Red Lentil Kibbeh (page 177), or Spicy Chicken Flautas (page 306).

1 Halve 1 avocado, remove pit, and scoop flesh into medium bowl. Add cilantro, jalapeño, onion, lime juice, garlic, salt, and cumin and mash with potato masher (or fork) until mostly smooth.

2 Halve, pit, and dice remaining 2 avocados. Add avocado cubes to bowl with mashed avocado mixture and gently mash until mixture is well combined but still coarse. Season with salt to taste, and serve.

Variations

Feta and Arugula Guacamole
Stir in ½ cup chopped baby arugula and 1 cup crumbled feta cheese before serving.

Habanero and Mango Guacamole
Substitute 1 stemmed, seeded, and minced habanero chile for jalapeño. Stir in ½ mango, peeled and cut into ¼-inch pieces, before serving.

ultracreamy hummus

2 (15-ounce) cans chickpeas, rinsed

½ teaspoon baking soda

4 garlic cloves, peeled

⅓ cup lemon juice (2 lemons), plus extra for seasoning

1 teaspoon table salt

¼ teaspoon ground cumin, plus extra for garnish

½ cup tahini, stirred well

2 tablespoons extra-virgin olive oil, plus extra for drizzling

1 tablespoon minced fresh parsley

Head Start

Refrigerate hummus for up to 5 days; let come to room temperature before serving. If necessary, stir in 1 tablespoon warm water to loosen texture.

Perfect Pair

Top hummus with one of the toppings on pages 100–101. For a simple meze platter, serve with marinated olives (page 26), Beet-Pickled Eggs (page 132), and Roasted Carrots and Shallots with Chermoula (page 229).

WHY THIS RECIPE WORKS It's not hard to find a perfectly good hummus (or several) conveniently premade and packaged at the grocery store, so why go to the trouble of making your own? After one taste of this deluxe, velvety-smooth hummus, we think you'll understand. Cooking the chickpeas with baking soda helps their grainy skins slide right off to yield a luxuriously creamy texture that will wow guests used to the store-bought stuff. Tahini made with heavily roasted seeds can contribute bitterness, so choose a light-colored tahini (avoid versions that look like peanut butter).

1 Combine chickpeas, baking soda, and 6 cups water in medium saucepan and bring to boil over high heat. Reduce heat to maintain simmer and cook, stirring occasionally, until chickpea skins begin to float to surface and chickpeas are creamy and very soft, 20 to 25 minutes.

2 While chickpeas cook, mince garlic. Measure out 1 tablespoon garlic and set aside; discard remaining garlic. Whisk lemon juice, salt, and reserved garlic together in small bowl and let sit for 10 minutes. Strain garlic-lemon mixture through fine-mesh strainer set over bowl, pressing on solids to extract as much liquid as possible; discard solids.

3 Drain chickpeas in colander and return to saucepan. Fill pan with cold water and gently swish chickpeas with your fingers to release skins. Pour off most of water into colander to collect skins, leaving chickpeas behind in saucepan. Repeat filling, swishing, and draining 3 or 4 times until most skins have been removed (this should yield about ¾ cup skins); discard skins. Transfer chickpeas to colander to drain.

4 Set aside 2 tablespoons whole chickpeas for garnish. Process garlic-lemon mixture, ¼ cup water, cumin, and remaining chickpeas in food processor until smooth, about 1 minute, scraping down sides of bowl as needed. Add tahini and oil and process until hummus is smooth, creamy, and light, about 1 minute, scraping down sides of bowl as needed. (Hummus should have pourable consistency similar to yogurt. If too thick, loosen with water, adding 1 teaspoon at a time.) Season with salt and extra lemon juice to taste. Transfer hummus to serving bowl and sprinkle with parsley, reserved chickpeas, and extra cumin. Drizzle with extra oil and serve.

sweet potato hummus

1 pound sweet potatoes, unpeeled

¼ cup tahini

3 tablespoons extra-virgin olive oil

¾ cup water

2 tablespoons lemon juice

1 garlic clove, minced

1 teaspoon paprika

¾ teaspoon table salt

½ teaspoon ground coriander

¼ teaspoon ground cumin

¼ teaspoon chipotle chile powder

WHY THIS RECIPE WORKS While we love traditional chickpea hummus, we thought it would be fun to create a new rendition that turned hummus on its head, keeping the familiar flavorings (tahini, olive oil, garlic, and lemon juice) but switching out the legumes for bright-hued sweet potatoes. Microwaving the sweet potatoes softens them quickly and concentrates their sweetness. Just ¼ cup of tahini is enough to stand up to the spuds without overwhelming the hummus. To round out the flavor, we add paprika, coriander, and cumin. The addition of chipotle chile and a clove of garlic curbs the spuds' sweetness with gentle warmth, while some lemon juice brings the flavors into focus.

1 Prick sweet potatoes several times with fork, place on plate, and microwave until very soft, about 12 minutes, flipping potatoes halfway through microwaving. Let potatoes cool for 5 minutes. Combine tahini and oil in small bowl.

2 Slice potatoes in half lengthwise and scoop flesh from skins; discard skins. Process sweet potato, water, lemon juice, garlic, paprika, salt, coriander, cumin, and chile powder in food processor until completely smooth, about 1 minute, scraping down sides of bowl as needed. With processor running, add tahini mixture in steady stream and process until hummus is smooth and creamy, about 15 seconds, scraping down bowl as needed. Season with salt and pepper to taste.

3 Transfer hummus to bowl, cover with plastic wrap, and let stand at room temperature until flavors meld, about 30 minutes. Serve.

Head Start

Refrigerate hummus for up to 5 days; let come to room temperature before serving. If necessary, stir in 1 tablespoon warm water to loosen texture.

Finish Line

Before serving, drizzle with extra-virgin olive oil and/or sprinkle with toasted sesame seeds and chipotle chile powder.

Perfect Pair

Top hummus with one of the toppings on pages 100–101. Serve with Pinto Bean, Ancho, and Beef Salad (page 204) or pan-seared scallops (see page 294).

butter bean and pea dip with mint

1 small garlic clove, minced

¼ teaspoon grated lemon zest plus 2 tablespoons juice

1 cup frozen baby peas, thawed and patted dry, divided

1 (15-ounce) can butter beans, 2 tablespoons liquid reserved, beans rinsed

1 scallion, white and light-green parts cut into ½-inch pieces, dark green part sliced thin on bias

¼ cup fresh mint leaves

¾ teaspoon table salt

¼ teaspoon ground coriander

   Pinch cayenne pepper

¼ cup plain Greek yogurt

WHY THIS RECIPE WORKS A light bean dip that highlights the beans' earthy-sweet flavors and their smooth, creamy texture isn't a hard thing to achieve—in fact, we came up with four flavorful versions that all fit the bill for delicious scoopability. Using canned beans makes the recipe a snap to throw together. To make the dip fresh, creamy, and complex tasting, we pair the starchy beans that make up the base of each dip with a more delicate add-in such as baby peas, edamame, or corn. By incorporating a lighter vegetable element, we avoid the pastiness of some bean-only dips. To further freshen the dip, we add creamy Greek yogurt, a healthy dose of lemon juice, and fresh herbs. We prefer these dips when made with whole Greek yogurt, but 2 percent or 0 percent varieties can be substituted.

1 Combine garlic and lemon zest and juice in small bowl; set aside for at least 15 minutes. Set aside 2 tablespoons peas for garnish.

2 Pulse butter beans, reserved liquid, scallion whites and light greens, mint, salt, coriander, cayenne, lemon juice mixture, and remaining peas in food processor until fully ground, 5 to 10 pulses. Scrape down sides of bowl, then continue to process until uniform paste forms, about 1 minute, scraping down sides of bowl twice. Add yogurt and continue to process until smooth and homogeneous, about 15 seconds, scraping down bowl as needed. Transfer to serving bowl, cover, and let stand at room temperature for at least 30 minutes.

3 Season with salt to taste. Sprinkle with scallion greens and reserved peas. Serve.

Variations

Cannellini Bean and Edamame Dip with Tarragon
Increase lemon zest to ½ teaspoon. Substitute frozen edamame for peas, cannellini beans for butter beans, and tarragon for mint. Omit coriander and increase yogurt to ⅓ cup.

Pinto Bean and Corn Dip with Cilantro
Substitute lime zest and juice for lemon, frozen corn for peas, pinto beans for butter beans, and cilantro for mint. Substitute ¼ teaspoon chipotle chile powder and ¼ teaspoon ground cumin for coriander.

Pink Bean and Lima Bean Dip with Parsley
Omit lemon zest. Substitute frozen lima beans for peas, pink beans for butter beans, and parsley for mint. Substitute ¼ teaspoon garam masala for coriander and increase yogurt to ⅓ cup.

Head Start

Refrigerate dip for up to 1 day; let stand at room temperature for 30 minutes before serving.

Perfect Pair

Serve with stuffed tomatoes (page 240), Gobi Manchurian (page 234), or Kataifi-Wrapped Feta with Tomatoes and Artichokes (page 357).

savory toppings for dips

A well-made dip doesn't have to be fancy to satisfy: a light drizzle of fruity extra-virgin olive oil or a sprinkling of chopped fresh herbs or toasted nuts is all the adornment most dips require. But to really up your dip game—whether you want to bulk up your favorite dip so it can stand on its own as a light meal, to add an extra wallop of flavor and texture, or to pull out all the stops to put together a dipping spread that's sure to impress guests—consider adding a savory topping. Hearty and satisfying, these toppings add irresistible intrigue to even the simplest of dips.

baharat beef topping

Serves 8 to 10 (makes about ¾ cup)
Active Time 25 minutes
Total Time 25 minutes

This topping is best enjoyed warm immediately after it's cooked, so prepare your dip of choice ahead of time. We like to serve the topping with one of the dips on pages 95–96.

- 2 teaspoons water
- ½ teaspoon table salt
- ¼ teaspoon baking soda
- 8 ounces 85 percent lean ground beef
- 1 tablespoon extra-virgin olive oil
- ¼ cup finely chopped onion
- 2 garlic cloves, minced
- 1 teaspoon smoked hot paprika
- 1 teaspoon ground cumin
- ¼ teaspoon pepper
- ¼ teaspoon ground coriander
- ⅛ teaspoon ground cloves
- ⅛ teaspoon ground cinnamon
- ⅓ cup pine nuts, toasted, divided
- 2 teaspoons lemon juice
- 1 recipe dip
- 1 teaspoon chopped fresh parsley

1 Combine water, salt, and baking soda in large bowl. Add beef and toss to combine. Let sit for 5 minutes.

2 Heat oil in 12-inch nonstick skillet over medium heat until shimmering. Add onion and garlic and cook, stirring occasionally, until onion is softened, 3 to 4 minutes. Add paprika, cumin, pepper, coriander, cloves, and cinnamon and cook, stirring constantly, until fragrant, about 30 seconds. Add beef and cook, breaking up meat with wooden spoon, until beef is no longer pink, about 5 minutes. Add ¼ cup pine nuts and lemon juice and toss to combine.

3 Top dip with beef mixture, parsley, and remaining pine nuts. Serve.

Variation

Baharat-Spiced Plant-Based Topping
Omit water, salt, and baking soda from topping and skip step 1. In step 2, substitute plant-based ground meat for beef and cook, breaking up meat with wooden spoon, until firm crumbles form, 2 to 3 minutes.

crispy mushroom and sumac topping

Serves 8 to 10 (makes about 2 cups)
Active Time 35 minutes
Total Time 35 minutes

You can substitute halved portobello mushrooms, sliced thin, for the oyster mushrooms, but note that the mushrooms will not become as crispy. This topping is best enjoyed warm immediately after cooking, so prepare your dip of choice ahead of time. We particularly like to serve the topping with one of the dips on pages 92–96.

12	ounces oyster mushrooms, trimmed and torn into 1½-inch pieces
¼	cup water
2	tablespoons extra-virgin olive oil, divided, plus extra for drizzling
⅛	teaspoon table salt
1	lemon, quartered
1	(15-ounce) can chickpeas, rinsed
2	teaspoons sumac, plus extra for serving
1	recipe dip
¼	cup fresh parsley leaves
2	tablespoons chopped toasted pistachios

1 Cook mushrooms and water in 12-inch nonstick skillet over high heat, stirring occasionally, until mushrooms begin to stick to bottom of skillet, 6 to 8 minutes. Reduce heat to medium-high and stir in 1 tablespoon oil and salt. Cook, stirring occasionally, until mushrooms are crispy and well browned, 8 to 12 minutes. Transfer to plate.

2 Add remaining 1 tablespoon oil and lemon quarters, cut sides down, to now-empty skillet and cook over medium-high heat until well browned on cut sides, 2 to 3 minutes; transfer to plate with mushrooms. Add chickpeas to oil left in again-empty skillet and cook until lightly browned, about 2 minutes. Off heat, add sumac and toss to coat. Season with salt and pepper to taste.

3 Top dip with mushrooms, chickpeas, parsley, and pistachios. Sprinkle with extra sumac and drizzle with extra oil. Serve with seared lemon quarters.

Perfect Pair

Use these toppings to bulk up one of hummuses on pages 95–96, or to top Pinto Bean and Corn Dip with Cilantro or Pink Bean and Lima Bean Dip with Parsley (page 99) in lieu of other garnishes. These toppings also pair nicely with Skordalia (page 109).

You may also choose to serve these toppings in separate bowls alongside a variety of dips, pickles, crudités, and crackers to allow guests to mix and match as they like.

muhammara

1 cup roasted red peppers, chopped

½ cup walnuts, toasted

⅓ cup cracker crumbs

3 scallions, chopped

¼ cup extra-virgin olive oil

1½ tablespoons pomegranate molasses

4 teaspoons lemon juice

1½ teaspoons paprika

1 teaspoon ground cumin

½ teaspoon table salt

⅛ teaspoon cayenne pepper

WHY THIS RECIPE WORKS Our quick version of this traditional Middle Eastern red pepper dip is simple to make and bursting with sweet, smoky, savory flavors. We start with roasted red peppers, which give the muhammara a sweet, smoky depth and velvety texture, and from there we spice things up with paprika, cumin, and cayenne. Toasted walnuts add a creamy richness that is balanced by the tartness of the pomegranate molasses and lemon juice. Cracker crumbs absorb the peppers' extra juices, so the finished dip is pleasingly thick and scoopable. We whir everything in the food processor for ease of preparation and a smooth consistency. Any type of lean cracker may be used for the crumbs. Crush the crackers in a zipper-lock bag using a rolling pin.

Process all ingredients in food processor until uniform coarse puree forms, about 15 seconds, scraping down sides of bowl halfway through processing. Transfer to bowl and serve.

Variation

Beet Muhammara
Microwave 8 ounces trimmed, peeled, and shredded beets in covered bowl, stirring often, until tender, about 4 minutes. Transfer beets to fine-mesh strainer set over bowl and let drain for 10 minutes. Add drained beets to food processor with other ingredients.

Head Start

Refrigerate muhammara, covered with plastic wrap, for up to 3 days.

Finish Line

Sprinkle dip with minced fresh parsley before serving. Muhammara adds color to all sorts of small plates; try dolloping it on simple grilled proteins such as chicken, scallops, or tofu to instantly add visual and textural interest.

Perfect Pair

Serve with Goat Cheese Log with Hazelnut-Nigella Dukkah (page 136), Chile-Marinated Pork Belly (page 280), or Kamut with Carrots and Pomegranate (page 195).

caponata

1½ pounds eggplant, cut into ½-inch pieces

½ teaspoon table salt

¾ cup V8 juice

¼ cup red wine vinegar, plus extra for seasoning

¼ cup chopped fresh parsley

2 tablespoons packed brown sugar

3 anchovy fillets, rinsed and minced

1 large tomato, cored, seeded, and chopped

¼ cup raisins

2 tablespoons minced black olives

6–7 teaspoons extra-virgin olive oil, divided

1 celery rib, chopped fine

1 red bell pepper, stemmed, seeded, and chopped fine

1 small onion, chopped fine

¼ cup pine nuts, toasted

WHY THIS RECIPE WORKS Caponata, a sweet-and-sour eggplant relish bolstered by the bold Mediterranean flavors of anchovies, olives, raisins, and pine nuts, is good enough to eat straight out of the bowl. Eggplant tends to absorb oil like a sponge, so we start by microwaving it on a bed of coffee filters, a technique that collapses the eggplant's cells and enables it to absorb the flavors of the other ingredients. We add concentrated tomato flavor in the form of V8 juice—an unlikely twist, but one that helps us avoid incorporating the pulpy texture of canned tomatoes. Although we prefer the flavor of V8 juice, tomato juice can be substituted. If coffee filters are not available, food-safe, undyed paper towels can be substituted. Be sure to remove the eggplant from the microwave immediately after microwaving so that the steam can escape.

1 Toss eggplant with salt in bowl. Line plate with double layer of coffee filters and lightly spray with vegetable oil spray. Spread eggplant in even layer on coffee filters. Microwave until eggplant is dry and shriveled to one-third of its original size, 8 to 15 minutes (eggplant should not brown). Transfer eggplant immediately to paper towel–lined plate.

2 Whisk V8 juice, vinegar, parsley, sugar, and anchovies together in bowl. Stir in tomato, raisins, and olives.

3 Heat 1 tablespoon oil in 12-inch nonstick skillet over medium-high heat until shimmering. Add eggplant and cook, stirring occasionally, until edges are browned, 4 to 8 minutes, adding 1 teaspoon more oil if skillet appears dry; transfer to bowl.

4 Add remaining 1 tablespoon oil to now-empty skillet and heat over medium-high heat until shimmering. Add celery, bell pepper, and onion and cook, stirring occasionally, until softened and edges are spotty brown, 6 to 8 minutes.

5 Reduce heat to medium-low and stir in eggplant and V8 juice mixture. Bring to simmer and cook until liquid is thickened and coats vegetables, 4 to 7 minutes. Transfer to serving bowl and let cool completely. Season with extra vinegar to taste and sprinkle with pine nuts before serving.

Head Start

Refrigerate caponata for up to 1 week; let it come to room temperature before serving.

Finish Line

Serve caponata with bruschetta or in a small bowl as an accent to antipasti or a meze spread.

Perfect Pair

Serve caponata with Pinchos Morunos (page 310) or Shrimp Rémoulade (page 263), or use as alternative topping for Grilled Polenta (page 52).

Serves 8 (makes about 2 cups) | **Active Time** 25 minutes
Total Time 1¼ hours, plus 1 hour chilling

baba ghanoush

2 eggplants (1 pound each), pricked all over with fork

2 tablespoons tahini

2 tablespoons extra-virgin olive oil, plus extra for drizzling

4 teaspoons lemon juice

1 small garlic clove, minced

¾ teaspoon table salt

¼ teaspoon pepper

2 teaspoons chopped fresh parsley

Head Start

Refrigerate baba ghanoush, covered tightly with plastic wrap, for up to 1 day; let sit at room temperature for 20 minutes before serving.

Perfect Pair

Serve with Crispy Lentil and Herb Salad (page 198), Chickpea Cakes (page 284), or Lamb Fatayer (page 340).

WHY THIS RECIPE WORKS Baba ghanoush is an eggplant-based meze staple across Israel, Lebanon, Palestine, and beyond. We love it in the summer as a chilled or room-temperature dip, and because it can be made in advance, it's also a great addition to a summertime party lineup. For the sake of convenience we prepare the eggplant in the oven rather than roasting it over an open flame as is traditional. We prick the eggplants' skin to help moisture evaporate during cooking and then roast them whole until the flesh is very soft and tender. To avoid a watery dip, we scoop the hot pulp into a colander to allow the excess moisture to drain before processing. Lemon juice, olive oil, garlic, and tahini flavor the dip. Look for eggplants with shiny, taut, and unbruised skins and an even shape (eggplants with a bulbous shape won't cook evenly).

1 Adjust oven rack to middle position and heat oven to 500 degrees. Place eggplants on aluminum foil–lined rimmed baking sheet and roast, turning eggplants every 15 minutes, until uniformly soft when pressed with tongs, 40 minutes to 1 hour. Let eggplants cool for 5 minutes on sheet.

2 Set colander over bowl. Trim top and bottom off each eggplant and cut eggplants in half lengthwise. Using spoon, scoop hot pulp into colander (you should have about 2 cups); discard skins. Let pulp drain for 3 minutes.

3 Transfer drained eggplant to food processor. Add tahini, oil, lemon juice, garlic, salt, and pepper. Pulse mixture to coarse puree, about 8 pulses. Season with salt and pepper to taste.

4 Transfer to serving bowl, cover tightly with plastic wrap, and refrigerate until chilled, about 1 hour. Season with salt and pepper to taste, drizzle with extra oil, and sprinkle with parsley before serving.

skordalia

1 large russet potato
(12 ounces), peeled and
sliced ½ inch thick

4 garlic cloves, peeled

2 teaspoons grated lemon zest
plus ¼ cup juice (2 lemons)

⅔ cup sliced almonds

½ cup extra-virgin olive oil, plus
extra for drizzling

¾ teaspoon table salt

2 teaspoons minced fresh
chives or parsley

Head Start

Refrigerate skordalia for up to
3 days; let stand, covered, at
room temperature for 30 minutes before serving.

Perfect Pair

Serve skordalia with Horiatiki
Salata (page 182); or use it as
condiment for Skillet-Roasted
Broccoli (page 224) or Gambas
a la Plancha (page 260).

WHY THIS RECIPE WORKS Skordalia, a garlicky Greek potato- or
bread-based spread, is often served as a condiment for meat or fish, but
it can also be served as a dip, perfect for scooping up with pita or crudités. Here we add garlic, its bite tempered by a soak in acidic lemon juice,
to a base of boiled potatoes. Almonds add earthy sweetness and richness
to the gloriously creamy puree. You will need a blender for this recipe. To
make a puree with the smoothest texture, you'll also need a potato ricer
or food mill equipped with a fine disk; if these aren't available, you can
mash the potato thoroughly with a potato masher, but the dip will have a
more rustic texture. We prefer a russet potato for its earthier flavor, but
a Yukon Gold works well, too. If a single large potato is unavailable, it's
fine to use two smaller potatoes that total 12 ounces. You can use either
blanched or skin-on almonds. A rasp-style grater makes quick work of
turning the garlic into a paste.

1 Place potato in medium saucepan and add cold water to cover by
1 inch. Bring to boil over high heat. Adjust heat to maintain simmer
and cook until paring knife can be easily slipped into and out of
potato, 18 to 22 minutes.

2 While potato cooks, mince garlic to fine paste. Transfer 1 tablespoon
garlic paste to small bowl; discard remaining garlic paste. Combine
lemon juice with garlic paste and let sit for 10 minutes.

3 Process garlic mixture, lemon zest, almonds, oil, ½ cup water, and
salt in blender until very smooth, about 45 seconds.

4 Drain potato. Set ricer or food mill over medium bowl. Working in
batches, transfer hot potato to hopper and process. Stir almond mixture into potato until smooth. Season with salt and pepper to taste
and transfer to serving bowl. Drizzle with extra oil and sprinkle with
chives. Serve warm or at room temperature.

slow-cooker dips

A flavorful dip shouldn't be hard to make. These slow-cooker dips are mostly hands-off and fuss-free, and thanks to the slow cooker's steady gentle heat, you can prepare them up to a few hours ahead of time and keep them warm until they're wanted.

spinach and artichoke dip

Serves 8 to 10 (makes about 5 cups)
Active Time 10 minutes
Cooking Time 1 to 2 hours on Low

We prefer the flavor and texture of jarred whole baby artichokes, but you can substitute 18 ounces frozen artichoke hearts, thawed and patted dry, for the jarred. The dip can be held on the warm or low setting for up to 2 hours.

- 6 ounces cream cheese, softened
- ½ cup mayonnaise
- 2 tablespoons water
- 1 tablespoon lemon juice
- 3 garlic cloves, minced
- ¼ teaspoon table salt
- ¼ teaspoon pepper
- 3 cups jarred whole baby artichokes packed in water, rinsed, patted dry, and chopped
- 10 ounces frozen spinach, thawed and squeezed dry
- 2 tablespoons minced fresh chives

1 Whisk cream cheese, mayonnaise, water, lemon juice, garlic, salt, and pepper in large bowl until well combined. Gently fold in artichokes and spinach.

2A **For 1½- to 5-quart slow cooker** Transfer mixture to slow cooker, cover, and cook until heated through, 1 to 2 hours on low.

2B **For 5½- to 7-quart slow cooker** Transfer mixture to 1½-quart soufflé dish. Set dish in slow cooker and pour water into slow cooker until it reaches about one-third up sides of dish (about 2 cups water). Cover and cook until heated through, 1 to 2 hours on low. Remove dish from slow cooker, if desired.

3 Gently stir dip to recombine. Sprinkle with chives, and serve.

chile con queso

Serves 8 to 10 (makes about 4 cups)
Active Time 15 minutes
Cooking Time 1 to 2 hours on Low

You can find block American cheese at the deli counter. Preshredded cheese will work, but the dip will be much thicker. If you prefer a mild chili con queso, omit the chipotle chile. The dip can be held on the warm or low setting for up to 2 hours. It will thicken slightly over time; adjust consistency with hot water as needed, adding 2 tablespoons at a time.

1 cup chicken or vegetable broth

4 ounces cream cheese

1 tablespoon cornstarch

1 tablespoon minced canned chipotle chile in adobo sauce

1 garlic clove, minced

¼ teaspoon pepper

8 ounces Monterey Jack cheese, shredded (2 cups)

4 ounces American cheese, shredded (1 cup)

1 (10-ounce) can Ro-tel Diced Tomatoes & Green Chilies, drained

1 Microwave broth, cream cheese, cornstarch, chipotle, garlic, and pepper in large bowl, whisking occasionally, until smooth and thickened, about 5 minutes. Stir in Monterey Jack and American cheeses until well combined.

2A **For 1½- to 5-quart slow cooker** Transfer mixture to slow cooker, cover, and cook until cheese is melted, 1 to 2 hours on low.

2B **For 5½- to 7-quart slow cooker** Transfer mixture to 1½-quart soufflé dish. Set dish in slow cooker and pour water into slow cooker until it reaches about one-third up sides of dish (about 2 cups water). Cover and cook until cheese is melted, 1 to 2 hours on low. Remove dish from slow cooker, if desired.

3 Whisk dip until smooth, then stir in tomatoes. Serve.

Perfect Pair

Both of these slow-cooker dips are great for scooping up with crackers, crostini, tortilla chips, or crudités. Take advantage of these dips' hands-off cooking time to prepare more time-consuming recipes, such as Shu Mai (page 346) or Crab Croquettes (page 272), to be served alongside. Or serve rich dips with lighter accompaniments such as Peach Caprese Salad (page 169) or Shaved Zucchini Salad (page 178).

sikil p'ak

1½ cups roasted, unhulled pumpkin seeds

1 pound plum tomatoes, cored and halved

¼ cup extra-virgin olive oil, divided

1 onion, chopped

2 tablespoons lime juice

1 habanero chile, stemmed, seeded, and chopped

2 ounces queso fresco, crumbled (½ cup)

2 tablespoons chopped fresh cilantro

Head Start

Refrigerate dip for up to 1 day.

Perfect Pair

Serve with Citrus and Radicchio Salad with Dates and Smoked Almonds (page 166), Southern Corn Fritters (page 212), or Molletes (page 333).

WHY THIS RECIPE WORKS Nothing against snacking on pumpkin seeds by the handful, but the ancient Mayans knew an even better use for them: They ground the seeds with tomatoes and spicy habanero chiles to make the earthy, toasty dip known as sikil p'ak. The dip features balanced spicy, tart, and roasty flavors, perfect for passing around on game day or enjoying as a midday snack. It's traditionally made with unhulled pumpkin seeds, which are still encased in their white shells. Since unhulled pumpkin seeds are almost always sold roasted and salted, we found it crucial to rinse off the salt before using the seeds. We then toast the seeds to a rich golden hue in a hot oven before processing them in a blender to break down the tough hulls into a smooth, scoopable dip. If using unsalted pumpkin seeds, skip the rinsing and drying in step 1 and instead start with the toasting.

1 Adjust 1 oven rack to middle position and second rack 6 inches from broiler element. Heat oven to 400 degrees. Rinse pumpkin seeds under warm water and dry thoroughly. Spread seeds on rimmed baking sheet, place sheet on lower rack, and toast seeds, stirring occasionally, until golden brown, 12 to 15 minutes. Set aside to cool and heat broiler.

2 Line second rimmed baking sheet with aluminum foil. Toss tomatoes with 1 tablespoon oil and arrange cut side down on prepared sheet. Place sheet on upper rack and broil until tomatoes are spotty brown, 7 to 10 minutes. Transfer tomatoes to blender and let cool completely.

3 Add onion, lime juice, habanero, pumpkin seeds, and remaining 3 tablespoons oil to blender and process until smooth, about 1 minute, scraping down sides of jar as needed. Transfer dip to serving bowl and refrigerate until completely chilled, at least 2 hours. Season with salt and pepper to taste. Sprinkle with queso fresco and cilantro before serving.

buffalo chicken dip

1 pound cream cheese

¾ cup hot sauce

1 (2½-pound) rotisserie chicken, skin and bones discarded; meat shredded into bite-size pieces (3 cups)

1 cup ranch dressing

4 ounces blue cheese, crumbled (1 cup)

2 teaspoons Worcestershire sauce

4 ounces sharp cheddar cheese, shredded (1 cup)

2 scallions, sliced thin

Head Start

Refrigerate assembled, unbaked dip for up to 2 days; let come to room temperature before continuing with step 2.

Perfect Pair

Serve with Pigs in Blankets (page 46), Green Chile Cheeseburger Sliders (page 66), or Honeydew Salad with Peanuts and Lime (page 173).

WHY THIS RECIPE WORKS Perfect for serving a crowd on game night, this dip has all the lip-tingling, tangy flavor of great buffalo wings (like those on page 61), but with less mess. Shredding the meat from a rotisserie chicken keeps the dip quick to assemble. Cream cheese provides a smooth base for the dip, and microwaving it with hot sauce loosens it so that stirring in chunky ingredients (chicken and blue cheese) is a snap. A cup of ranch dressing, a couple teaspoons of Worcestershire sauce, and a sprinkling of cheddar cheese and scallions heighten the dip's zesty tang. If you have only a 2-quart baking dish, extend the baking time to 45 minutes. We prefer Frank's RedHot Original Cayenne Pepper Sauce here, but other hot sauces will work.

1 Adjust oven rack to middle position and heat oven to 350 degrees. Combine cream cheese and hot sauce in medium bowl and microwave until cream cheese is very soft, about 2 minutes, whisking halfway through microwaving. Whisk until smooth and no lumps of cream cheese remain. Stir in chicken, ranch dressing, blue cheese, and Worcestershire until combined (visible bits of blue cheese are OK).

2 Transfer dip to shallow 3-quart baking dish and bake for 10 minutes. Remove dish from oven, stir, and sprinkle with cheddar. Return dish to oven and continue to bake until cheddar is melted and dip is bubbling around edges, about 10 minutes. Sprinkle with scallions and serve.

Serves 8 to 10 (makes about 2 cups) | **Active Time** 30 minutes
Total Time 30 minutes, plus 6½ hours chilling and standing

chicken liver pâté

8 tablespoons unsalted butter

3 large shallots, sliced

1 tablespoon minced
  fresh thyme

¼ teaspoon table salt

1 pound chicken livers, rinsed,
  patted dry, and trimmed

¾ cup dry vermouth

2 teaspoons brandy

Head Start

Refrigerate pâté, with plastic wrap pressed flush against surface, for up to 2 days; let soften at room temperature for 30 minutes before serving.

Finish Line

For a sophisticated presentation, transfer pâté to small ramekins or one larger ramekin.

Perfect Pair

Serve as part of charcuterie or cheese plate with pickles (see pages 76–80), Prosciutto-Wrapped Figs with Gorgonzola (page 42), Baked Goat Cheese (page 139), and/or albóndigas (see pages 276–278).

WHY THIS RECIPE WORKS A good chicken liver pâté has a smooth, mellow flavor and a velvety texture that seems to melt on the tongue, but bad renditions are all too common. Our recipe circumvents all the potential pitfalls and results in a pâté that is buttery, rich, and very easy to make. Searing the livers to develop their flavor and then gently poaching them in vermouth ensures a moist pâté. A dash of brandy unifies the flavors. It is important to cook the livers until just rosy in the center in order to avoid the telltale chalky flavor that results from overcooking. Pressing plastic wrap flush against the surface of the pâté minimizes discoloration due to oxidation.

1 Melt butter in 12-inch skillet over medium-high heat. Add shallots, thyme, and salt and cook until shallots are lightly browned, about 5 minutes. Add chicken livers and cook, stirring constantly, about 1 minute. Add vermouth and simmer until livers are cooked but still have rosy interiors, 4 to 6 minutes.

2 Using slotted spoon, transfer livers and shallots to food processor, leaving liquid in skillet. Continue to simmer liquid over medium-high heat until slightly syrupy, about 2 minutes, then add to processor.

3 Add brandy to processor and process mixture until very smooth, about 2 minutes, stopping to scrape down sides of bowl as needed. Season with salt and pepper to taste, then transfer to serving bowl and smooth top. Press plastic wrap flush against surface of pâté and refrigerate until firm, at least 6 hours. Let soften at room temperature for 30 minutes before serving.

smoked trout pâté

⅓ cup sour cream

2 ounces cream cheese, softened

2 teaspoons fresh lemon juice

8 ounces smoked trout, skin removed, broken into 1-inch pieces

3 tablespoons minced fresh chives

WHY THIS RECIPE WORKS This creamy, beautiful pâté allows the flavor of smoked trout to shine. Using just enough cream cheese and sour cream to create a luscious base for 8 ounces of smoked trout allows the smoky, flaky, savory fish to take center stage. A food processor makes quick work of turning the ingredients into a smooth mixture; we pulse the ingredients until finely chopped but still retaining a bit of textural variation. Fresh chives add more flavor and color, and lemon juice contributes brightness. To soften cream cheese quickly, microwave it for 20 to 30 seconds.

Process sour cream, cream cheese, and lemon juice in food processor until smooth, about 30 seconds, scraping down sides of bowl as needed. Add trout and pulse until finely chopped and incorporated, about 6 pulses. Transfer pâté to serving bowl, fold in chives, and season with salt and pepper to taste. Serve.

Head Start

Refrigerate pâté, with plastic wrap pressed flush against surface, for up to 3 days; season pâté with additional lemon juice, salt, and pepper to taste before serving.

Finish Line

Spread pâté on sliced cucumbers or red bell pepper or serve alongside seeded crackers or bagel chips.

Perfect Pair

Serve with Blue Cheese Log with Walnuts and Honey (page 135), Fava Bean and Radish Salad (page 178), Latkes (page 236), or Blini (page 322).

easy mushroom pâté

1 ounce dried porcini mushrooms, rinsed

1 pound white mushrooms, trimmed and halved

3 tablespoons unsalted butter

2 large shallots, minced

¾ teaspoon table salt

3 garlic cloves, minced

1½ teaspoons minced fresh thyme

2 ounces cream cheese, softened

2 tablespoons heavy cream

1 tablespoon minced fresh parsley

1½ teaspoons lemon juice

Head Start

Refrigerate pâté, with plastic wrap pressed flush against surface, for up to 3 days; season with salt and pepper to taste and let soften at room temperature before serving.

Perfect Pair

Serve as part of vegetarian spread with Herb Salad (page 155) or Seared Tempeh with Tomato Jam (page 288).

WHY THIS RECIPE WORKS This vegetarian pâté is redolent with heady, earthy mushroom flavor that belies its utter ease of preparation. We supplement everyday white mushrooms with dried porcini, which are intensely flavored and widely available year-round. After rehydrating the dried porcini, we reserve some of the flavorful soaking liquid to add back to the pâté after processing it, locking in the liquid's mushroom flavor and thinning the pâté to our preferred consistency. We process the mushrooms before cooking them and leave them slightly chunky rather than aiming for a completely smooth texture. Cream cheese and a couple of tablespoons of heavy cream provide creaminess, while sautéed shallots, garlic, and thyme contribute deep flavor. Lemon juice and parsley offset the earthy flavors with some brightness. To soften cream cheese quickly, microwave it for 20 to 30 seconds.

1 Microwave 1 cup water and porcini mushrooms in covered bowl until steaming, about 1 minute. Let sit until softened, about 5 minutes. Drain porcini in fine-mesh strainer lined with coffee filter set over bowl. Reserve ⅓ cup liquid. Pulse porcini and white mushrooms in food processor until finely chopped and all pieces are pea-size or smaller, about 10 pulses, scraping down sides of bowl as needed.

2 Melt butter in 12-inch skillet over medium heat. Add shallots and salt and cook until shallots are softened, 3 to 5 minutes. Stir in garlic and thyme and cook until fragrant, 30 seconds. Stir in mushrooms and cook, stirring occasionally, until liquid released from mushrooms evaporates and mushrooms begin to brown, 10 to 12 minutes.

3 Stir in reserved porcini liquid and cook until nearly evaporated, about 1 minute. Off heat, stir in cream cheese, cream, parsley, and lemon juice, and season with salt and pepper to taste. Transfer to serving bowl and smooth top. Press plastic wrap flush to surface of pâté and refrigerate until firm, at least 2 hours. Let pâté soften at room temperature for 30 minutes before serving.

cheese and eggs

frico friabile

1 pound Montasio or aged
Asiago cheese, shredded
(4 cups)

WHY THIS RECIPE WORKS Frico friabile is a one-ingredient wonder and a delightful antipasto—especially alongside a chilled glass of wine. Nothing more than grated cheese that is melted and then browned to create a light, airy, crisp, and impressively sized wafer, this simple snack highlights the intense flavor of Montasio cheese. Some recipes cook the cheese in butter or olive oil, but using a 10-inch nonstick skillet eliminates the need for any fat. To flip the round without it tearing or stretching, we remove the pan from the heat for several seconds to cool; allowing a few moments for the cheese wafer to set up makes it easy to flip. Cooking the cheese at high heat causes it to brown too fast and become bitter, but at low heat it takes too long and dries out, so medium-high heat is best. Montasio cheese is worth tracking down; if you can't find it, substitute aged Asiago.

Sprinkle ½ cup cheese over bottom of 10-inch nonstick skillet. Cook over medium-high heat, shaking skillet occasionally to ensure even distribution of cheese over bottom of skillet, until edges are lacy and toasted, about 4 minutes. As cheese begins to melt, use spatula to tidy lacy outer edges of cheese and prevent them from burning. Remove skillet from heat and allow cheese to set, about 30 seconds. Using fork and spatula, carefully flip cheese wafer over and return skillet to medium-high heat. Cook until second side is golden brown, about 2 minutes. Slide cheese wafer out of skillet onto plate. Repeat with remaining cheese. Serve.

Head Start

Store frico in airtight container at room temperature for up to 1 day.

Finish Line

Break frico into halves or quarters before serving it.

Perfect Pair

Serve frico with marinated olives (see page 26) or Pink Pickled Turnips (page 77). Add heartier fare such as Spiralized Sweet Potatoes with Crispy Shallots, Pistachios, and Urfa (page 250). Frico is also good crouton-style, crumbled onto salads such as Shaved Zucchini Salad with Pepitas (page 155).

marinated manchego

¾ cup extra-virgin olive oil, plus extra as needed

8 garlic cloves, smashed and peeled

6 (3-inch) strips orange zest

8 sprigs fresh thyme

3 bay leaves

½ teaspoon table salt

¼ teaspoon red pepper flakes

8 ounces Manchego cheese, cut into rough ¾-inch cubes

WHY THIS RECIPE WORKS Marinating Manchego is a way to add more depth to an already flavorful cheese. It's great to serve as a small plate, and you get the added bonus of making an infused oil that can be used in a salad dressing or for sautéing vegetables. To make it, we gently heat garlic, orange zest, thyme, bay leaves, and pepper flakes in oil. The garlic softens slightly and infuses the oil with nutty-sweet flavor. Once the mixture cools, we pour it over the Manchego so the cheese can marinate in that deeply flavored oil. Use a good-quality extra-virgin olive oil here. Remove the strips of orange zest with a vegetable peeler. You can serve the marinating oil with bread for dipping.

1 Combine oil, garlic, orange zest, thyme sprigs, bay leaves, salt, and pepper flakes in small saucepan and cook over medium-low heat until garlic begins to turn golden, about 10 minutes. Set aside and let cool completely.

2 Place Manchego in 16-ounce jar with tight-fitting lid. Using tongs or fork, transfer garlic, orange zest, thyme sprigs, and bay leaves to jar with Manchego. Pour oil mixture over Manchego, pressing down cheese as needed to submerge it. If needed, add extra oil to cover cheese. Cover jar with lid and refrigerate for at least 24 hours. Let come to room temperature before serving.

Head Start

Marinate cheese for up to 1 week before serving.

Finish Line

Let cheese come to room temperature before serving to ensure that marinating oil isn't cloudy.

Perfect Pair

Serve cheese with Tomato Salad with Capers and Parsley (page 154) or Marinated Zucchini (page 292).

deviled eggs

This brunch and picnic classic makes a wonderful small bite. Perfectly cooked egg-white nests cradle a creamy filling, made with simple ingredients quickly whipped together. We start with hard-cooked eggs, then add a filling made of mashed yolks, mayonnaise, herbs, and spices. For some eggs, we also add finely chopped bacon to the filling. In others, we let smoked trout or salmon do the talking.

easy-peel hard-cooked eggs

Makes 6 eggs
Active Time 20 minutes
Total Time 35 minutes

You can use this method for fewer than six eggs without altering the timing. You can also double this recipe as long as you use a pot and steamer basket large enough to hold the eggs in a single layer. The eggs can be refrigerated in their shells in an airtight container for up to 5 days and peeled when needed.

6 large eggs

1 Bring 1 inch water to rolling boil in medium saucepan over high heat. Place eggs in steamer basket in a single layer. Transfer basket to saucepan. Cover, reduce heat to medium-low, and cook eggs for 13 minutes.

2 When eggs are almost finished cooking, combine 2 cups ice cubes and 2 cups cold water in medium bowl. Using tongs or spoon, transfer eggs to ice bath; let cool for 15 minutes.

Perfect Pair

Serve with Kamut with Carrots and Pomegranate (page 195) or Bruschetta with Arugula Pesto and Goat Cheese Topping (page 331). Add Watermelon-Lime Agua Fresca (page 385) if the weather is warm.

curried deviled eggs

Serves 10 to 12
Active Time 15 minutes
Total Time 15 minutes

- 6 hard-cooked eggs, halved, yolks separated (page 128)
- 3 tablespoons mayonnaise
- 1 tablespoon minced parsley, plus 12 small whole parsley leaves for garnishing
- 1½ teaspoons lemon juice
- 1 teaspoon Dijon mustard
- 1 teaspoon curry powder
- Pinch cayenne pepper

1 Mash yolks with fork until no large lumps remain. Add mayonnaise and use rubber spatula to smear mixture against side of bowl until thick, smooth paste forms, 1 to 2 minutes. Add minced parsley, lemon juice, mustard, curry powder, and cayenne and mix until fully incorporated.

2 Transfer yolk mixture to small, heavy-duty plastic bag. Press mixture into 1 corner and twist top of bag. Using scissors, snip ½ inch off filled corner. Squeezing bag, distribute yolk mixture evenly among egg white halves. Garnish each egg half with parsley leaf and serve.

Variation

Bacon and Chive Deviled Eggs
Cook 2 finely chopped slices bacon in 10-inch skillet over medium heat until crispy, 5 to 7 minutes. Using slotted spoon, transfer bacon to paper towel–lined plate. Reserve 1 tablespoon fat. Make filling, reducing mayonnaise to 2 tablespoons. Add reserved fat and ⅛ teaspoon salt. Substitute fresh chives for parsley and 2 teaspoons distilled white vinegar for lemon juice. Stir in three-quarters of bacon and sprinkle remaining bacon on filled eggs. Serve.

smoked trout deviled eggs

Serves 10 to 12
Active Time 15 minutes
Total Time 15 minutes

- 6 hard-cooked eggs, halved, yolks separated (page 128)
- 2½ ounces smoked trout, skin removed, divided (2 ounces chopped fine, ½ ounce flaked)
- 3 tablespoons yogurt
- 1 tablespoon capers, rinsed and chopped fine
- 1 tablespoon chopped fresh chives, divided
- 2 teaspoons mayonnaise
- 1½ teaspoons lemon juice
- ¾ teaspoon whole-grain mustard
- ¼ teaspoon ground turmeric

1 Mash yolks with fork until no large lumps remain. Stir in chopped trout, yogurt, capers, 2 teaspoons chives, mayonnaise, lemon juice, mustard, and turmeric, mashing mixture against side of bowl until well incorporated.

2 Transfer yolk mixture to small, heavy-duty plastic bag. Press mixture into one corner and twist top of bag. Using scissors, snip ½ inch off filled corner. Squeezing bag, distribute yolk mixture evenly among egg white halves, mounding filling above flat surface of whites. Top each egg with piece of flaked trout and sprinkle with remaining 1 teaspoon chives. Serve immediately.

Variation

Smoked Salmon Deviled Eggs
Substitute smoked salmon for trout and chopped fresh dill for chives.

soy-marinated eggs

1 cup soy sauce

¼ cup mirin

2 scallions, sliced thin

2 tablespoons grated fresh ginger

2 tablespoons sugar

2 garlic cloves, minced

8 large eggs

Head Start

Refrigerate eggs, removed from marinade, for up to 2 days. Leftover marinade can be reused to marinate up to three batches of eggs; it can be refrigerated for up to 1 week or frozen for up to 1 month.

Perfect Pair

To serve more people, cut eggs in half. Serve with Loaded Sweet Potato Wedges with Tempeh (page 249), bruschetta (see pages 330–331), or Sung Choy Bao (page 296).

WHY THIS RECIPE WORKS These soft-cooked and marinated eggs make a delicious small bite, snack, or even a tasty addition to a lunchbox. For perfectly seasoned eggs full of complex, savory flavor, we marinate them for 3 to 4 hours in a mix of soy sauce, mirin, garlic, ginger, and scallions. A bit of sugar helps balance the salty soy sauce, and adding water to the potent marinade ensures that the eggs don't end up too salty.

1 Combine soy sauce, mirin, scallions, ginger, sugar, and garlic in small saucepan and bring to simmer over medium-high heat. Remove from heat and stir in 1 cup cold water; set aside.

2 Bring 3 quarts water to boil in large saucepan over high heat. Fill large bowl halfway with ice and water.

3 Using spider skimmer or slotted spoon, gently lower eggs into boiling water and cook for 7 minutes. Transfer eggs to ice bath and let cool for 5 minutes.

4 Gently tap eggs on counter to crack shells. Begin peeling off shell at wider end of egg, making sure to break membrane between shell and egg white. Working under gently running water, carefully peel membranes and shells off eggs.

5 Combine soy sauce mixture and eggs in large zipper-lock bag and place bag in medium bowl. Press out as much air as possible from bag so eggs are fully submerged in marinade, then seal bag. Refrigerate for at least 3 hours or up to 4 hours (any longer and eggs may become too salty). Remove eggs from marinade using slotted spoon. Serve.

beet-pickled eggs

2 cups distilled white vinegar

1⅓ cups sugar

1 cup water

½ onion, halved and sliced thin

3¾ teaspoons kosher salt

8 whole cloves

12 large eggs

1 beet, peeled and cut into 1-inch pieces

WHY THIS RECIPE WORKS Eyecatching and make-ahead, these eggs are perfect for an Easter small plates brunch or any time you want color on your table. Seasoned with cloves and onion, these fuchsia colored eggs are also packed with flavor. We gently shake hard-cooked eggs back and forth in their pan to crack the shells. Then we shock the lightly cracked eggs in ice water, which seeps underneath the shells and makes them easier to peel. To stain our pickled eggs vibrant purple, we pack them with pieces of beet, which leach their color into the brine. Let the brine cool completely before adding the eggs. The egg white's membrane toughens when pickled, so be sure to peel this off completely before pickling. To help eggs stay fully submerged, place a bag of brine on top of a round of parchment paper to weigh them down.

Head Start

Make these eggs at least 3 days before serving. Refrigerate pickled eggs for up to 4 days longer, but note that they must be discarded 7 days after being made.

Finish Line

Cut pickled eggs into halves or quarters to yield daintier portions.

Perfect Pair

Serve eggs with Herb Salad (page 155), Moroccan-Style Carrot Salad with Harissa and Feta (page 159), or Apple-Fennel Rémoulade (page 162).

1 Bring vinegar, sugar, water, onion, salt, and cloves to boil in small saucepan over medium-high heat; remove from heat.

2 Cut out parchment paper round to match diameter of ½-gallon wide-mouth jar. Measure out 1 cup brine (without onions); set aside. Using funnel and ladle, pour remaining brine with onions into jar; let cool for 1 hour.

3 Meanwhile, place eggs in large saucepan, cover with 1 inch water, and bring to boil. Remove pan from heat, cover, and let stand 10 minutes. Fill large bowl with ice water. Pour off hot water from saucepan and gently shake pan back and forth to crack shells. Transfer eggs to ice water with slotted spoon, let cool for 5 minutes, then peel.

4 Gently add peeled eggs and beets to jar, distributing beet pieces evenly throughout jar. Press parchment round flush against surface of brine.

5 Fill 1-quart zipper-lock bag with 1 cup reserved brine, squeeze out air, and seal well. Place bag of brine on top of parchment and gently press down to submerge eggs. Cover jar with lid and refrigerate for 3 days before serving.

cheddar cheese log with chives

6 ounces extra-sharp yellow cheddar cheese, shredded (1½ cups)

6 ounces cream cheese

¼ cup mayonnaise

1 tablespoon prepared horseradish, drained

2 teaspoons Worcestershire sauce

1 small garlic clove, minced

½ teaspoon pepper

½ cup minced fresh chives

WHY THIS RECIPE WORKS Buying cheese to serve is the quick and easy way to go. But if you have time to spare, make this impressive but deliciously easy and flavorful, shareable bite ahead of time. For a cheese log that is firm enough to hold its shape but soft enough to easily drag a cracker through at room temperature, we use a simple mixture of half cheddar cheese and half cream cheese and some creamy mayonnaise. To flavor our cheddar-based log, we stir in a bit of horseradish, some Worcestershire sauce, and minced garlic. Our cheese mixture can be easily shaped in plastic wrap, and after a trip to the freezer it firms up enough to be easily rolled in minced chives. Then the cheese log can be wrapped tightly in plastic wrap and refrigerated for up to two days. For flavor variations, we use ingredients as far-ranging as tortilla chips and bacon. Buy refrigerated prepared horseradish, not the shelf-stable kind, which contains preservatives and additives.

1 Process cheddar, cream cheese, mayonnaise, horseradish, Worcestershire, garlic, and pepper in food processor until smooth, about 1 minute, scraping down sides of bowl as needed.

2 Lay 18 by 11-inch sheet of plastic wrap on counter with long side parallel to counter edge. Transfer cheese mixture to center of plastic and shape into approximate 9-inch log with long side parallel to counter edge. Fold plastic over log and roll up. Pinch plastic at ends of log and roll log on counter to form tight cylinder. Tuck ends of plastic underneath. Freeze until completely firm, 1½ to 2 hours.

3 Spread chives on large plate. Unwrap cheese log and roll in chives to evenly coat. Transfer to serving dish and let come to room temperature, about 1 hour. Serve.

Variations

Pimento Cheese Log with Bacon
Omit horseradish. Add 1 minced small shallot and ¼ teaspoon cayenne pepper to food processor with cheese. After processing, add ½ cup jarred chopped pimentos, patted dry, and pulse to combine, about 3 pulses. Substitute 8 slices finely chopped cooked bacon for chives.

Chile Cheese Log with Tortilla Chips

Substitute Monterey Jack cheese for cheddar, 2 tablespoons minced canned chipotle chile in adobo sauce for horseradish, and lime juice for Worcestershire sauce. After processing, add ⅓ cup drained canned chopped green chiles and pulse to combine, about 3 pulses. Substitute crushed blue corn tortilla chips for chives.

Blue Cheese Log with Walnuts and Honey

Omit mayonnaise, horseradish, Worcestershire, and garlic. Substitute 1½ cups soft, mild blue cheese for cheddar. Increase pepper to 1 teaspoon. Substitute a mixture of ¼ cup walnuts, toasted and chopped fine, and ¼ cup chopped pitted dates for chives. Drizzle cheese log with 2 tablespoons honey before serving.

Head Start

Refrigerate uncoated cheese log, wrapped tightly in plastic wrap, for up to 2 days.

Finish Line

Bring coated log to room temperature before serving on a wooden cheese board with slices of baguette or mild crackers.

Perfect Pair

Quick pickles (see pages 76–77) make a tangy accompaniment. Gobi Manchurian (page 234) or Southern Corn Fritters (page 212) are more filling pairings.

goat cheese log with hazelnut-nigella dukkah

Cheese

- 6 ounces goat cheese
- 6 ounces cream cheese
- 1 small garlic clove, minced
- ½ teaspoon pepper

Dukkah

- 1 teaspoon fennel seeds, toasted
- 1 teaspoon coriander seeds, toasted
- 1½ tablespoons raw sunflower seeds, toasted
- 1 tablespoon sesame seeds, toasted
- 1½ teaspoons nigella seeds
- 3 tablespoons hazelnuts, toasted, skinned, and chopped fine
- 1½ teaspoons paprika
- ½ teaspoon flake sea salt
- 2 tablespoons extra-virgin olive oil

WHY THIS RECIPE WORKS Sprinkling a spice, herb, and seed blend on a dish adds bright flavor and appealing crunch. Here we use dukkah to flavor our goat cheese, making an easy snack to pull out when unexpected guests stop by. Made with nuts and spices such as anise-like fennel seeds, coconutty coriander seeds, and crunchy-oniony nigella seeds, the condiment adds oomph to our goat cheese log. Spread on crackers, it brings a burst of complex tastes to your guests' palates.

1 **For the cheese** Process all ingredients in food processor until smooth, about 1 minute, scraping down sides of bowl as needed.

2 Place 18 by 11-inch sheet of plastic wrap on counter with long side parallel to counter edge. Transfer cheese mixture to center of plastic and shape into log with long side parallel to counter edge (log should be about 9 inches long). Fold plastic over log and roll up. Pinch plastic at ends of log and roll on counter to form tight cylinder. Tuck ends of plastic underneath log and freeze until completely firm, 1½ to 2 hours.

3 **For the dukkah** Grind fennel seeds and coriander seeds in spice grinder until finely ground, about 30 seconds. Add sunflower seeds, sesame seeds, and nigella seeds and pulse until coarsely ground, about 4 pulses; transfer to small bowl. Stir in hazelnuts, paprika, and salt.

4 Unwrap cheese log and let sit until outside is slightly tacky to touch, about 10 minutes. Spread dukkah into even layer on large plate and roll cheese log in dukkah to evenly coat, pressing gently to adhere. Transfer to serving platter and let sit at room temperature until softened, about 1 hour. Drizzle with oil and serve.

Head Start

Freeze uncoated cheese log for up to 1 week. Refrigerate coated cheese log, wrapped tightly in plastic wrap, for up to 2 days. Refrigerate dukkah in airtight container for up to 3 months.

Finish Line

To vary log's flavor, try mixing finely chopped dates or dried figs into cheese mixture before rolling into log, or substituting Pistachio Dukkah (page 20) for hazelnut-nigella dukkah.

Perfect Pair

Serve, accompanied by Roasted Carrots and Shallots with Chermoula (page 229) or Pressure-Cooker Winter Squash with Halloumi and Brussels Sprouts (page 252).

baked goat cheese

3 tablespoons extra-virgin olive oil, plus extra for drizzling

1 onion, chopped fine

¾ teaspoon table salt

3 garlic cloves, sliced thin

2 teaspoons smoked paprika

1 teaspoon ground cumin

¼ teaspoon red pepper flakes

¼ teaspoon pepper

1 (28-ounce) can crushed tomatoes

1 (8- to 10-ounce) log goat cheese, softened

2 tablespoons coarsely chopped fresh cilantro

1 teaspoon grated lemon zest

WHY THIS RECIPE WORKS There is one thing you can count on at holiday cocktail parties: small plates featuring melted cheese. Put out a dish of cheesy buffalo dip, a bowl of queso fundido, or a wheel of baked Brie, and your guests will cluster around it, spooning soft, warm morsels onto chips or bread, tucking spiderweb strands of cheese into their mouths, smiling and nodding in appreciation as they go. This warm goat cheese broiled in a baking dish with a mildly spicy tomato sauce combines tangy cheese with a smoky, sweet sauce. Goat cheese logs come in different sizes. Any size from 8 to 10 ounces will work in this recipe. If you can find only small logs of goat cheese (around 4 ounces), you can press two smaller logs together.

1 Heat oil in medium saucepan over medium heat until shimmering. Add onion and salt and cook, stirring occasionally, until golden brown, about 10 minutes. Add garlic, paprika, cumin, pepper flakes, and pepper and cook until fragrant, about 1 minute. Add tomatoes and bring to boil. Reduce heat to medium-low and simmer for 15 minutes. Season with salt to taste.

2 Adjust oven rack 6 inches from broiler element and heat broiler. Place goat cheese between 2 sheets of plastic wrap. Flatten goat cheese into 1-inch-thick disk, 3 to 4 inches in diameter, cupping your hands around outside of disk as needed to make compact shape.

3 Transfer tomato sauce to shallow 2-quart broiler-safe dish. Place goat cheese in center. Broil until goat cheese is well browned, about 10 minutes. Sprinkle cilantro and lemon zest over sauce and drizzle with extra oil. Serve.

Head Start

Refrigerate sauce in airtight container for up to 3 days, and goat cheese disk, wrapped tightly in plastic wrap, for up to 1 day. To finish dish, increase broiling time to 12 to 15 minutes.

Perfect Pair

Serve alongside Watermelon Salad (page 172) or Cóctel de Camarón (page 266).

baked brie with honeyed apricots

¼ cup chopped dried apricots

¼ cup honey, divided

1 teaspoon minced fresh rosemary

¼ teaspoon table salt

¼ teaspoon pepper

2 (8-ounce) wheels firm Brie cheese, rind removed, cheese cut into 1-inch pieces

1 tablespoon minced fresh chives

Perfect Pair

Tomato Salad (page 154) or Skillet-Roasted Broccoli with Smoky Sunflower Seed Topping (page 225) make excellent fresh counterpoints.

WHY THIS RECIPE WORKS When Brie is warmed, it becomes rich and gooey, and pairing it with sweet fruit or jam brings out its savory notes. For sweet and creamy flavor in this small bite, we reengineer the traditional whole wheel of baked Brie by trimming off the rind (which doesn't melt that well) and cutting the cheese into cubes. This allows our honey-apricot mixture to be evenly distributed throughout this deconstructed version of the dish, not just spooned on top. We bake the cheese in a cast-iron skillet; since cast iron holds on to heat so well, it keeps the cheese in the ideal luscious, fluid state for serving, too. An extra drizzle of honey and some minced chives at the finish reinforce the sweet-savory flavor profile. Be sure to use a firm, fairly unripe Brie for this recipe.

1 Adjust oven rack to middle position and heat oven to 400 degrees. Microwave apricots, 2 tablespoons honey, rosemary, salt, and pepper in medium bowl until apricots are softened and mixture is fragrant, about 1 minute, stirring halfway through microwaving. Add Brie and toss to combine.

2 Transfer mixture to 10-inch cast-iron skillet and bake until cheese is melted, 10 to 15 minutes. Drizzle with remaining 2 tablespoons honey and sprinkle with chives. Serve immediately.

saganaki

2 tablespoons cornmeal

1 tablespoon all-purpose flour

1 (8-ounce) block halloumi cheese, sliced into ½-inch-thick slabs

2 tablespoons extra-virgin olive oil

Lemon wedges

Finish Line

Saganaki is wonderful drizzled with honey.

Perfect Pair

Serve with Brown Rice Salad with Fennel, Mushrooms, and Walnuts (page 190), roasted chickpeas (see page 31), or Pan-Seared Shrimp with Pistachios, Cumin, and Parsley (page 264).

WHY THIS RECIPE WORKS Named for the small frying pan traditionally used to prepare this dish, Greek saganaki is made by pan-searing slabs of firm cheese until they develop a crisp, golden brown exterior and a satisfyingly warm, chewy interior; a wonderful dish to make after your guests have arrived. The cheese of choice is often halloumi, a brined cheese originally from Cyprus but now popular throughout the eastern Mediterranean. Made from cow's, sheep's, or goat's milk (or a combination), halloumi has an elastic quality similar to that of mozzarella, but it's firmer. It has a mild though usually quite salty flavor, and you'll often find it packed in brine and sold in blocks. Because of how it's made, halloumi has a very strong protein network—which means that when it's heated, it softens but doesn't melt. To achieve the classic crisp, golden exterior, dust the halloumi with a mixture of flour and cornmeal before pan-frying. A squeeze of lemon juice offers a bright, tangy finish.

1 Combine cornmeal and flour in shallow dish. Working with one piece of cheese at a time, coat both wide sides with cornmeal mixture, pressing to help coating adhere; transfer to plate.

2 Heat oil in 12-inch nonstick skillet over medium heat until shimmering. Arrange halloumi in single layer in skillet and cook until golden brown on both sides, 2 to 4 minutes per side. Transfer to platter and serve with lemon wedges.

Variation

Saganaki with Garlic-Parsley Sauce
After frying halloumi, discard oil left in skillet and wipe out skillet with paper towels. Add 2 tablespoons extra-virgin olive oil to now-empty skillet and heat over medium heat until shimmering. Add 1 thinly sliced garlic clove, 2 tablespoons chopped fresh parsley, and ¼ teaspoon red pepper flakes and cook until garlic is golden brown and fragrant, about 1 minute. Drizzle sauce over pan-fried halloumi and serve with lemon wedges.

egg roulade with spinach and gruyére

12 large eggs

 1 garlic clove, minced to paste

¼ teaspoon table salt

⅛ teaspoon pepper

¼ cup half-and-half

 2 tablespoons all-purpose flour

 8 ounces frozen chopped spinach, thawed and squeezed dry

 4 ounces Gruyére cheese, shredded (1 cup)

Finish Line

Cut roulade into even slices and present on large serving platter, sprinkled with chopped parsley or chives.

Perfect Pair

Serve with Red Pepper Mayonnaise (page 17) and Cajun Pickled Okra (page 80), Fresh Fig Salad (page 174), or Baguette with Radishes, Butter, and Herbs (page 327).

WHY THIS RECIPE WORKS An egg roulade or rolled soufflé omelet is light and airy and can feed many people at once, making it an ideal—and easy—egg dish for Sunday brunch. Roll the cooked roulade into a spiral on a baking sheet with the aid of parchment paper to prevent tearing. (Following the instructions for lining the baking sheet with overhanging parchment paper is crucial to the success of this dish.) To remove excess water from the thawed spinach before adding it to the eggs, wrap it in a clean dish towel or cheesecloth and squeeze firmly.

1 Adjust oven rack to middle position and heat oven to 375 degrees. Grease rimmed baking sheet with vegetable oil spray, then line with overhanging sheet of parchment paper and grease parchment with vegetable oil spray.

2 Whisk eggs, garlic, salt, and pepper together in large bowl. In separate bowl, whisk half-and-half and flour together, then slowly whisk into egg mixture until uniform. Carefully pour egg mixture into prepared baking sheet and sprinkle spinach over top. Bake until eggs are just set, about 9 minutes, rotating baking sheet halfway through baking.

3 Remove pan from oven and immediately sprinkle Gruyére over top. Using parchment paper, roll egg over itself into tight cylinder. Use parchment paper to transfer roulade to cutting board. Slice and serve.

breakfast buttercups

10 medium eggs

10 slices hearty white sandwich bread, crusts removed

4 tablespoons unsalted butter, melted

10 thin slices deli Swiss or cheddar cheese (about 5 ounces)

5 thin slices deli Black Forest ham (about 5 ounces), halved crosswise

Finish Line

If you like, garnish each buttercup with freshly cracked black pepper and/or minced chives.

Perfect Pair

Serve with Tomato and Burrata Salad with Pangrattato and Basil (page 170), Pressure-Cooker Braised Radishes and Snap Peas (page 223), or Baked Brie with Honeyed Apricots (page 140).

WHY THIS RECIPE WORKS Breakfast buttercups give you eggs, meat, and toast for 10 people in one fell swoop, and you can make them any time of day. The dish is made by rolling bread thin and pressing it into muffin tins or ramekins, lining each muffin cup with ham and cheese, cracking eggs into the centers, and baking until eggs are just set and the toast cups are golden. While most of our recipes call for large eggs, medium eggs are needed here in order to fit in the muffin tins.

1 Adjust oven rack to upper-middle position and heat oven to 375 degrees. Place eggs in large bowl and cover with hot tap water. Let sit 10 minutes.

2 Meanwhile, roll bread as thin as possible with rolling pin and press into 10 perimeter cups of 12-cup muffin tin, leaving 2 center cups empty. Brush bread cups with melted butter and bake until light golden brown, 5 to 7 minutes.

3 Top each cheese slice with ham slice. Make cut from center to 1 side of each stack. Fold each ham and cheese stack into a cone and press into toasted bread cup. Crack 1 egg into each cup and season with salt and pepper.

4 Return muffin tin to oven and bake until egg whites are barely set and still appear slightly moist, 14 to 18 minutes. Transfer pan to wire rack and cover tightly with aluminum foil. Let sit 5 minutes. Serve immediately.

spanish tortilla

6 tablespoons plus 1 teaspoon extra-virgin olive oil, divided

1½ pounds Yukon Gold potatoes, peeled, quartered, and cut into ⅛-inch-thick slices

1 small onion, halved and sliced thin

1 teaspoon table salt, divided

¼ teaspoon pepper

8 large eggs

½ cup jarred roasted red peppers, rinsed, patted dry, and cut into ½-inch pieces

½ cup frozen peas, thawed

1 recipe Aioli (page 16)

WHY THIS RECIPE WORKS Boasting meltingly tender potatoes in a dense, creamy omelet, a Spanish tortilla is an immensely appealing tapas bar favorite. It's also very easy to make at home. Garlic is often included in the omelet, but we like the idea of topping the tortilla with a garlicky aïoli instead, the creaminess of which beautifully complements the potatoes and eggs. We up the flavor ante of the tortilla even further by adding green peas and roasted red peppers. To flip the tortilla, we slide it onto a plate, put another plate on top before inverting it, and then slide the flipped tortilla back into the skillet—a potentially messy task made foolproof. Letting the tortilla cool on a clean dish towel ensures that it doesn't turn soggy and fall apart. You will need a 10-inch nonstick skillet with a tight-fitting lid for this recipe.

1 Toss ¼ cup oil, potatoes, onion, ½ teaspoon salt, and pepper together in large bowl. Heat 2 tablespoons oil in 10-inch nonstick skillet over medium-high heat until shimmering. Add potato mixture to skillet and reduce heat to medium-low. Cover and cook, stirring every 5 minutes, until potatoes are tender, about 25 minutes.

2 Whisk eggs and remaining ½ teaspoon salt together in now-empty bowl, then gently fold in cooked potato mixture, red peppers, and peas. Make sure to scrape all of potato mixture out of skillet.

3 Heat remaining 1 teaspoon oil in now-empty skillet over medium-high heat until just smoking. Add potato-egg mixture and cook, shaking skillet and folding mixture constantly for 15 seconds. Smooth top of mixture, reduce heat to medium, cover, and cook, gently shaking skillet every 30 seconds, until bottom is golden brown and top is lightly set, about 2 minutes.

4 Off heat, run heat-resistant rubber spatula around edge of skillet and shake skillet gently to loosen tortilla; it should slide around freely in skillet. Slide tortilla onto large plate, then invert onto second large plate and slide back into skillet, browned side up. Tuck edges of tortilla into skillet with rubber spatula. Continue to cook over medium heat, gently shaking skillet every 30 seconds, until second side is golden brown, about 2 minutes. Slide tortilla onto clean dish towel and let cool slightly. Serve warm or at room temperature with aioli.

Head Start

Refrigerate tortilla, wrapped tightly in plastic wrap, for up to 1 day.

Finish Line

To serve a larger number of guests or transform this heartier bite into a little bite, cut tortilla into small squares; otherwise, stick with traditional wedges.

Perfect Pair

Add Black Olive Tapenade (page 84), Prosciutto-Wrapped Figs with Gorgonzola (page 42), or Cantaloupe Salad with Olives and Red Onion (page 172) to your spread.

quesadillas for a crowd

3 tablespoons vegetable oil

8 ounces provolone cheese, shredded (2 cups)

8 ounces whole-milk mozzarella cheese, shredded (2 cups)

¼ cup minced jarred jalapeño chiles

4 (10-inch) flour tortillas

WHY THIS RECIPE WORKS Quesadillas are a great cheesy snack, given heft by tortillas. To make enough of these treats to feed a large group of people at a single go, we like to bake them instead of cooking them in a skillet. To prevent the cheese from liquefying and running onto the baking sheet, we add it only after the first side of each tortilla has been browned. This arrangement on the baking sheet isn't random. It's the best way to fit four large quesadillas at once. For these grownup quesadillas, we add jalapeños for a hint of heat that also cuts the cheese's richness. Letting the quesadillas cool before cutting them is important; straight from the oven the cheese is molten and will ooze out.

Finish Line

Serve quesadillas with sour cream and garnish with chopped cilantro.

Perfect Pair

Add pineapple salsa (see page 14), Habanero and Mango Guacamole (page 92), or Esquites (page 177) for a flavorful, Mexican-inspired spread.

1 Adjust oven rack to middle position and heat oven to 450 degrees. Brush rimmed baking sheet with oil.

2 Combine provolone, mozzarella, and jalapeños in bowl. Fold tortillas in half. Arrange folded tortillas in single layer on prepared sheet with rounded edges facing center of sheet.

3 Bake until tortilla tops and edges begin to turn spotty brown, 5 to 7 minutes. Remove sheet from oven. Flip tortillas over. Using tongs, open each tortilla and fill each with equal amount cheese mixture (about 1 cup each), leaving 1-inch border. Close tortillas and press firmly with spatula to compact.

4 Return quesadillas to oven and continue to bake until crisp around edges and golden brown on second side, 4 to 6 minutes longer. Remove from oven and press quesadillas gently with spatula to deflate any air bubbles. Transfer to wire rack and let cool for 5 minutes. Slice each quesadilla into 8 wedges and serve.

salads for sharing

simple layerable salads

Almost anything can be a small plate, but a pop of color and contrasting texture is what sets a truly memorable plate apart. That's where these quick and easy salads come in. Layer any of them beneath a basic protein, and you instantly have a composed small plate that's much greater than the sum of its parts.

tomato salad

Serves 6
Active Time 10 minutes
Total Time 10 minutes

The success of this summery salad depends on using ripe, in-season tomatoes.

1½ pounds mixed ripe tomatoes, cored and sliced ¼ inch thick

3 tablespoons extra-virgin olive oil

1 tablespoon minced shallot

1 teaspoon lemon juice

½ teaspoon table salt

¼ teaspoon pepper

2 tablespoons pine nuts, toasted

1 tablespoon torn fresh basil leaves or chopped fresh chives

Arrange tomatoes on large platter. Whisk oil, shallot, lemon juice, salt, and pepper together in small bowl. Spoon dressing over tomatoes. Sprinkle with pine nuts and basil. Serve immediately.

Variations

Tomato Salad with Capers and Parsley

Omit pine nuts. Add 1 tablespoon rinsed capers, 1 rinsed and minced anchovy fillet, and ⅛ teaspoon red pepper flakes to dressing. Substitute chopped fresh parsley for basil.

Tomato Salad with Pecorino Romano and Oregano

Add ½ teaspoon grated lemon zest and ⅛ teaspoon red pepper flakes to dressing. Substitute 1 ounce shaved Pecorino Romano or Parmesan cheese for pine nuts and 2 teaspoons chopped fresh oregano for basil.

shaved zucchini salad with pepitas

Serves 6
Active Time 15 minutes
Total Time 15 minutes

Using in-season zucchini and good olive oil is crucial here. Look for small zucchini, which are younger and have thinner skins. Be ready to serve this dish quickly after it is assembled.

1½ pounds zucchini or summer squash

2 tablespoons extra-virgin olive oil

½ teaspoon grated lime zest plus
   1 tablespoon juice

1 garlic clove, minced

¾ teaspoon table salt

¼ teaspoon pepper

½ cup chopped fresh cilantro or parsley

2 ounces queso fresco or feta cheese,
   crumbled (½ cup)

¼ cup pepitas or sunflower seeds, toasted

Using vegetable peeler, shave zucchini lengthwise into very thin ribbons. Whisk oil, lime zest and juice, garlic, salt, and pepper together in large bowl. Add zucchini, cilantro, and queso fresco and toss to combine. Season with salt and pepper to taste. Sprinkle with pepitas and serve immediately.

herb salad

Serves 6
Active Time 10 minutes
Total Time 10 minutes

Delicate herbs such as basil, parsley, cilantro, dill, mint, chives, and tarragon are delicious raw, and we suggest any combination for this salad. Wash and dry the herbs thoroughly; excess liquid can wilt the leaves and dilute the dressing. To introduce more dynamic color, texture, and bulk, add up to ½ cup of thinly sliced vegetables, such as radishes, shallots, fennel, or celery.

3 tablespoons extra-virgin olive oil

¼ teaspoon grated lemon zest plus
   1 tablespoon juice

¼ teaspoon kosher salt

2 cups fresh parsley leaves

2 cups mixed tender herb leaves

Add oil, lemon zest and juice, and salt to large bowl. Season with pepper to taste, and whisk to thoroughly combine. Add parsley and herb leaves and toss until evenly coated with dressing. Season with salt to taste. Serve immediately.

Perfect Pair

We especially enjoy these salads when layered beneath a simple protein. Try them with grilled meat such as Chicken Satay (page 308), or with chilled seafood such as Shrimp Rémoulade (page 267). They're also great with Chinese Barbecue Spare Ribs (page 314). For a vegetarian option, try topping them with saganaki (see page 143) or sprinkling with crumbled Frico Friabile (page 124).

pai huang gua

2 English cucumbers

1½ teaspoons kosher salt

4 teaspoons Chinese black vinegar

1 teaspoon garlic, minced to paste

1 tablespoon soy sauce

2 teaspoons toasted sesame oil

1 teaspoon sugar

1 teaspoon sesame seeds, toasted

Perfect Pair

Serve with Sichuan Chili Oil (page 19), Tempeh with Sambal Sauce (page 291), or Fritto Misto di Mare (page 275). Or try serving these cucumbers on a cheese board instead of cornichons.

WHY THIS RECIPE WORKS In the Chinese province of Sichuan, pai huang gua (smashed cucumbers) is traditionally served as a cooling counterpoint to rich, spicy dishes. Easy to portion and lacking delicate greens that would quickly wilt if left to sit for any length of time, the salad is also a great candidate for a small plate. A brief salting encourages the smashed cucumbers to quickly release the extra liquid that might otherwise dilute their flavor, and the craggy edges readily hold on to the pungent dressing of black vinegar, soy sauce, and toasted sesame oil. We recommend using Chinese Chinkiang (or Zhenjiang) black vinegar for this dish. If you can't find it, you can substitute 2 teaspoons of unseasoned rice vinegar and 1 teaspoon of balsamic vinegar. A rasp-style grater makes quick work of turning the garlic into a paste.

1 Trim and discard ends from cucumbers. Cut cucumbers crosswise into 3 equal lengths. Place pieces in large zipper-lock bag and seal bag. Using small skillet or rolling pin, firmly but gently smash cucumber pieces until flattened and split lengthwise into 3 to 4 spears each. Tear spears into rough 1- to 1½-inch pieces and transfer to colander set in large bowl. Toss cucumber pieces with salt and let drain for at least 15 minutes or up to 30 minutes.

2 While cucumbers sit, whisk vinegar and garlic together in small bowl; let sit for at least 5 minutes or up to 15 minutes.

3 Whisk soy sauce, oil, and sugar into vinegar mixture until sugar has dissolved. Transfer cucumbers to medium bowl, discarding any extracted liquid. Add dressing and sesame seeds to cucumbers and toss to combine. Serve immediately.

moroccan-style carrot salad

2 oranges

1 tablespoon lemon juice

1 teaspoon honey

¾ teaspoon ground cumin

½ teaspoon table salt

⅛ teaspoon cayenne pepper

⅛ teaspoon ground cinnamon

1 pound carrots, peeled and shredded

3 tablespoons minced fresh cilantro

3 tablespoons extra-virgin olive oil

Head Start

Refrigerate salad for up to 1 day. Let come to room temperature, drain, and stir in cilantro and oil just before serving.

Perfect Pair

Serve with Oven-Baked Buffalo Wings (page 61), Beet-Pickled Eggs (page 132), Breakfast Buttercups (page 147), or Lop Cheung Bao (page 352).

WHY THIS RECIPE WORKS Colorful carrots serve as the foundation of this easy salad, made even easier thanks to the fact that it can be made up to a day ahead of time without losing its vibrancy. Inspired by the flavors of Morocco, we combine grated carrots with fruity olive oil, floral honey, and warmly fragrant cumin, cinnamon, and cayenne pepper. To complement the earthy-sweet carrots, we add juicy orange segments, reserving some of the orange juice for the salad dressing. A squeeze of tangier lemon juice keeps the salad's sweetness in check. To add freshness, we stir in some minced cilantro before serving. Use the large holes of a box grater to shred the carrots.

1 Cut away peel and pith from oranges. Holding fruit over bowl, use paring knife to slice between membranes to release segments. Cut segments in half crosswise and let drain in fine-mesh strainer set over large bowl, reserving juice.

2 Whisk lemon juice, honey, cumin, salt, cayenne, and cinnamon into reserved orange juice. Add drained oranges and carrots and toss gently to coat. Let sit until liquid starts to pool in bottom of bowl, 3 to 5 minutes.

3 Drain salad in fine-mesh strainer and return to now-empty bowl. Stir in cilantro and oil and season with salt and pepper to taste. Serve.

Variation

Moroccan-Style Carrot Salad with Harissa and Feta

Substitute 2 tablespoons harissa for cumin, cayenne pepper, and cinnamon. Substitute 2 tablespoons chopped fresh mint for cilantro. Stir ½ cup crumbled feta cheese into salad with mint.

gajarachi koshimbir

Salad

12 ounces carrot noodles, cut into 3-inch lengths

3 tablespoons sugar

¾ teaspoon table salt

½ onion, chopped fine (optional)

2 tablespoons lime juice

6 tablespoons dry-roasted peanuts, chopped fine

¼ cup chopped fresh cilantro leaves and stems

¼ cup shredded fresh coconut

Spiced Seasoning Oil

1 tablespoon vegetable oil

2 teaspoons black mustard seeds

1 Thai chile, halved lengthwise

⅛ teaspoon ground turmeric

⅛ teaspoon ground asafetida

10 fresh curry leaves

WHY THIS RECIPE WORKS Sweet, spicy, acidic, crunchy, and aromatic, this traditional salad from the state of Maharashtra in western India combines carrots with coconut, peanuts, cilantro, and a spiced oil. Spiralized carrots are the right thickness for pairing with the spiced dressing; salting and sugaring them intensifies their flavor and sweetness. We prefer to spiralize the carrots ourselves for the best flavor, but you can use store-bought carrot noodles or matchstick carrots. You will need 1 pound of carrots to yield 12 ounces of noodles. Black mustard seeds, turmeric, asafetida, and curry leaves can be found at Indian markets, spice purveyors, or online. We prefer to shred fresh coconut on the large holes of a box grater. You can also use frozen unsweetened, shredded coconut from Indian or Asian markets. Mustard seeds will jump out of the pan and curry leaves will spatter when added to hot oil; consider covering the saucepan with either a splatter screen or a lid during cooking. If you prefer, you can add ¼ teaspoon of cayenne pepper to the carrot mixture with the lime juice in step 1 in place of the Thai chile used in step 2.

1 **For the salad** Toss carrot noodles with sugar and salt in salad spinner and let sit until partially wilted and reduced in volume by one-third, about 15 minutes. Spin carrots until excess liquid is removed, 10 to 20 seconds. Transfer carrots to large bowl and toss with onion, if using, and lime juice.

2 **For the spiced seasoning oil** Heat oil in small saucepan or seasoning wok over medium-high heat until just smoking. (Test temperature of oil by adding 1 mustard seed; mustard seed should sizzle and pop immediately; if it does not, continue to heat oil and repeat testing.) Carefully add mustard seeds, then reduce heat to low. Stir in Thai chile, turmeric, and asafetida and cook until fragrant, about 5 seconds. Off heat, carefully stir in curry leaves and cook until leaves sizzle and are translucent in spots, 5 to 10 seconds.

3 Pour hot oil mixture into carrot mixture and let sit for 15 minutes. Stir in peanuts, then sprinkle with cilantro and coconut. Serve.

Head Start

Refrigerate spiced seasoning oil for up to
6 hours. Prior to adding peanuts, cilantro, and
coconut, refrigerate salad for up to 6 hours.
Stir in peanuts and garnish with cilantro and
coconut before serving.

Perfect Pair

Serve with Spanish Tortilla (page 148),
Pakoras (page 49) and Cilantro-Mint Chutney
(page 18), or Dakgangjeong (page 299).

apple-fennel rémoulade

¼ cup mayonnaise

2 tablespoons whole-grain mustard

2 tablespoons lemon juice

2 tablespoons capers, rinsed, plus 1 tablespoon brine

4 celery ribs, sliced thin on bias

1 fennel bulb, 1 tablespoon fronds minced, stalks discarded, bulb halved, cored, and sliced thin crosswise

1 apple, cored and cut into 2-inch-long matchsticks

WHY THIS RECIPE WORKS This light salad lets apples shine in a savory application alongside fennel and celery, with creamy richness from a dollop of mayonnaise and a pop of tang from mustard and lemon juice. Simple but versatile, as a standalone small plate it teases the palate with its combination of bright flavors and delicate, crisp textures. These qualities also make this salad an excellent pairing for a variety of heavier small plates—for a restaurant-worthy presentation you can even use it as a bed for a simply cooked protein such as chicken or pork. You can use any variety of apple here, but crisp-sweet varieties, including Fuji, Gala, and Honeycrisp, work especially well.

Whisk mayonnaise, mustard, lemon juice, and caper brine together in large bowl. Add capers, celery, fennel bulb, and apple and toss to combine. Season with salt and pepper to taste. Top with fennel fronds and serve.

Head Start

Refrigerate rémoulade for up to 1 day; stir salad to recombine before serving.

Perfect Pair

Serve rémoulade with sliced bratwurst, stuffed mushrooms (see pages 216–217), Pretzel-Crusted Chicken Fingers with Honey Mustard (page 300), or Latkes (page 236).

fennel, orange, and olive salad

2 blood oranges

1 fennel bulb, stalks discarded, bulb halved, cored, and sliced thin

¼ cup pitted brine-cured black olives, sliced thin

3 tablespoons extra-virgin olive oil

2 tablespoons coarsely chopped fresh mint

2 teaspoons lemon juice

WHY THIS RECIPE WORKS The eye-catching colors of this light, bright Sicilian salad mean that it never fades into the background, even when it's just one element of a larger spread. And even better, its complementary assortment of flavors and textures—crisp, anise-scented fennel; juicy blood oranges; tender and briny black olives—make this one salad that's every bit as enjoyable to eat as it is to look at. To ensure that the crimson blood oranges are evenly distributed in the salad, we cut the segments into bite-size pieces and toss the salad gently to keep the small pieces from falling apart. To finish our salad, we add some oil-cured black olives for salty contrast, plus fresh mint, lemon juice, olive oil, salt, and pepper.

Cut away peel and pith from oranges. Quarter oranges, then slice crosswise into ½-inch-thick pieces. Combine oranges and any accumulated juice, fennel, olives, oil, mint, and lemon juice in bowl. Season with salt and pepper to taste. Serve.

Head Start

Refrigerate salad for up to 1 day. Let come to room temperature and stir in mint and oil just before serving.

Perfect Pair

Serve with socca (see pages 50–51), Marinated Manchego (page 127), or Lamb Fatayer (page 340).

citrus and radicchio salad with dates and smoked almonds

2 red grapefruits

3 oranges

1 teaspoon sugar

½ teaspoon table salt

3 tablespoons extra-virgin olive oil

1 small shallot, minced

1 teaspoon Dijon mustard

1 small head radicchio (6 ounces), halved, cored, and sliced thin

⅔ cup chopped pitted dates, divided

½ cup smoked almonds, chopped, divided

WHY THIS RECIPE WORKS This composed salad will brighten up any table. We start building the salad on a base of grapefruit and orange slices, topping the citrus with sliced purple-red radicchio for an attractive presentation. To tame the bitterness of the grapefruit and prevent its ample juice from drowning the salad in liquid, we treat the grapefruit (and the oranges) with sugar and salt and let them drain for a quarter of an hour before layering them on the serving plate, reserving some of the juice for a vinaigrette. Salty smoked almonds add mellow richness, and dates contribute sweetness. We prefer to use navel oranges, tangelos, or Cara Caras here.

1 Cut away peel and pith from grapefruits and oranges. Cut each fruit in half pole to pole, then slice crosswise ¼ inch thick. Transfer to bowl, toss with sugar and salt, and let sit for 15 minutes.

2 Drain fruit in fine-mesh strainer set over bowl, reserving 2 tablespoons juice. Arrange fruit in even layer on serving platter and drizzle with oil. Whisk reserved citrus juice, shallot, and mustard together in medium bowl. Add radicchio, ⅓ cup dates, and ¼ cup almonds and toss gently to coat. Season with salt and pepper to taste. Arrange radicchio mixture over fruit, leaving 1-inch border of fruit around edges. Sprinkle with remaining ⅓ cup dates and remaining ¼ cup almonds. Serve.

Finish Line

To ensure that radicchio doesn't wilt, be sure to arrange citrus slices on bottom of plate before topping them with radicchio.

Perfect Pair

Serve salad with Saganaki (page 143), Pressure-Cooker Winter Squash with Halloumi and Brussels Sprouts (page 252), or Potato-Cheddar Pierogi (page 348).

peach caprese salad

3 tablespoons extra-virgin olive oil

1½ tablespoons lemon juice

¼ teaspoon table salt

⅛ teaspoon pepper

1 pound ripe but slightly firm peaches, quartered and pitted, each quarter cut into 4 slices

12 ounces fresh mozzarella cheese, balls halved and sliced ¼ inch thick

6 large fresh basil or mint leaves, torn into small pieces

WHY THIS RECIPE WORKS A traditional caprese salad shows off the simple but compelling combination of ripe tomatoes and fresh mozzarella. Throw in some good-quality extra-virgin olive oil and sweet balsamic vinegar, and you've got a guaranteed summer cookout winner. We wanted to preserve a caprese's purity while featuring another of summer's juicy gems: ripe fresh peaches. In this salad we prefer the way that fresh lemon juice, instead of balsamic vinegar, enhances and complements the flavor of the sweet peaches. Tossing the peach slices with the dressing before assembling the salad ensures that each bite is fully coated and seasoned. For the best results, use high-quality, ripe, in-season peaches with a fragrant aroma and flesh that yields slightly when gently pressed. We like using 4-ounce balls of fresh mozzarella in this recipe.

1 Whisk oil, lemon juice, salt, and pepper together in large bowl. Add peaches and toss gently to coat.

2 Shingle peaches and mozzarella on serving platter. Drizzle any remaining dressing from bowl over top. Sprinkle with basil. Season with salt and pepper to taste. Serve.

Finish Line

When plating salad, alternate slices of mozzarella with peaches to create a pleasing pattern.

Perfect Pair

Serve salad with an antipasto platter, arepas (see pages 350–351) or Shrimp Tostadas with Coconut and Pineapple Slaw (page 292).

Serves 6 to 8 | **Active Time** 35 minutes
Total Time 35 minutes, plus 30 minutes draining

tomato and burrata salad with pangrattato and basil

1½ pounds ripe tomatoes, cored and cut into 1-inch pieces

8 ounces ripe cherry tomatoes, halved

½ teaspoon plus pinch table salt, divided

3 ounces rustic Italian bread, cut into 1-inch pieces (1 cup)

6 tablespoons extra-virgin olive oil, divided

Pinch pepper

1 garlic clove, minced

1 shallot, halved and sliced thin

1½ tablespoons white balsamic vinegar

½ cup chopped fresh basil

8 ounces burrata cheese, room temperature

WHY THIS RECIPE WORKS The best small plates feature eye-catching color, bold flavor, and textural variation in every bite. This reimagined rendition of caprese salad does all of the above, starring summer's best tomatoes alongside rich and buttery burrata, a deluxe version of fresh mozzarella. Since burrata is so much richer than regular fresh mozzarella, the other ingredients need to be intensified so they can hold their own. Salting standard tomatoes and cherry tomatoes draws out their watery juices and concentrates their flavor. Shallot and white balsamic vinegar make a bold vinaigrette (you could use red balsamic vinegar, but it will stain the beautiful, creamy cheese). A topping of Italian pangrattato (rustic garlicky bread crumbs) soaks up the tomato juices and the burrata cream. The success of this dish depends on using ripe, in-season tomatoes and very fresh, high-quality burrata.

1 Toss tomatoes with ¼ teaspoon salt and let drain in colander for 30 minutes.

2 Meanwhile, pulse bread in food processor into large crumbs measuring between ⅛ and ¼ inch, about 10 pulses. Combine crumbs, 2 tablespoons oil, pinch salt, and pepper in 12-inch nonstick skillet. Cook over medium heat, stirring often, until crumbs are crispy and golden, about 10 minutes. Clear center of skillet, add garlic, and cook, mashing garlic into skillet, until fragrant, about 30 seconds. Stir garlic into crumbs. Transfer to plate and let cool slightly.

3 Whisk shallot, vinegar, and remaining ¼ teaspoon salt together in large bowl. Whisking constantly, slowly drizzle in remaining ¼ cup oil. Add tomatoes and basil and toss gently to combine. Season with salt and pepper to taste, and arrange on serving platter. Cut burrata into 1-inch pieces, collecting creamy liquid. Sprinkle burrata over tomatoes and drizzle with creamy liquid. Sprinkle with bread crumbs and serve immediately.

Finish Line

For an even more colorful salad, use a combination of yellow, orange, and red cherry tomatoes and/or a variety of colorful heirloom tomatoes. If you like, garnish salad with a handful of whole basil leaves.

Perfect Pair

Serve with Pinchos Morunos (page 310), Chickpea Cakes (page 284), or grilled flatbread (see pages 336-337).

watermelon salad with cotija and serrano chiles

⅓ cup lime juice (3 limes)

2 scallions, white and green parts separated and sliced thin

2 serrano chiles, stemmed, halved, seeded, and sliced thin crosswise

1–2 tablespoons sugar (optional)

¾ teaspoon table salt

6 cups 1½-inch seedless watermelon pieces

3 ounces cotija cheese, crumbled (¾ cup), divided

5 tablespoons chopped fresh cilantro, divided

5 tablespoons chopped roasted, salted pepitas, divided

WHY THIS RECIPE WORKS Juicy and sweet and made up of large chunks of brightly colored melon, this salad and its variations have all the makings of a striking small plate. Our watermelon version features an intense dressing of lime juice, scallions, chiles, and cilantro that resists being diluted by the watermelon's abundant moisture. Some roasted pepitas offer subtle crunch, and the nuts in combination with a sprinkling of cotija cheese add richness in lieu of oil (which would only be repelled by the watermelon's surface moisture). The two variations substitute cantaloupe and honeydew for the watermelon and switch up the flavors of the dressings and garnishes. Taste your melon as you cut it up: If it's very sweet, omit the sugar; if it's less sweet, add the sugar to the dressing. Jalapeños can be substituted for the serranos. If cotija cheese is unavailable, substitute feta cheese.

Combine lime juice, scallion whites, and serranos in large bowl and let sit for 5 minutes. Stir in sugar, if using, and salt. Add watermelon, ½ cup cotija, ¼ cup cilantro, ¼ cup pepitas, and scallion greens and stir to combine. Transfer to shallow serving bowl. Sprinkle with remaining ¼ cup cotija, remaining 1 tablespoon cilantro, and remaining 1 tablespoon pepitas and serve.

Variations

Cantaloupe Salad with Olives and Red Onion

Omit serranos, sugar, cotija, and cilantro. Reduce salt to ½ teaspoon. Substitute lemon juice and ½ thinly sliced red onion for lime juice and scallions. Add 1–3 tablespoons honey (optional), 1 teaspoon ground dried Aleppo pepper, and salt to lemon juice mixture. Substitute 1 cantaloupe, cut into 1½-inch chunks (about 6 cups), for watermelon, and stir in ¼ cup chopped fresh parsley, ¼ cup chopped fresh mint, and 3 tablespoons finely chopped pitted oil-cured olives along with cantaloupe. Transfer to serving bowl and sprinkle with additional 1 tablespoon parsley, 1 tablespoon mint, and 1 tablespoon olives before serving.

Honeydew Salad with Peanuts and Lime

Omit serranos and cotija. Substitute 1 thinly sliced shallot for scallions, 1 honeydew melon, cut into 1½-inch chunks (about 6 cups), for watermelon, and chopped salted dry-roasted peanuts for pepitas. Reduce salt to ½ teaspoon. Using mortar and pestle (or on cutting board using flat side of chef's knife), mash 2 stemmed, seeded, and minced Thai chiles, 1 minced garlic clove, and salt to fine paste. Add chile paste and 1 tablespoon fish sauce to bowl with shallot mixture. Add ¼ cup chopped fresh mint to bowl with honeydew. Transfer to shallow serving bowl and sprinkle with additional 1 tablespoon mint along with cilantro and peanuts before serving.

Perfect Pair

Serve salad with Sung Choy Bao (page 296), Cóctel de Camarón (page 266), or Easy Mini Chicken Empanadas (page 338).

fresh fig salad

3 tablespoons balsamic vinegar

2 tablespoons ruby port

¾ cup baby arugula, chopped coarse

8 ounces figs, halved (about 2 cups)

4 ounces goat cheese, crumbled

2 ounces thinly sliced mortadella, torn

½ teaspoon flake sea salt

½ teaspoon cracked pepper

2 tablespoons extra-virgin olive oil

2 tablespoons chopped toasted pistachios

WHY THIS RECIPE WORKS For a composed salad that showcases jewel-like fresh figs—and wouldn't look out of place at even the fanciest dinner party—we start by cooking down port wine and balsamic vinegar into a syrup. We then drizzle this flavorful mixture over a bed of spicy arugula, halved fresh figs, goat cheese, and torn mortadella slices. Some flake sea salt, cracked black pepper, olive oil, and chopped toasted pistachios on top round out this elegant plated salad. You can substitute prosciutto for the mortadella if you like. We prefer small figs here. If you can find only large figs, quarter them. For a nonalcoholic version, omit the port and increase the balsamic vinegar to 5 tablespoons. For the best results, we suggest buying a log of good-quality goat cheese.

1 Combine vinegar and port in small saucepan. Bring to boil over medium-high heat. Cook until thickened and just becoming syrupy (mixture should measure scant 2 tablespoons), about 3 minutes. Let cool for at least 5 minutes.

2 Arrange arugula on serving platter and top with figs, goat cheese, and mortadella. Sprinkle with salt and pepper. Drizzle with oil and balsamic mixture. Top with pistachios. Serve.

Finish Line

For an attractive presentation, spread salad in a single layer on a wide serving platter or individual plates, and be sure to turn figs cut side up.

Perfect Pair

Serve with Olives all'Ascolana (page 36), Chicken Liver Pâté (page 116), French Bread Pizzas (page 354), or Gougères (page 324).

esquites

3 tablespoons lime juice, plus extra for seasoning (2 limes)

3 tablespoons sour cream

1 tablespoon mayonnaise

1–2 serrano chiles, stemmed and cut into ⅛-inch-thick rings

¾ teaspoon table salt, divided

2 tablespoons plus 1 teaspoon vegetable oil, divided

6 ears corn, kernels cut from cobs (6 cups), divided

2 garlic cloves, minced

½ teaspoon chili powder

4 ounces cotija cheese, crumbled (1 cup)

¾ cup coarsely chopped fresh cilantro

3 scallions, sliced thin

Perfect Pair

Serve salad with Peruvian Ceviche with Radishes and Orange (page 270) or Green Chile Cheeseburger Sliders (page 66).

WHY THIS RECIPE WORKS This Mexican corn salad features nutty-sweet charred kernels and a delightfully creamy, tangy dressing. We first char the corn in a covered skillet in two batches to allow plenty of the kernels to make contact with the skillet and brown. We then use the leftover hot oil in the skillet to bloom chili powder and lightly cook some garlic. Letting the corn cool before adding chopped cilantro and spicy serrano chiles preserves their bright colors and fresh flavors. If desired, substitute plain Greek yogurt for the sour cream. We like serrano chiles here, but you can substitute a jalapeño chile that has been halved length-wise and sliced into ⅛-inch-thick half-moons. Adjust the amount of chiles to suit your taste. If cotija cheese is unavailable, substitute feta cheese.

1 Combine lime juice, sour cream, mayonnaise, serrano(s), and ¼ teaspoon salt in large bowl. Set aside.

2 Heat 1 tablespoon oil in 12-inch nonstick skillet over high heat until shimmering. Add half of corn and spread into even layer. Sprinkle with ¼ teaspoon salt. Cover and cook, without stirring, until corn touching skillet is charred, about 3 minutes. Remove skillet from heat and let stand, covered, for 15 seconds, until any popping subsides. Transfer corn to bowl with sour cream mixture. Repeat with 1 tablespoon oil, remaining ¼ teaspoon salt, and remaining corn.

3 Return now-empty skillet to medium heat and add remaining 1 teaspoon oil, garlic, and chili powder. Cook, stirring constantly, until fragrant, about 30 seconds. Transfer garlic mixture to bowl with corn mixture and toss to combine. Let cool for at least 15 minutes.

4 Add cotija, cilantro, and scallions and toss to combine. Season salad with salt and up to 1 tablespoon extra lime juice to taste. Serve.

fava bean and radish salad

3 pounds fava beans, shucked (3 cups)

¼ cup extra-virgin olive oil

3 tablespoons lemon juice

2 garlic cloves, minced

½ teaspoon table salt

¼ teaspoon pepper

¼ teaspoon ground coriander

10 radishes, trimmed, halved, and sliced thin

1½ ounces (1½ cups) pea shoots or microgreens

¼ cup chopped fresh basil or mint

Head Start

Blanch and shell fava beans up to 1 day ahead; resume with step 2 when ready to assemble salad.

Perfect Pair

Serve salad with toasted almonds (see page 33), Easy Mushroom Pâté (page 120), Smoked Trout Deviled Eggs (page 129), or Egg Roulade with Spinach and Gruyére (page 144).

WHY THIS RECIPE WORKS Every bite of this vibrant, flavorful salad featuring fava beans, radishes, and pea shoots is a celebration of springtime. The fava beans are creamy and tender, the fresh pea shoots supply a delicate texture and a bit of natural sweetness, and thin half-moons of peppery radishes provide crunchy, spicy bite and flecks of contrasting red and white to our otherwise green salad. Fresh basil and a lemony dressing add a zesty herbal finishing note. This recipe works best with fresh fava beans, but if you can't find them, you can substitute 1 pound (3 cups) of frozen shucked fava beans, thawed. Skip step 1 if using frozen favas. Be sure to set up the ice bath before cooking the fava beans, as plunging them immediately into the cold water after blanching is what helps them retain their bright-green color and ensures that they don't overcook.

1 Bring 4 quarts water to boil in large pot over high heat. Fill large bowl halfway with ice and water. Add fava beans to boiling water and cook for 1 minute. Using slotted spoon, transfer fava beans to ice bath and let cool, about 2 minutes. Transfer fava beans to triple layer of paper towels and dry well. Using paring knife, make small cut along edge of each bean through waxy sheath, then gently squeeze sheath to release bean; discard sheath.

2 Whisk oil, lemon juice, garlic, salt, pepper, and coriander together in large bowl. Add radishes, pea shoots, basil, and fava beans and toss gently to coat. Serve immediately.

som tam

2 tablespoons packed brown sugar, divided

2–4 Thai chiles, stemmed and sliced thin

2 tablespoons minced dried shrimp (optional)

1 garlic clove, minced

3 tablespoons lime juice (2 limes), plus extra for seasoning

2 tablespoons fish sauce, plus extra for seasoning

1 green papaya (2 pounds), peeled, halved lengthwise, and seeded

4 ounces green beans, trimmed and cut into 1-inch lengths on bias

3 ounces cherry tomatoes, quartered

3 tablespoons chopped dry-roasted peanuts

Head Start

Marinate papaya in dressing for up to 4 hours.

Perfect Pair

Serve salad with Jalapeño Poppers (page 45), Spinach and Edamame Brown Rice Cakes (page 64), or Chile Marinated Pork Belly (page 313).

WHY THIS RECIPE WORKS Som tam ("sour pounding"), a crunchy, tart-spicy northeastern Thai salad made with green papaya, brings the crisp-fresh contrast needed to balance a meal of heavier dishes. The firm flesh of a papaya can be hard to chew, so traditionally the fruit is shredded with a machete-size knife and then pounded using a mortar and pestle until softened. We use a box grater to do the shredding and then, rather than relying on mechanical pounding, we soften the papaya by macerating it in a garlic, lime juice, fish sauce, brown sugar, and Thai chile dressing. Green beans and tomatoes add crisp crunch, as does a finishing sprinkle of roasted peanuts. Do not use ripe papaya; it will not work here. Substitute 1½ pounds jicama (peeled, quartered, and shredded) for the papaya if desired. You can substitute 1–2 serrano chiles or ½–1 jalapeño chile for the Thai chiles. For a spicier dish, use the larger number of chiles.

1 Using mortar and pestle (or on cutting board using flat side of chef's knife), mash 1 tablespoon sugar; Thai chiles; shrimp, if using; and garlic to fine paste; transfer to large bowl. Whisk in lime juice, fish sauce, and remaining 1 tablespoon sugar until sugar has dissolved. Quarter each papaya half. Using large holes of box grater or shredding disk of food processor, shred papaya. Transfer papaya to bowl with dressing and toss to coat. Let stand for at least 30 minutes, tossing occasionally.

2 Microwave green beans and 1 tablespoon water in covered bowl, stirring occasionally, until tender, about 4 minutes. Drain green beans and immediately rinse with cold water. Once cool, drain again and dry thoroughly with paper towels. Add green beans and tomatoes to papaya mixture and toss to combine. Season with extra lime juice and fish sauce to taste. Transfer salad to serving platter and sprinkle with peanuts. Serve.

horiatiki salata

1¾ pounds ripe tomatoes, cored

1¼ teaspoons table salt, divided

½ red onion, sliced thin

2 tablespoons red wine vinegar

1 teaspoon dried oregano, plus extra for seasoning

½ teaspoon pepper

1 English cucumber, quartered lengthwise and cut into ¾-inch pieces

1 green bell pepper, stemmed, seeded, and cut into 2 by ½-inch strips

1 cup pitted kalamata olives

2 tablespoons capers, rinsed

¼ cup extra-virgin olive oil, plus extra for drizzling

1 (8-ounce) block feta cheese, sliced into ½-inch-thick triangles

WHY THIS RECIPE WORKS Bites of sweet tomatoes, briny olives, savory onion, crunchy cucumber, and tangy slabs of feta make up this classic Greek salad. Using ripe, peak-season tomatoes is a must here; we start by tossing halved tomato wedges with salt and setting them in a colander to drain away their excess moisture. Soaking the onion slices in ice water tempers their bite. A creamy Greek feta brings richness to the lean vegetables. Dried oregano is the traditional choice for the dressing: Its delicate flavor complements the vegetables and doesn't upstage them like fresh oregano could. It is customary to dress horiatiki salata with drizzles of oil and vinegar, but we tweak the custom by tossing the vegetables with vinegar before drizzling them with oil to ensure even coverage. Use only large, round tomatoes here, not Roma or cherry tomatoes.

1 Cut tomatoes into ½-inch-thick wedges. Cut wedges in half crosswise. Toss tomatoes and ½ teaspoon salt together in colander set in large bowl. Let drain for 30 minutes. Place onion in small bowl, cover with ice water, and let sit for 15 minutes. Whisk vinegar, oregano, pepper, and remaining ¾ teaspoon salt together in second small bowl.

2 Discard tomato juice and transfer tomatoes to now-empty bowl. Drain onion and add to bowl with tomatoes. Add vinegar mixture, cucumber, bell pepper, olives, and capers and toss to combine. Drizzle with oil and toss gently to coat. Season with salt and pepper to taste. Transfer to serving platter and top with feta. Season each slice of feta with extra oregano to taste, and drizzle with extra oil. Serve.

Perfect Pair

For a spread featuring the flavors of the Mediterranean, serve with Muhammara (see page 103), Lamb Rib Chops with Mint-Rosemary Relish (page 283), or Keftedes (page 280).

butternut squash and apple fattoush

2 (8-inch) pita breads

½ cup extra-virgin olive oil, divided

⅛ plus ¾ teaspoon table salt, divided

⅛ teaspoon pepper

2 pounds butternut squash, peeled, seeded, and cut into ½-inch pieces

3 tablespoons lemon juice

4 teaspoons ground sumac, plus extra for serving

1 garlic clove, minced

1 apple, cored and cut into ½-inch pieces

¼ head radicchio, cored and chopped (1 cup)

½ cup chopped fresh parsley

4 scallions, sliced thin

Head Start

Store toasted pita in airtight container at room temperature for up to 2 days.

Perfect Pair

Serve salad with sliders (see pages 66–68), Skordalia (page 109), or Pork and Ricotta Meatballs (page 278).

WHY THIS RECIPE WORKS Pita bread salad, or fattoush, typically features peak summertime produce such as ripe tomatoes and cucumber. This twist on the classic employs ingredients that are more readily available the other half of the year, but no less pleasing to the eye and palate: crisp apples, sweet roasted butternut squash, and pleasantly bitter radicchio. Tossed with toasted pita and a dressing loaded with lemon juice and citrusy sumac, the bright, punchy flavor of this salad makes every bite a multilayered experience that doesn't get overshadowed even when the salad is paired with a variety of other dishes.

1 Adjust oven racks to middle and lowest positions and heat oven to 375 degrees. Using kitchen shears, cut around perimeter of each pita and separate into 2 thin rounds. Cut each round in half. Place pitas smooth side down on wire rack set in rimmed baking sheet. Brush rough side of pitas evenly with 3 tablespoons oil, then sprinkle with ⅛ teaspoon salt and pepper. (Pitas do not need to be uniformly coated with oil.) Bake on middle rack until pitas are crispy and pale golden brown, 10 to 14 minutes. Let cool completely.

2 Increase oven temperature to 450 degrees. Toss squash with 1 tablespoon oil and ½ teaspoon salt. Spread in even layer on rimmed baking sheet and roast on bottom rack until browned and tender, 20 to 25 minutes, stirring halfway through. Set aside to cool slightly, about 10 minutes.

3 Meanwhile, whisk lemon juice, sumac, garlic, and remaining ¼ teaspoon salt together in small bowl and let sit for 10 minutes. Whisking constantly, slowly drizzle in remaining ¼ cup oil.

4 Break cooled pitas into ½-inch pieces and place in large bowl. Add roasted squash, apple, radicchio, parsley, and scallions. Drizzle dressing over salad and toss gently to coat. Season with salt and pepper to taste. Serve, sprinkling individual portions with extra sumac.

fingerling potato salad with sun-dried tomato dressing

2 pounds fingerling potatoes, unpeeled, halved lengthwise

¼ cup extra-virgin olive oil, divided

1½ teaspoons table salt

1 teaspoon pepper

1 teaspoon herbes de Provence

⅓ cup oil-packed sun-dried tomatoes, minced

¼ cup pitted kalamata olives, chopped fine

¼ cup chopped fresh parsley

3 tablespoons finely chopped shallot

2 teaspoons grated lemon zest plus 1 tablespoon juice

1 garlic clove, minced

½ teaspoon red pepper flakes

WHY THIS RECIPE WORKS Fingerling potatoes have an earthy, mildly nutty flavor and a slender shape that makes them the perfect option for a potato salad that feels grown-up and elegant. Inspired by the flavors of France, we toss the potatoes with fruity extra-virgin olive oil and herbes de Provence before roasting them to tenderness. Dressing the potatoes while still hot allows the spuds to more readily soak up the dressing's zingy flavors. This salad can be served warm, room temperature, or cold. Try to find fingerling potatoes that are consistently 2 to 3 inches long and 1 inch in diameter. It is important to toss the potatoes with the dressing while they're still hot.

1 Adjust oven rack to middle position and heat oven to 450 degrees. Toss potatoes, 2 tablespoons oil, salt, pepper, and herbes de Provence in large bowl until potatoes are well coated. Arrange potatoes cut side down in single layer on rimmed baking sheet. Roast until potatoes are tender and cut sides are golden brown, about 20 minutes.

2 Meanwhile, wipe bowl clean with paper towels. Add tomatoes, olives, parsley, shallot, lemon zest and juice, garlic, pepper flakes, and remaining 2 tablespoons oil to now-empty bowl.

3 Transfer hot potatoes to tomato mixture and toss to combine. Let sit for 30 minutes, tossing occasionally. Transfer to platter and serve.

Head Start

Let potato salad sit at room temperature for up to 2 hours, or refrigerate for up to 1 day.

Finish Line

Sprinkle potatoes with additional chopped fresh parsley before serving.

Perfect Pair

Serve with aioli (see page 16), Roasted Asparagus with Mustard-Dill Hollandaise (page 226), Keftedes (page 280), or Seared Tempeh with Tomato Jam (page 288).

Serves 6 to 8 | **Active Time** 30 minutes

Total Time 1 hour, plus 30 minutes cooling

sweet potato salad with cumin, smoked paprika, and almonds

3 pounds sweet potatoes, peeled and cut into ¾-inch pieces

3 tablespoons plus ¼ cup extra-virgin olive oil, divided

2 teaspoons table salt

3 scallions, sliced thin

3 tablespoons lime juice (2 limes)

1 jalapeño chile, stemmed, seeded, and minced

1 garlic clove, minced

1 teaspoon ground cumin

1 teaspoon smoked paprika

1 teaspoon pepper

½ teaspoon ground allspice

½ cup coarsely chopped fresh cilantro leaves and stems

½ cup whole almonds, toasted and chopped

WHY THIS RECIPE WORKS Vibrant sweet potatoes take on new small plate–worthy dimension when roasted until tender and lightly caramelized and combined with warm spices, fresh herbs, and crunchy nuts. Cooking the potatoes in a hot oven develops a golden exterior while the insides bake up fluffy and tender. We let the roasted potatoes cool down (to protect their structural integrity) before tossing them with a bold vinaigrette made with scallions, jalapeño, lime juice, and garlic and scented with earthy cumin and smoky paprika. We then finish the dressed sweet potatoes with a flourish of fresh cilantro, plus toasted almonds for nutty crunch. We prefer using a high-quality extra-virgin olive oil to add depth and complexity here.

1 Adjust oven rack to middle position and heat oven to 450 degrees. Toss potatoes with 3 tablespoons oil and salt in bowl. Transfer to rimmed baking sheet and spread into even layer. Roast until potatoes are tender and just beginning to brown, 30 to 40 minutes, stirring halfway through roasting. Let potatoes cool for 30 minutes.

2 Meanwhile, combine scallions, lime juice, jalapeño, garlic, cumin, paprika, pepper, allspice, and remaining ¼ cup oil in large bowl.

3 Add cilantro, almonds, and potatoes to bowl with scallion mixture and toss to combine. Serve.

Variation

Sweet Potato Salad with Soy Sauce, Sriracha, and Peanuts

Substitute 1 tablespoon soy sauce, 1 tablespoon sriracha, 1 teaspoon sugar, and 1 teaspoon grated fresh ginger for cumin, smoked paprika, pepper, and allspice. Substitute salted dry-roasted peanuts for almonds.

Head Start

Refrigerate cooked sweet potatoes and scallion mixture separately for up to 1 day. Let both come to room temperature before proceeding with recipe.

Perfect Pair

Serve salad with Bacon and Chive Deviled Eggs (page 129), Skillet Roasted Brussels Sprouts with Chorizo and Manchego Cheese (page 245), or Kombdi, Jira Galun (page 304).

brown rice salad with fennel, mushrooms, and walnuts

1½ cups long-grain brown rice

1¼ teaspoons table salt, divided, plus salt for cooking rice

3 tablespoons white wine vinegar, divided

¼ cup extra-virgin olive oil, divided

1 pound white or cremini mushrooms, trimmed and quartered

1 large fennel bulb, stalks discarded, bulb halved, cored, and sliced thin

1 shallot, minced

½ teaspoon pepper

⅔ cup walnuts or whole almonds, toasted and chopped coarse, divided

2 tablespoons minced fresh tarragon or chives

2 tablespoons minced fresh parsley or dill, divided

WHY THIS RECIPE WORKS The irresistible earthiness of brown rice is shown off to great advantage in this whole-grain salad, where the nutty rice is enhanced by aromatic fennel, crunchy walnuts, and chewy, savory mushrooms. Using the pasta method to cook the brown rice (boiling it in a large quantity of water and then draining away the excess) ensures evenly cooked, tender grains. To finish, we season the salad with a piquant vinaigrette of white wine vinegar, shallot, and extra-virgin olive oil.

1 Bring 3 quarts water to boil in large pot. Add rice and 2 teaspoons salt and cook, stirring occasionally, until rice is tender, 22 to 25 minutes. Drain rice, spread onto rimmed baking sheet, and drizzle with 1 tablespoon vinegar. Let rice cool completely, about 15 minutes; transfer to large bowl.

2 Heat 1 tablespoon oil in 12-inch skillet over medium-high heat until shimmering. Add mushrooms and ½ teaspoon salt and cook, stirring occasionally, until skillet is dry and mushrooms are browned, 6 to 8 minutes; transfer to plate and let cool.

3 Heat 1 tablespoon oil in now-empty skillet over medium-high heat until shimmering. Add fennel and ¼ teaspoon salt and cook, stirring occasionally, until just browned and crisp-tender, 3 to 4 minutes; transfer to plate with mushrooms and let cool.

4 Whisk shallot, pepper, remaining ½ teaspoon salt, remaining 2 tablespoons vinegar, and remaining 2 tablespoons oil together in small bowl, then drizzle over rice. Add mushrooms and fennel and toss to combine. Let sit until flavors meld, about 10 minutes.

5 Add ½ cup walnuts, tarragon, and 1 tablespoon parsley and toss to combine. Season with salt and pepper to taste. Sprinkle with remaining walnuts and remaining 1 tablespoon parsley and serve.

Head Start

Refrigerate cooked rice in airtight container for up to 3 days.

Finish Line

Serve salad with Spiralized Sweet Potatoes with Crispy Shallots, Pistachios, and Urfa (page 250) or Tuna and Heirloom Tomato Salad with Olives and Parsley (page 201).

farro salad with sugar snap peas and white beans

12 ounces sugar snap peas, strings removed, cut into 1-inch lengths

¼ teaspoon table salt, plus salt for cooking snap peas and farro

1½ cups whole farro

3 tablespoons extra-virgin olive oil

2 tablespoons lemon juice

2 tablespoons minced shallot

1 teaspoon Dijon mustard

¼ teaspoon pepper

1 (15-ounce) can cannellini beans, rinsed

6 ounces cherry tomatoes, halved

⅓ cup chopped pitted kalamata olives

2 tablespoons chopped fresh dill

WHY THIS RECIPE WORKS In this salad, nutty, pleasantly chewy farro is set off by crisp-tender fresh summer vegetables. As in our brown rice salad (see page 190), we use the pasta method to cook the farro to yield firm but tender grains. A lemon-dill dressing serves as a citrusy, herbal complement to the earthy farro and crunchy blanched snap peas. To add a little more substance to the salad, we also throw in a few cherry tomatoes, meaty kalamata olives, and creamy cannellini beans. We prefer the flavor and texture of whole-grain farro; pearled farro can be used in this dish, but the texture may be softer. We found a wide range of cooking times among various brands of farro, so start checking for doneness after 10 minutes. Do not use quick-cooking farro here.

1 Bring 4 quarts water to boil in large pot. Add snap peas and 1 tablespoon salt and cook until crisp-tender, about 2 minutes. Using slotted spoon, transfer snap peas to large plate and let cool completely, about 15 minutes.

2 Add farro to water, return to boil, and cook until grains are tender with slight chew, 15 to 30 minutes. Drain farro, spread on rimmed baking sheet, and let cool completely, about 15 minutes.

3 Whisk oil, lemon juice, shallot, mustard, pepper, and salt together in large bowl. Add snap peas, farro, beans, tomatoes, olives, and dill and toss to combine. Season with salt and pepper to taste, and serve.

Head Start

Refrigerate cooked farro in airtight container for up to 3 days.

Perfect Pair

Serve with Roasted Carrots and Shallots with Chermoula (page 229) or Albóndigas en Salsa de Almendras (page 276).

kamut with carrots and pomegranate

1 cup kamut, rinsed and drained

¼ teaspoon table salt, plus salt for cooking kamut

2 tablespoons vegetable oil

2 carrots, peeled and cut into ¼-inch pieces

2 garlic cloves, minced

¾ teaspoon garam masala

¼ cup shelled pistachios, lightly toasted and chopped coarse, divided

3 tablespoons chopped fresh cilantro, divided

1 teaspoon lemon juice

¼ cup pomegranate seeds

WHY THIS RECIPE WORKS With an earthy, nutty flavor and firm chew, kamut makes a delicious base for a whole-grain salad. We cook the kamut like pasta, simmering the kernels in a pot of water until they're tender but still chewy and then draining away the extra water. Sautéing the cooked kamut in a skillet with garlic, carrots, and garam masala yields a pilaf-like dish full of vibrant color and a variety of textures, especially after the addition of a handful of pistachios, jewel-like pomegranate seeds, and cilantro. Kamut is also sold as khorasan wheat. You can substitute barley or wheat berries for kamut, if desired; reduce cooking time to 20 to 40 minutes for barley.

1 Bring 2 quarts water to boil in large saucepan. Stir in kamut and 2 teaspoons salt. Return to boil; reduce heat; and simmer until tender, 55 minutes to 1¼ hours. Drain well. Spread on rimmed baking sheet and let cool for at least 15 minutes.

2 Heat oil in 12-inch skillet over medium heat until shimmering. Add carrots and salt and cook, stirring frequently, until carrots are softened and lightly browned, 4 to 6 minutes. Add garlic and garam masala and cook, stirring constantly, until fragrant, about 1 minute. Add kamut and cook until warmed through, 2 to 5 minutes. Off heat, stir in half of pistachios, 2 tablespoons cilantro, and lemon juice. Season with salt and pepper to taste. Transfer to serving bowl and sprinkle with pomegranate seeds, remaining pistachios, and remaining 1 tablespoon cilantro. Serve.

Head Start

Soak kamut in water overnight to shorten cooking time to 35 to 50 minutes. Refrigerate cooked kamut in airtight container for up to 2 days.

Perfect Pair

Serve with Braised Eggplant with Paprika, Coriander, and Yogurt (page 243), Lamb Rib Chops with Mint-Rosemary Relish (page 283), or Tuna Poke (page 269).

texas caviar

⅓ cup red wine vinegar

3 tablespoons vegetable oil

1 tablespoon sugar

2 garlic cloves, minced

1 teaspoon table salt

½ teaspoon pepper

2 (15-ounce) cans black-eyed peas, rinsed

6 scallions, sliced thin

1 red bell pepper, stemmed, seeded, and chopped

1 green bell pepper, stemmed, seeded, and chopped

2 jalapeño chiles, stemmed, seeded, and minced

1 celery rib, chopped fine

¼ cup chopped fresh cilantro

¼ cup chopped fresh parsley

WHY THIS RECIPE WORKS Contrary to what its name suggests, this salad is composed of "pickled" black-eyed peas, not fish roe. But Texas caviar, like its fancier namesake, is right at home in a party spread—its bright colors and creamy-crisp texture make it an excellent accompaniment to a variety of dishes, and even better, it can be prepared well in advance. To make it, we add scallions to a base of canned black-eyed peas, plus red and green bell peppers for sweetness and color, celery for vegetal crunch, and two jalapeños for heat. A hearty dose of chopped parsley and cilantro freshens up the canned beans. Red wine vinegar provides the punchy acidity in Texas caviar's hallmark dressing. Note that the salad needs to sit for at least 1 hour for the flavors to meld, but the longer it sits, the better it will taste. If you prefer a spicier salad, reserve and stir in some of the jalapeño seeds.

1 Whisk vinegar, oil, sugar, garlic, salt, and pepper together in large bowl.

2 Add black-eyed peas, scallions, bell peppers, jalapeños, celery, cilantro, and parsley and toss to combine. Season with salt and pepper to taste. Let sit for at least 1 hour before serving.

Head Start

Refrigerate salad for up to 5 days.

Perfect Pair

Serve with Quesadillas for a Crowd (page 151), Pan-Seared Scallops with Mango-Cucumber Salad (page 295), or Fried Green Tomatoes (page 215).

crispy lentil and herb salad

1 teaspoon table salt for brining

½ cup dried lentilles du Puy, picked over and rinsed

⅓ cup vegetable oil for frying

½ teaspoon ground cumin

¼ teaspoon plus pinch table salt, divided

1 cup plain Greek yogurt

3 tablespoons extra-virgin olive oil, divided

1 teaspoon grated lemon zest plus 1 teaspoon juice

1 garlic clove, minced

½ cup fresh parsley leaves

½ cup torn fresh dill

½ cup fresh cilantro leaves

¼ cup dried cherries, chopped

Pomegranate molasses

WHY THIS RECIPE WORKS This crispy, herby lentil salad can be served on individual plates as a beautiful composed salad or scooped up with pita like an elaborately topped dip—either way, it's tailor-made for sharing. The firm texture of small lentilles du Puy means that they hold up well to frying; soaking the lentils before frying ensures that they turn tender and lightly crispy without burning. Instead of simply tossing all of the salad components together with a dressing, we use yogurt as an anchor for the other ingredients, spreading it on a platter and then topping it with a lightly dressed mix of fresh herbs tossed with the crunchy lentils and a handful of sweet dried cherries. You can substitute brown lentils for the lentilles du Puy. Be sure to use a large saucepan to fry the lentils, as the oil will bubble and steam.

1 Dissolve 1 teaspoon salt in 1 quart water in bowl. Add lentils and let sit at room temperature for at least 1 hour. Drain well and pat dry with paper towels.

2 Heat vegetable oil in large saucepan over medium heat until shimmering. Add lentils and cook, stirring constantly, until crispy and golden in spots, 8 to 12 minutes (oil should bubble vigorously throughout; adjust heat as needed). Carefully drain lentils in fine-mesh strainer set over bowl, then transfer lentils to paper towel–lined plate. Discard oil. Sprinkle with cumin and ¼ teaspoon salt and toss to combine; set aside.

3 Whisk yogurt, 2 tablespoons olive oil, lemon zest and juice, and garlic together in bowl and season with salt and pepper to taste. Spread yogurt mixture over serving platter. Toss parsley, dill, cilantro, remaining pinch salt, and remaining 1 tablespoon olive oil together in bowl, then gently stir in lentils and cherries and arrange on top of yogurt mixture, leaving 1-inch border. Drizzle with pomegranate molasses and serve.

Head Start

Salt-soak lentils for up to 1 day. Store cooled fried lentils in airtight container at room temperature for up to 1 day.

Perfect Pair

Serve salad with quick pickles (see pages 76–77), Pai Huang Gua (page 156), or Roasted King Trumpet Mushrooms (page 219).

tuna and heirloom tomato salad with olives and parsley

4 heirloom tomatoes, cored and sliced ½ inch thick

1¼ teaspoons table salt, divided

⅓ cup extra-virgin olive oil

1½ tablespoons lemon juice

1 tablespoon Dijon mustard

1 garlic clove, minced

¼ teaspoon pepper

3 (6-ounce) jars oil-packed tuna, drained (1½ cups)

1 cup fresh parsley leaves

½ cup pitted kalamata olives, halved

1 shallot, sliced thin

WHY THIS RECIPE WORKS Made with bright, sweet heirloom tomatoes, topped with a mound of rich tuna, and lightly dressed with a lemony, herby, mustard-spiked dressing, this composed salad is made for laid-back summertime entertaining. And better yet, it looks every bit as gorgeous as a restaurant small plate while coming together in mere minutes. Using high-quality oil-packed tuna adds richness and superior flavor. Kalamata olives add yet more briny richness as well as pops of contrasting color, and a single shallot contributes a hint of bite. You can substitute vine-ripened tomatoes for the heirloom tomatoes, if desired.

1 Shingle tomatoes on small dinner plates and sprinkle with ½ teaspoon salt.

2 Whisk oil, lemon juice, mustard, garlic, pepper, and remaining ¾ teaspoon salt together in large bowl. Reserve 2 tablespoons vinaigrette.

3 Add tuna, parsley, olives, and shallot to remaining vinaigrette in bowl and toss gently to combine. Divide salad evenly among plates on top of tomatoes. Drizzle reserved vinaigrette over salads. Serve.

Finish Line

For an even more colorful salad, use combination of yellow, orange, and/or red heirloom tomatoes.

Perfect Pair

Serve with Butter Bean and Pea Dip with Mint (page 98) or topped naan (see page 334).

crab and mizuna salad

12 ounces lump crabmeat, picked over for shells

½ cup mayonnaise

2 scallions, white parts minced, green parts sliced thin

2 tablespoons minced fresh shiso

2 tablespoons unseasoned rice vinegar, divided

4 teaspoons minced pickled ginger

2 teaspoons wasabi paste, divided

¼ cup extra-virgin olive oil

¼ teaspoon table salt

8 ounces (8 cups) mizuna or baby arugula

1 cup Quick Pickled Daikon Radish and Carrot (page 20)

WHY THIS RECIPE WORKS Fresh greens topped with dollops of sweet crabmeat spiced with fiery ginger and wasabi are a recipe for a visually arresting and tastebud-pleasing composed salad. Mizuna, pickled ginger, and wasabi contribute varied texture and spicy bite; mayonnaise adds tangy richness; and shiso leaves bring a bold, almost indescribable flavor that combines hints of mint, cilantro, basil, and tarragon. Mizuna, a Japanese mustard green, serves well for the salad's leafy component. We stir more wasabi into a simple vinaigrette of olive oil, scallion whites, and rice vinegar, and for a little more crunch, we top each salad with a handful of pickled daikon radish and carrot. Note that this recipe calls for unseasoned rice vinegar; we don't recommend using seasoned rice vinegar in its place.

Press crab dry with paper towels, then toss gently with mayonnaise, scallion greens, shiso, 2 teaspoons vinegar, pickled ginger, and ½ teaspoon wasabi in bowl; season with salt to taste. Whisk oil, salt, scallion whites, remaining 4 teaspoons vinegar, and remaining 1½ teaspoons wasabi together in large bowl. Add mizuna and pickled vegetables and toss gently to combine, then divide among individual plates. Serve, topping individual portions with crab mixture.

Head Start

Refrigerate crab mixture for up to 1 day before assembling rest of salad.

Perfect Pair

Serve with Curried Deviled Eggs (page 129), Patatas Bravas (page 210), or Blini (page 322).

pinto bean, ancho, and beef salad

1 cup red wine vinegar

⅓ cup sugar

1¼ teaspoons table salt, divided

4 ounces poblano chiles, stemmed, seeded, and sliced ⅛ inch thick

1 (1-pound) skirt steak, trimmed and cut into thirds

2 teaspoons ancho chile powder

¾ teaspoon pepper, divided

2 tablespoons vegetable oil, divided

2 (15-ounce) cans pinto beans, rinsed

12 ounces jicama, peeled and grated (1½ cups)

½ cup finely chopped red onion

¼ cup chopped fresh cilantro leaves and stems, plus extra for sprinkling

3 tablespoons lime juice (2 limes)

1½ ounces cotija cheese, crumbled (⅓ cup)

½ ounce unsweetened chocolate, chopped fine (optional)

WHY THIS RECIPE WORKS This shareable salad pays homage to the Mexican ingredients that inspired its creation. Ancho chiles, frequently used in Mexican cuisine, are dried poblanos; we employ both fresh and dried forms, using ancho chile powder as a rub for our steak and quick-pickling poblanos for sweet-sour spiciness. Grated jicama brings crunch to our salad of pinto beans, red onion, cilantro, and lime juice. The dressed salad makes a refreshing counterpoint to the rich, spice-rubbed skirt steak, which we sear in a skillet. Crumbled cotija gives the dish an umami, salty bite. Finally, a sprinkle of finely chopped unsweetened chocolate lends complex bitterness and aroma. Be sure to slice the steak thin against the grain or it will be very chewy. It is important to chop the chocolate fine, as bigger pieces of chocolate will be overpoweringly bitter.

1 Microwave vinegar, sugar, and ¼ teaspoon salt in medium bowl until simmering, 3 to 4 minutes. Whisk to dissolve any residual sugar and salt, then stir in poblanos. Let sit, stirring occasionally, for 30 minutes. Drain and set aside.

2 Meanwhile, pat steak dry with paper towels, then sprinkle with chile powder, ¼ teaspoon pepper, and ½ teaspoon salt. Heat 1 tablespoon oil in 12-inch skillet over medium-high heat until just smoking. Add steak and cook until well browned and meat registers 120 to 125 degrees (for medium-rare), about 2 minutes per side. Transfer steak to cutting board, tent with aluminum foil, and let rest for 5 minutes.

3 Gently toss beans, jicama, onion, cilantro, lime juice, remaining ½ teaspoon salt, remaining ½ teaspoon pepper, and remaining 1 tablespoon oil to combine, then transfer to serving platter. Slice steak thin against grain and arrange over top of salad. Sprinkle with cotija; chocolate, if using; poblanos; and extra cilantro. Serve.

Head Start

Refrigerate bean-jicama mixture, without cilantro, for up to 1 day. Toss in cilantro and top with steak just before serving.

Finish Line

For a more classic small plate presentation, portion bean mixture onto individual plates and top with a small amount of beef before sprinkling with garnishes.

Perfect Pair

Serve salad with Cajun Pickled Okra (page 31) or Tomato Salad (page 154) and refreshing Watermelon-Lime Aguas Frescas (page 385).

dressed-up vegetables

marinated vegetables

Marinated vegetables are pretty much the perfect small plate. Each bite offers the bold flavors of extra-virgin olive oil, vinegar or lemon juice, garlic, and fresh herbs and spices. These tangy dishes go with everything and also look appealing. They can be made ahead and refrigerated. Pull out marinated vegetables and let them sit for 1 hour before serving at room temperature.

marinated zucchini

Serves 6 to 8
Active Time 30 minutes
Total Time 35 minutes, plus 1 hour marinating

Buy medium zucchini that weigh about 8 ounces each. Refrigerate marinated zucchini for up to 1 day.

- 5 tablespoons extra-virgin olive oil, divided
- 1 shallot, minced
- 1½ tablespoons lemon juice
- 1½ teaspoons table salt
- 1 teaspoon chopped fresh thyme
- 1 garlic clove, minced
- ⅛ teaspoon red pepper flakes
- 1½ pounds zucchini, trimmed and halved lengthwise
- 1½ ounces Parmesan cheese, shaved with vegetable peeler (about ⅔ cup)

1 Combine ¼ cup oil, shallot, lemon juice, salt, thyme, garlic, and pepper flakes in medium bowl.

2 Pat zucchini dry with paper towels. Heat remaining 1 tablespoon oil in 12-inch nonstick skillet over medium heat until shimmering. Add half of zucchini to skillet cut side down and cook until browned, about 3 minutes. Flip and cook until skin side is spotty brown, about 3 minutes. Transfer to large plate. Repeat with remaining zucchini. Let cool for 5 minutes.

3 Slice zucchini crosswise ¼ inch thick. Transfer zucchini to bowl with oil mixture and toss to evenly coat. Marinate for at least 1 hour or up to 24 hours. (If marinating longer than 1 hour, cover with plastic wrap and refrigerate. Let sit at room temperature for 1 hour before serving.)

4 Season with salt to taste. Transfer zucchini to shallow platter and sprinkle with Parmesan. Serve.

marinated eggplant with capers and mint

Serves 6 to 8
Active Time 30 minutes
Total Time 1 hour, plus 1 hour marinating

Refrigerate marinated eggplant for up to 3 days.

1½ pounds Italian eggplant, sliced into
    1-inch-thick rounds

½ teaspoon kosher salt

¼ cup extra-virgin olive oil, divided

4 teaspoons red wine vinegar

1 tablespoon capers, rinsed and minced

1 garlic clove, minced

½ teaspoon grated lemon zest

½ teaspoon minced fresh oregano

¼ teaspoon pepper

3 tablespoons minced fresh mint

1 Arrange eggplant on paper towel–lined rimmed baking sheet, sprinkle both sides with salt, and let sit for 30 minutes.

2 Adjust oven rack 4 inches from broiler element and heat broiler. Thoroughly pat eggplant dry with paper towels, arrange on aluminum foil–lined rimmed baking sheet in single layer, and lightly brush both sides with 1 tablespoon oil. Broil eggplant until mahogany brown and lightly charred, 6 to 8 minutes per side.

3 Whisk remaining 3 tablespoons oil, vinegar, capers, garlic, lemon zest, oregano, and pepper together in large bowl. Add eggplant and mint and toss gently to combine. Let eggplant cool to room temperature, about 1 hour. Season with pepper to taste, and serve.

marinated cauliflower

Serves 6 to 8
Active Time 35 minutes
Total Time 35 minutes, plus 4 hours marinating

Refrigerate marinated cauliflower for up to 3 days.

½ head cauliflower (1 pound), cored and
   cut into 1-inch florets

1½ teaspoons table salt, plus salt for
    cooking cauliflower

¼ cup hot water

⅛ teaspoon saffron threads, crumbled

⅓ cup extra-virgin olive oil

5 garlic cloves, peeled and smashed

1½ teaspoons sugar

1½ teaspoons smoked paprika

1 small sprig fresh rosemary

2 tablespoons sherry vinegar

¼ teaspoon pepper

1 cup canned chickpeas, rinsed

½ lemon, sliced thin

1 tablespoon minced fresh parsley

1 Bring 2 quarts water to boil in large saucepan. Add cauliflower and 1 tablespoon salt and cook until florets begin to soften, about 3 minutes. Drain cauliflower and transfer to paper towel–lined rimmed baking sheet.

2 Combine hot water and saffron in bowl; set aside. Heat oil and garlic in small saucepan over medium-low heat until fragrant and beginning to sizzle but not brown, 4 to 6 minutes. Stir in sugar, paprika, and rosemary and cook until fragrant, about 30 seconds. Off heat, stir in saffron mixture, vinegar, pepper, and salt.

Combine cauliflower, saffron mixture, chickpeas, and lemon in large bowl. Cover and refrigerate, stirring occasionally, about 4 hours. To serve, discard rosemary sprig, transfer cauliflower and chickpeas to serving bowl, and sprinkle with parsley.

patatas bravas

Sauce

1 tablespoon vegetable oil

2 teaspoons garlic, minced to paste

1 teaspoon sweet smoked paprika

½ teaspoon kosher salt

½–¾ teaspoon cayenne pepper

Pinch red pepper flakes

¼ cup tomato paste

½ cup water

2 teaspoons sherry vinegar

¼ cup mayonnaise

Potatoes

2¼ pounds russet potatoes, peeled and cut into 1-inch pieces

½ teaspoon baking soda

1½ teaspoons kosher salt

3 cups vegetable oil for frying

WHY THIS RECIPE WORKS Patatas bravas is a tapas classic that showcases crispy, well-browned potatoes served with a smoky, spicy tomato-based sauce. To create an ultracrispy crust without the need for double frying, we first parboil russet potatoes with baking soda, which helps their exteriors break down and develop a thick crust when fried. We toss the parcooked potatoes with kosher salt, which roughs up the surfaces of the potatoes, creating nooks and crannies that trap oil, helping to make an even more substantial crunchy crust. Tomato paste, cayenne, sweet smoked paprika, garlic, and water make a smooth and spicy sauce, while sherry vinegar adds tang and mayo creaminess. Traditionally served hot, patatas bravas can also be served at room temperature. Use a Dutch oven that holds 6 quarts or more.

1 For the sauce Heat oil in small saucepan over medium-low heat until shimmering. Add garlic, paprika, salt, cayenne, and pepper flakes and cook until fragrant, about 30 seconds. Add tomato paste and cook for 30 seconds. Whisk in water and bring to boil over high heat. Reduce heat to medium-low and simmer until slightly thickened, 4 to 5 minutes. Transfer sauce to bowl, stir in vinegar, and let cool completely. Once cool, whisk in mayonnaise.

2 For the potatoes Bring 8 cups water to boil in large saucepan over high heat. Add potatoes and baking soda. Return to boil and cook for 1 minute. Drain potatoes.

3 Return potatoes to saucepan and place over low heat. Cook, shaking saucepan occasionally, until any surface moisture has evaporated, 30 seconds to 1 minute. Remove from heat. Add salt and stir with rubber spatula until potatoes are coated with thick, starchy paste, about 30 seconds. Transfer potatoes to rimmed baking sheet in single layer to cool. (Potatoes can stand at room temperature for up to 2 hours.)

4 Heat oil in large Dutch oven over high heat to 375 degrees. Add all potatoes (they should be just submerged in oil) and cook, stirring occasionally with wire skimmer or slotted spoon, until deep golden brown and crispy, 20 to 25 minutes.

5 Transfer potatoes to paper towel–lined wire rack set in rimmed baking sheet. Season with salt to taste. Spoon ½ cup sauce onto bottom of large platter or 1½ tablespoons sauce onto individual plates. Arrange potatoes over sauce and serve immediately, passing remaining sauce separately.

Head Start

Make sauce up to 1 day ahead and refrigerate until needed; let come to room temperature before serving.

Finish Line

Use bittersweet or hot smoked paprika instead of sweet paprika in sauce, if desired. Be sure to taste sauce before deciding how much cayenne to add, if any.

Perfect Pair

Serve with Oven-Baked Buffalo Wings (page 61) and Shaved Zucchini Salad with Pepitas (page 155).

southern corn fritters

4 ears corn, kernels cut from cobs (3 cups), divided

1 teaspoon plus ½ cup vegetable oil, divided

⅛ plus ¼ teaspoon table salt, divided

¼ cup all-purpose flour

¼ cup finely minced fresh chives, divided

2 tablespoons grated Parmesan cheese

1 tablespoon cornstarch

⅛ teaspoon pepper

Pinch cayenne pepper

1 large egg, lightly beaten

Head Start

Shuck corn and strip kernels a few hours ahead of preparing fritters.

Finish Line

Serve with sour cream or a flavored aioli or mayonnaise (see pages 16–17).

Perfect Pair

For a late-summer vibe, serve Tomato and Burrata Salad with Pangrattato and Basil (page 170) and Sweet Glazed Peaches (page 373) alongside.

WHY THIS RECIPE WORKS These savory fritters have a proper balance of corn, batter, and flavorings. To let the fresh corn flavor shine, we process some of the kernels to use as a thickener rather than adding more flour or cornmeal. Browning the corn kernels and puree in a skillet drives off excess moisture and concentrates their flavor. Adding cayenne, nutty Parmesan, and oniony chives contrasts with the corn's sweetness, and a little cornstarch helps to crisp the exteriors.

1 Process 1½ cups corn kernels in food processor to uniformly coarse puree, 15 to 20 seconds, scraping down sides of bowl halfway through processing. Set aside.

2 Heat 1 teaspoon oil in 12-inch nonstick skillet over medium-high heat until shimmering. Add remaining 1½ cups corn kernels and ⅛ teaspoon salt and cook, stirring frequently, until light golden, 3 to 4 minutes. Transfer to medium bowl.

3 Return skillet to medium heat, add corn puree and cook, stirring frequently with heatproof spatula, until puree is consistency of thick oatmeal (puree clings to spatula rather than dripping off), about 5 minutes. Transfer puree to bowl with kernels and stir to combine. Rinse skillet and dry with paper towels.

4 Stir flour, 3 tablespoons chives, Parmesan, cornstarch, pepper, cayenne, and remaining ¼ teaspoon salt into corn mixture until well combined. Gently stir in egg until incorporated.

5 Line rimmed baking sheet with paper towels. Heat remaining ½ cup oil in now-empty skillet over medium heat until shimmering. Drop six 2-tablespoon portions batter into skillet. Press with spatula to flatten into 2½- to 3-inch disks. Fry until deep golden brown on both sides, 2 to 3 minutes per side. Transfer fritters to prepared sheet. Repeat with remaining batter.

6 Transfer fritters to large plate or platter, sprinkle with remaining 1 tablespoon chives, and serve immediately.

fried green tomatoes

1½ pounds green tomatoes, cored and sliced ¼ inch thick

⅔ cup finely ground cornmeal, divided

⅓ cup all-purpose flour

1½ teaspoons table salt

½ teaspoon pepper

⅛ teaspoon cayenne pepper

⅔ cup buttermilk

1 large egg

2 cups peanut or vegetable oil for frying

WHY THIS RECIPE WORKS This classic Southern recipe makes a delightful small plate. Juicy slices of tart green tomatoes are encased in a crisp cornmeal coating with just a hint of cayenne heat. We drain the tomatoes on paper towels to rid them of excess liquid, which allows the coating to better adhere. Finely ground cornmeal ensures a coating with a light texture.

1 Line rimmed baking sheet with triple layer of paper towels. Place tomatoes on prepared sheet, then cover with another triple layer of paper towels. Let tomatoes sit for 20 minutes, then press dry. Meanwhile, process ⅓ cup cornmeal in blender until very finely ground, about 1 minute. Combine flour, salt, pepper, cayenne, processed cornmeal, and remaining ⅓ cup cornmeal in shallow dish. Whisk buttermilk and egg together in second shallow dish.

2 Working with one slice at a time, dip tomatoes in buttermilk mixture, then dredge in cornmeal mixture, pressing firmly to adhere; transfer to clean rimmed baking sheet.

3 Set wire rack on another rimmed baking sheet. Heat oil in 12-inch skillet over medium-high heat to 350 degrees. Place 4 tomato slices in skillet and cook until golden brown on both sides, 4 to 6 minutes. Transfer slices to prepared rack and let drain. Return oil to 350 degrees and repeat with remaining tomato slices. Serve.

Head Start

Mix cornmeal coating up to 1 day ahead and refrigerate until needed.

Finish Line

Dollop each fried slice with mayonnaise (page 17) or store-bought ranch dressing. Serve with lemon wedges on the side.

Perfect Pair

For some down-home comfort, serve with Chile con Queso (page 111), Texas Caviar (page 196), or Quesadillas for a Crowd (page 151). Offer some sweet tea too.

Serves 6 to 8 (makes 24 stuffed mushrooms) | **Active Time** 25 minutes
Total Time 1¼ hours

sausage-and-cheddar-stuffed mushrooms

24 white mushrooms (1½ to 2 inches in diameter)

2 tablespoons extra-virgin olive oil

2 tablespoons balsamic vinegar

1¼ teaspoons table salt, divided

1 teaspoon pepper, divided

12 ounces hot Italian sausage, casings removed

3 ounces extra-sharp cheddar cheese, shredded (¾ cup)

4 scallions, sliced thin

¼ cup panko bread crumbs

3 tablespoons white wine

1 tablespoon chopped fresh thyme

3 garlic cloves, minced

¼ cup grated Parmesan cheese

WHY THIS RECIPE WORKS An enduring small plate favorite, these stuffed mushrooms have serious mushroom flavor and an irresistible savory filling. We chose hot Italian sausage as the stuffing base and happily found that it doesn't need to be cooked first. We combine the raw sausage with tangy extra-sharp cheddar, scallions, panko to bind, a few splashes of white wine for acidity, fresh thyme, and minced garlic and use this mixture to fill the caps. Then we roast the mushrooms in a skillet in the oven. Using a skillet rather than a baking sheet to roast the mushrooms captures and concentrates the mushrooms' juice, resulting in deeper flavor as the mushrooms reabsorb this potent liquid. You will need about 1½ pounds of mushrooms to yield 24 filled mushrooms.

1 Adjust oven rack to middle position and heat oven to 425 degrees. Remove stems from mushrooms and chop half of stems fine; discard remaining stems. Whisk oil, vinegar, 1 teaspoon salt, and ½ teaspoon pepper together in medium bowl. Add mushroom caps and toss to coat with oil mixture; set aside.

2 Using your hands, thoroughly combine sausage, cheddar, scallions, panko, wine, thyme, garlic, mushroom stems, remaining ¼ teaspoon salt, and remaining ½ teaspoon pepper in bowl.

3 Spray 12-inch ovensafe skillet (or 13 by 9-inch baking dish) with vegetable oil spray. Fill mushroom caps with sausage mixture and place in prepared skillet. Sprinkle tops of filled mushrooms with Parmesan.

4 Bake until cooked through and lightly browned on top, about 35 minutes. Let cool for 10 minutes. Transfer to platter and serve.

Variation

Pizza-Flavored Stuffed Mushrooms
Substitute whole-milk mozzarella for cheddar, ¼ cup chopped fresh basil for scallions, and ½ teaspoon dried Italian seasoning for thyme. Add ¼ cup finely chopped pepperoni and 1 tablespoon tomato paste to sausage mixture.

Head Start

Stuff mushrooms, cover with plastic wrap, and refrigerate for up to 24 hours before baking.

Perfect Pair

Serve with Tempeh with Sambal Sauce (page 291), Gobi Manchurian (page 234), or Stir-Fried En Choy with Garlic (page 220).

roasted king trumpet mushrooms

1¾ pounds king trumpet mushrooms

½ teaspoon table salt

4 tablespoons unsalted butter, melted

Lemon wedges

WHY THIS RECIPE WORKS King trumpet mushrooms, also called king oyster mushrooms, have little aroma or flavor when raw, but when cooked they become deeply savory, with the texture of squid or tender octopus. They make an elegant and meaty small plate, and they couldn't be simpler to cook. We halve them lengthwise to preserve their dramatic shape; cross-hatch each mushroom, creating attractive "fillets"; and then salt them. Roasting the mushrooms in a hot oven gives them a nicely browned exterior crust and a plump, juicy, and well-seasoned interior. Look for trumpet mushrooms that weigh 3 to 4 ounces.

1 Adjust oven rack to lowest position and heat oven to 500 degrees. Trim bottom ½ inch of mushroom stems, then halve mushrooms lengthwise. Cut 1/16-inch-deep slits on cut side of mushrooms, spaced ½ inch apart, in crosshatch pattern. Sprinkle cut side of mushrooms with salt and let sit for 15 minutes.

2 Brush mushrooms evenly with melted butter, season with pepper to taste, and arrange cut side down on rimmed baking sheet. Roast until mushrooms are browned on cut side, 20 to 24 minutes. Transfer to serving platter. Serve immediately, with lemon wedges.

Finish Line

The mushrooms are delicious with just a squeeze of lemon or Red Wine–Miso Sauce (page 15) or Browned Butter–Lemon Vinaigrette (page 16).

Perfect Pair

Play up the mushrooms' earthiness by serving with Farro Salad with Sugar Snap Peas and White Beans (page 192) or Caramel Tofu (page 259).

stir-fried en choy with garlic

4 teaspoons vegetable oil, divided

2 garlic cloves, chopped, divided

1 pound red or green en choy, flat-leaf spinach, watercress, or ong choy, trimmed, divided

¼ teaspoon table salt, divided

WHY THIS RECIPE WORKS These very simple tender greens with garlic cook quickly, and their light seasoning makes them a small plate that goes with everything. They are also pretty; the high heat turns the greens a vivid bright green. Be sure to wait until they are slightly wilted to add the salt, so that it adheres better. We use en choy (Chinese spinach) for this stir-fry, but you can substitute flat-leaf spinach, watercress, or ong choy (water spinach). You will need a 14-inch flat-bottomed wok or 12-inch nonstick skillet for this recipe. You can easily double this recipe.

1 Heat 2 teaspoons oil in 14-inch flat-bottomed wok or 12-inch nonstick skillet over medium-high heat until just smoking. Add half of garlic, then immediately add half of en choy and increase heat to high. Cook, tossing spinach slowly but constantly, until just beginning to wilt, about 30 seconds. Sprinkle with ⅛ teaspoon salt and continue to cook until spinach is bright green and just tender, 30 seconds to 2 minutes; transfer to bowl.

2 Repeat with remaining 2 teaspoons oil, remaining garlic, remaining spinach, and remaining ⅛ teaspoon salt. Off heat, return first batch of en choy to pan and toss to combine. Serve.

Finish Line

These quick-cooking greens are best made at the last minute, after guests arrive.

Perfect Pair

Serve with Chinese Barbecue Spareribs (page 314) or Chicken Satay (page 303).

pressure-cooker braised radishes and snap peas

¼ cup extra-virgin olive oil, divided

1 shallot, sliced thin

3 garlic cloves, sliced thin

1½ pounds radishes, 2 cups greens reserved, radishes trimmed and halved if small or quartered if large

½ cup water

½ teaspoon table salt

8 ounces sugar snap peas, strings removed, sliced thin on bias

8 ounces cremini mushrooms, trimmed and sliced thin

2 teaspoons grated lemon zest plus 1 teaspoon juice

1 cup plain Greek yogurt

½ cup fresh cilantro leaves

3 tablespoons Pistachio Dukkah (page 20

WHY THIS RECIPE WORKS Crisp radishes have their place on a crudités plate, but braising them quickly in a pressure cooker turns them sweet and meaty. Pairing them with sliced cremini and sugar snap peas makes them even more special. We flavor the braising liquid with shallot and garlic along with some lemon zest for brightness. A swoosh of Greek yogurt makes a creamy bed for the vegetables, while a sprinkle of dukkah, the Egyptian spice blend, adds a final layer of flavor and crunch. If your radishes do not come with greens, substitute baby arugula. We prefer to make our own dukkah, but you can substitute store-bought dukkah. This recipe will work only in an electric pressure cooker.

1 Using highest sauté function, heat 2 tablespoons oil in electric pressure cooker until shimmering. Add shallot and cook until softened, about 2 minutes. Stir in garlic and cook until fragrant, about 30 seconds. Stir in radishes, water, and salt. Lock lid in place and close pressure release valve. Select high pressure cook function and cook for 1 minute.

2 Turn off pressure cooker and quick-release pressure. Carefully remove lid, allowing steam to escape away from you. Stir in snap peas, cover, and let sit until heated through, about 3 minutes. Add radish greens, mushrooms, lemon zest and juice, and remaining 2 tablespoons oil and toss gently to combine. Season with salt and pepper to taste.

3 Spread yogurt over bottom of serving platter. Using slotted spoon, arrange vegetable mixture on top. Sprinkle with cilantro and dukkah and serve.

Head Start

Prep radishes and snap peas up to 1 day ahead; refrigerate covered until needed.

Perfect Pair

Serve with Pork and Cabbage Potstickers (page 344) or Naan with Roasted Red Peppers, Feta, and Olives (page 334).

skillet-roasted broccoli with sesame and orange topping

Sesame and Orange Topping

2 tablespoons toasted sesame seeds, divided

½ teaspoon grated orange zest

¼ teaspoon kosher salt

Broccoli

1¼ pounds broccoli crowns

5 tablespoons vegetable oil

¾ teaspoon kosher salt

2 tablespoons water

WHY THIS RECIPE WORKS Skillet roasting turns everyday broccoli into a dynamite small plate. Deeply browning the broccoli enhances the meaty stems and delicate florets, giving them a nutty flavor and crisp texture. The umami-rich crunchy topping is our take on the Japanese dry condiment gomasio. We cut broccoli crowns into wedges to create flat sides to sit flush with the surface of the skillet. Once the broccoli is softened, the oil fills any gaps between the broccoli and the skillet. We developed this recipe with Diamond Crystal kosher salt, which has large grains. If using smaller-grained Morton's kosher salt, use only ½ teaspoon with the broccoli. Do not adjust the small amount of salt in the topping.

1 **For the sesame and orange topping** Using spice grinder or mortar and pestle, grind 1 tablespoon sesame seeds, orange zest, and salt to powder. Transfer to small bowl. Add remaining 1 tablespoon sesame seeds and toss with your fingers until sesame seeds are evenly distributed. Sprinkle one-third of topping onto platter.

2 **For the broccoli** Cut broccoli into 4 wedges if crowns are 3 to 4 inches in diameter or 6 wedges if 4 to 5 inches in diameter. Add oil to 12-inch nonstick skillet and tilt skillet until oil covers surface. Add broccoli, cut side down (pieces will fit snugly; if a few pieces don't fit in bottom layer, place on top). Sprinkle evenly with salt and drizzle with water. Cover and cook over high heat, without moving broccoli, until broccoli is bright green, about 4 minutes.

3 Uncover and press gently on broccoli with back of spatula. Cover and cook until undersides of broccoli are deeply charred and stems are crisp-tender, 4 to 6 minutes. Off heat, uncover and turn broccoli so second cut side is touching skillet. Move any pieces that were on top so they are flush with skillet surface. Continue to cook, uncovered, pressing gently on broccoli with back of spatula, until second cut side is deeply browned, 3 to 5 minutes longer. Transfer to platter, sprinkle with remaining topping, and serve.

Variations

Skillet-Roasted Broccoli with Smoky Sunflower Seed Topping
Nutritional yeast is a flaky, golden, nonleavening form of yeast with a nutty, tangy flavor; look for it in natural foods stores.

Using spice grinder or mortar and pestle, grind 2 tablespoons toasted sunflower seeds, 1 tablespoon nutritional yeast, ½ teaspoon grated lemon zest, ¼ teaspoon smoked paprika, and ¼ teaspoon kosher salt to coarse powder. Substitute for Sesame and Orange Topping.

Skillet-Roasted Broccoli with Parmesan and Black Pepper Topping
Using your fingers, mix ½ teaspoon pepper and ½ teaspoon grated lemon zest in small bowl until evenly combined. Add ½ cup grated Parmesan cheese and toss until lemon zest and pepper are evenly distributed. Substitute for Sesame and Orange Topping.

Finish Line
Drizzle Sichuan Chili Oil (page 19) over broccoli if you like.

Perfect Pair
For a lighter small plate selection, serve with Pink Bean and Lima Bean Dip with Parsley (page 99) and Baked Goat Cheese (page 139). Or pair with Arrosticini (page 317) or Lamb Rib Chops with Mint-Rosemary Relish (page 283).

roasted asparagus with mustard-dill hollandaise

Asparagus

- 2 pounds thick asparagus, trimmed
- 2 tablespoons extra-virgin olive oil
- ½ teaspoon table salt
- ¼ teaspoon pepper

Mustard-Dill Hollandaise

- 3 large egg yolks
- 2 tablespoons lemon juice
- ¼ teaspoon table salt

  Pinch cayenne pepper, plus extra for seasoning
- 16 tablespoons unsalted butter, melted and still hot (180 degrees)
- 1 tablespoon whole-grain mustard
- 1 tablespoon minced fresh dill

Perfect Pair

Serve with Breakfast Buttercups (page 147) or Spiralized Sweet Potatoes with Crispy Shallots, Pistachios, and Urfa (page 250).

WHY THIS RECIPE WORKS Asparagus is one of the easiest vegetables to roast. Add a foolproof, rich hollandaise sauce that's made in the blender and you have a simple yet elegant small plate that would be perfect for brunch or dinner. To ensure a hard sear on the asparagus, preheat the baking sheet and resist the urge to shake it during roasting. This recipe works best with thick asparagus spears that are between ½ and ¾ inch in diameter. Do not use pencil-thin asparagus; it overcooks too easily. For the hollandaise, it's important to make sure the butter is still hot (about 180 degrees) so that the egg yolks cook sufficiently.

1 **For the asparagus** Adjust oven rack to lowest position, place rimmed baking sheet on rack, and heat oven to 500 degrees. Peel bottom halves of asparagus spears until white flesh is exposed, then toss with oil, salt, and pepper in bowl.

2 Transfer asparagus to preheated sheet and spread into single layer. Roast, without moving asparagus, until undersides of spears are browned, tops are bright green, and tip of paring knife inserted at base of largest spear meets little resistance, 8 to 10 minutes.

3 **For the mustard-dill hollandaise** Meanwhile, process egg yolks, lemon juice, salt, and cayenne in blender until frothy, about 10 seconds, scraping bottom and sides of blender jar as needed. With blender running, slowly add hot butter and process until hollandaise is emulsified, about 2 minutes. Adjust consistency with hot water as needed until sauce slowly drips from spoon. Season with salt and extra cayenne to taste. Add mustard and dill to hollandaise and blend until combined but not smooth.

4 Transfer asparagus to serving dish and drizzle with hollandaise. Serve.

roasted carrots and shallots with chermoula

Carrots

1½ pounds carrots, peeled and halved lengthwise

4 large shallots, peeled and halved through root end

2 tablespoons refined coconut oil or unsalted butter, melted

½ teaspoon table salt

¼ teaspoon pepper

2 tablespoons coarsely chopped toasted pine nuts

Chermoula

¾ cup fresh cilantro leaves

2 tablespoons lemon juice

4 garlic cloves, minced

1 serrano chile, stemmed, seeded, and minced

½ teaspoon ground cumin

½ teaspoon table salt

⅛ teaspoon cayenne pepper

¼ cup extra-virgin olive oil

WHY THIS RECIPE WORKS Roasting carrots with shallots and topping them with a garlicky herb sauce takes them from side dish to small plate sensation. We coat the carrots with fat and roast them on the lowest oven rack for a tender, sweet, and almost caramel-like result. We then spice them up with an intense green chermoula and plenty of toasted pine nuts. Choose carrots that are about 1½ inches in diameter at the thicker end. If your carrots are smaller, leave them whole; if they're larger, extend the roasting time slightly.

1 **For the carrots** Adjust oven rack to lowest position and heat oven to 450 degrees. Toss carrots, shallots, melted oil, salt, and pepper together in bowl to coat. Spread carrot-shallot mixture in even layer on rimmed baking sheet, cut sides down. Roast until tender and cut sides are well browned, 15 to 25 minutes.

2 **For the chermoula** Meanwhile, process cilantro, lemon juice, garlic, serrano, cumin, salt, and cayenne in food processor until finely chopped, about 1 minute, scraping down sides of bowl as needed. With processor running, slowly add oil until incorporated. Transfer to small bowl.

3 Transfer carrots and shallots to serving platter and season with salt to taste. Drizzle with chermoula and sprinkle with pine nuts. Serve.

Perfect Pair

Butternut Squash and Apple Fattoush (page 185) or Pizza-Flavored Stuffed Mushrooms (page 217) are hearty pairings.

grilled vegetables

When you are grilling a protein, you can easily grill a vegetable as well. These recipes offer easy, flavorful ways to make small plate grilled vegetables, and our chart has other vegetables to grill. You can also add a savory sauce or spice garnish (see pages 14–21) to dress up the vegetables even more.

grilled radicchio

Serves 8 to 12
Active Time 10 minutes
Total Time 10 minutes

Turning the wedges during cooking ensures that all sides, including the rounded one, spend time facing the fire.

- 3 heads radicchio (10 ounces each), quartered
- ¼ cup extra-virgin olive oil
- Balsamic vinegar

1 Place radicchio on rimmed baking sheet, brush with oil, and season with salt and pepper to taste.

2A **For a charcoal grill** Open bottom vent completely. Light large chimney starter filled with charcoal briquettes (6 quarts). When top coals are partially covered with ash, pour evenly over grill. Set cooking grate in place, cover, and open lid vent completely. Heat grill until hot, about 5 minutes.

2B **For a gas grill** Turn all burners to high, cover, and heat grill until hot, about 15 minutes. Turn all burners to medium-high.

3 Clean and oil cooking grate. Grill radicchio (covered if using gas), turning every 1½ minutes, until edges are browned and wilted but centers are still slightly firm, about 5 minutes. Transfer radicchio to serving dish, drizzle with vinegar, and serve.

Perfect Pair

Serve grilled vegetables with Arrosticini (page 317), Pinchos Morunos (page 310), or any proteins and breads you are grilling.

grilled prosciutto-wrapped asparagus

Serves 4 to 6
Active time 20 minutes
Total time 30 minutes

For the best results, look for spears that are bright green in color and firm to the touch, with tightly closed tips. If you are using asparagus spears that are thicker than ½ inch in diameter, you may have to increase the grilling time. Do not use asparagus that is thinner than ½ inch in diameter. This recipe can be easily doubled.

16 (½-inch-thick) asparagus spears, trimmed

8 thin slices prosciutto (4 ounces)

2 tablespoons extra-virgin olive oil

Pepper

Lemon wedges

1 Working with 2 asparagus spears at a time, tightly wrap 1 slice prosciutto around middle of spears to create bundle. (If prosciutto rips, slightly overlap ripped pieces and press with your fingers to stick it back together.) Brush bundles on both sides with oil and season with pepper.

2A **For a charcoal grill** Open bottom vent completely. Light large chimney starter filled with charcoal briquettes (6 quarts). When top coals are partially covered with ash, pour evenly over grill. Set cooking grate in place, cover, and open lid vent completely. Heat grill until hot, about 5 minutes.

2B **For a gas grill** Turn all burners to high, cover, and heat grill until hot, about 15 minutes. Turn all burners to medium.

3 Clean and oil cooking grate. Grill asparagus bundles (covered if using gas) until prosciutto is spotty brown and paring knife slips easily in and out of asparagus, 6 to 8 minutes, flipping bundles halfway through cooking. Transfer asparagus bundles to platter. Serve warm or at room temperature with lemon wedges.

How to Grill Vegetables

To easily grill a simple vegetable for a small plate spread, use this chart as a guide. Brush or toss the vegetables with oil and sprinkle with salt and pepper before grilling. Grill vegetables over a moderate fire (you can comfortably hold your hand 5 inches above the cooking grate for 3 to 4 seconds).

Vegetable	Preparation	Grilling Directions
Asparagus	Trim ends.	Grill, turning once, until streaked with light grill marks, 5 to 7 minutes.
Bell Pepper	Core, seed, and cut into large wedges.	Grill, turning often, until streaked with dark grill marks, 8 to 10 minutes.
Eggplant	Remove ends. Cut into ¾-inch-thick rounds or strips.	Grill, turning once, until flesh is darkly colored, 8 to 10 minutes.
Endive	Halve lengthwise through stem end.	Grill, flat side down, until streaked with dark grill marks, 5 to 7 minutes.
Portobello Mushrooms	Discard stems; wipe caps clean.	Grill, turning once, until streaked with dark grill marks and quite soft, 7 to 9 minutes.
White or Cremini Mushrooms	Trim thin slice from stems, then thread onto skewers.	Grill, turning several times, until golden brown, 6 to 7 minutes.
Cherry Tomatoes	Remove stems, then thread onto skewers.	Grill, turning often, until streaked with dark grill marks, 3 to 6 minutes.
Plum Tomatoes	Halve lengthwise and seed, if desired.	Grill, turning once, until streaked with dark grill marks, about 6 minutes.
Zucchini or Yellow Summer Squash	Remove ends. Slice lengthwise into ½-inch-thick strips.	Grill, turning once, until streaked with dark grill marks, 8 to 10 minutes.

carciofi alla giudia

4 artichokes (10 to 12 ounces each)

6 cups vegetable oil or peanut oil for frying

2 cups extra-virgin olive oil for frying

Lemon wedges

Flake sea salt

Head Start

Prepare artichokes through step 3 up to 1 day ahead; wrap them well and refrigerate until needed. Reserve oil and reuse to finish cooking artichokes.

Finish Line

Serve with Aioli (page 16) and lemon wedges.

Perfect Pair

The fresh flavors of Fennel, Orange, and Olive Salad (page 165) and Bruschetta with Artichoke Hearts and Basil (page 330) are a cheeky complement to these fried artichokes.

WHY THIS RECIPE WORKS These beautiful fried artichokes make an elegant small plate. They are crunchy, crispy, and creamy. Our double frying method ensures good browning and superb texture. Artichokes discolor as you prep them, but that won't be visible after frying. If your large saucepan holds less than 4 quarts, use a large Dutch oven (add 2 cups more vegetable oil so the artichokes are completely covered). Look for artichokes that are uniformly green, have tightly closed leaves, feel heavy for their size, and squeak a little when squeezed. Avoid any that are browning and dried out.

1 Working with one artichoke at a time, snap off tough outer leaves until you reach tender inner leaves (they'll be pale yellow at their base). Trim stem to 1½-inches. Peel stem and base with paring or bird's beak knife to remove dark-green layer. Starting halfway up leaves, use chef's knife to make 45-degree angled cut toward top of artichoke to remove tips of leaves. Repeat same cut three more times, rotating artichoke quarter turn before each cut.

2 Set wire rack on rimmed baking sheet and line with double layer of paper towels. Heat vegetable oil and olive oil in large saucepan over medium-high heat to 275 degrees. Cut each artichoke in half through stem.

3 Using spider skimmer or slotted spoon, carefully add artichokes to oil. Cook until paring knife slipped into thickest part of base meets little resistance and leaves are medium brown, 10 to 12 minutes. Remove from heat. Transfer artichokes to prepared rack, cut side down, to drain. Let cool for 15 minutes.

4 Using spoon, scoop out choke from center of each artichoke half, being careful not to dislodge leaves attached to base. Replace paper towels with double layer of fresh paper towels. Heat oil over high heat to 350 degrees.

5 Place two artichoke halves cut side down in oil and, using spider skimmer or slotted spoon, lightly press on artichokes to submerge. Cook until outer leaves are dark brown, 45 to 60 seconds. Transfer to prepared rack, cut side down, to drain. Return oil to 350 degrees and repeat with remaining artichoke halves in three batches. Sprinkle artichokes on both sides with flake sea salt to taste.

gobi manchurian

Cauliflower

- 1 cup water
- ⅔ cup cornstarch
- ⅔ cup all-purpose flour
- 1 teaspoon table salt
- 1 teaspoon baking powder
- 1 pound (1½-inch) cauliflower florets (4 cups)
- 2 quarts peanut or vegetable oil for frying

Sauce

- ¼ cup ketchup
- 3 tablespoons water
- 2 tablespoons soy sauce
- 1 tablespoon chili-garlic sauce
- 2 teaspoons lime juice, plus lime wedges for serving
- ¾ teaspoon pepper
- ½ teaspoon ground cumin
- 2 tablespoons vegetable oil
- 3 scallions, white and green parts separated and sliced thin
- 1 tablespoon grated fresh ginger
- 3 garlic cloves, minced

WHY THIS RECIPE WORKS Gobi Manchurian is a multinational dish with roots in the Chinese immigrant communities in Kolkata, India. It features cauliflower florets battered and deep fried until crisp and then tossed in a rich, spicy sauce, making a satisfying, multitextured dish that is perfect for sharing. The fried florets stay crispy even after being dressed in the sauce. A spritz of fresh lime juice adds brightness to the dish. A 2½-pound head of cauliflower should yield 1 pound of florets. You can also buy precut florets if available. Use a Dutch oven that holds 6 quarts or more.

1 **For the cauliflower** Whisk water, cornstarch, flour, salt, and baking powder in large bowl until smooth. Add cauliflower to batter and toss with rubber spatula to evenly coat; set aside.

2 Line rimmed baking sheet with triple layer of paper towels. Add oil to large Dutch oven until it measures about 1½ inches deep and heat over medium-high heat to 375 degrees.

3 Using tongs, add cauliflower to hot oil one piece at a time. Cook, stirring occasionally to prevent cauliflower from sticking, until coating is firm and very lightly golden, about 5 minutes. (Adjust burner, if necessary, to maintain oil temperature between 300 and 325 degrees.) Using spider skimmer, transfer cauliflower to prepared sheet.

4 **For the sauce** Combine ketchup, water, soy sauce, chili-garlic sauce, lime juice, pepper, and cumin in bowl. Heat oil in small saucepan over medium-high heat until shimmering. Add scallion whites, ginger, and garlic and cook, stirring frequently, until fragrant, about 1½ minutes. Stir in ketchup mixture and bring to simmer, scraping up any bits of ginger mixture from bottom of saucepan. Transfer sauce to clean large bowl.

5 Add cauliflower and scallion greens to bowl with sauce and toss to combine. Transfer to platter and serve with lime wedges.

Head Start

Make sauce up to 1 day ahead and refrigerate; reheat in microwave before tossing with cauliflower.

Perfect Pair

Serve with Masala Chai (page 387), Quick Carrot Pickles (page 76), or Easy Cheese Straws (page 320). Try leftover sauce with Pakoras (page 49) or dumplings (see pages 342–345).

latkes

2 pounds russet potatoes, unpeeled, scrubbed, and shredded

½ cup grated onion

1 teaspoon table salt

2 large eggs, lightly beaten

2 teaspoons minced fresh parsley

¼ teaspoon pepper

Vegetable oil for frying

WHY THIS RECIPE WORKS Potato pancakes are the ideal vehicle for all manner of toppings, making them a super-versatile small plates pick. We keep our latkes light and crisp by removing as much water as possible from the potato shreds. We prefer shredding the potatoes on the large holes of a box grater, but you can also use the large shredding disk of a food processor. Cut the potatoes into 2-inch lengths first so you are left with short shreds.

1 Adjust oven rack to middle position, place rimmed baking sheet on rack, and heat oven to 200 degrees. Toss potatoes, onion, and salt in bowl. Place half of mixture in center of dish towel. Gather ends together and twist tightly to drain as much liquid as possible, reserving liquid in liquid measuring cup. Transfer drained mixture to second bowl and repeat process with remaining mixture. Set potato liquid aside and let stand so starch settles to bottom, at least 5 minutes.

2 Cover potato mixture and microwave until just warmed through but not hot, 1 to 2 minutes, stirring with fork every 30 seconds. Spread mixture evenly over second rimmed baking sheet and let cool for 10 minutes. Don't wash bowl.

3 Pour off water from reserved potato liquid, leaving potato starch in measuring cup. Add eggs and stir until smooth. Return cooled potato mixture to bowl. Add parsley, pepper, and potato starch mixture and toss until evenly combined.

4 Set wire rack on clean rimmed baking sheet and line with triple layer of paper towels. Add oil to 12-inch skillet until it measures about ¼ inch deep and heat over medium-high heat until shimmering but not smoking (350 degrees). Place ¼-cup mound of potato mixture in oil and press with nonstick spatula into ⅓-inch-thick disk. Repeat until 5 latkes are in pan. Cook, adjusting heat so fat bubbles around latke edges, until golden brown on bottom, about 3 minutes. Turn and continue cooking until golden brown on second side, about 3 minutes longer. Drain on paper towels and transfer to baking sheet in oven. Repeat with remaining potato mixture, adding oil to maintain ¼-inch depth and returning oil to 350 degrees between batches. Season with salt and pepper to taste, and serve immediately.

Head Start

Cover cooled latkes loosely with plastic wrap and hold at room temperature for up to 4 hours. Alternatively, freeze latkes on baking sheet until firm, transfer to zipper-lock bag, and keep frozen for up to 1 month. Reheat latkes in 375-degree oven until crispy and hot, 3 minutes per side for room-temperature and 6 minutes per side for frozen.

Finish Line

Serve with applesauce, sour cream, smoked salmon, and/or caviar.

Perfect Pair

Beet Muhammara (page 103), Bacon and Chive Deviled Eggs (page 129), or Crab Croquettes (page 272) are great accompaniments.

samosas

Filling

- 2 pounds russet potatoes, peeled and cut into 1-inch pieces
- 1 teaspoon table salt, plus salt for cooking potatoes
- 3 tablespoons vegetable oil
- 1 teaspoon fennel seeds
- 1 teaspoon cumin seeds
- 1 teaspoon brown mustard seeds
- ¼ teaspoon ground fenugreek
- ¼ teaspoon ground turmeric
- ⅛ teaspoon red pepper flakes
- 1 onion, chopped fine
- 3 garlic cloves, minced
- 1½ teaspoons grated fresh ginger
- ½ cup frozen peas, thawed
- ¼ cup minced fresh cilantro
- 1½ teaspoons lemon juice

Dough

- 2 cups (10 ounces) all-purpose flour
- ½ teaspoon table salt
- 3 tablespoons vegetable oil
- 2 tablespoons plain whole-milk yogurt
- 4–6 tablespoons ice water

- 3 quarts vegetable oil for frying

WHY THIS RECIPE WORKS We think that samosas, an Indian fried snack, often with a pungently spiced potato filling in a thin, crispy pastry shell, make a wonderful small plate. We parcook potatoes and then fry them with spices such as cumin, mustard seeds, and fenugreek until the edges are crisp and browned and their flavors have bloomed. Peas, cilantro, and lemon juice round out the filling. Our dough includes yogurt and vegetable oil to make it pliable and easy to work with; as a bonus, the fat turns it crispy and golden when cooked. If necessary, you can substitute ½ teaspoon of ground fennel and ½ teaspoon of ground cumin for the whole spices. We prefer whole-milk yogurt in the dough, but you can substitute low-fat yogurt (do not use nonfat). Be sure to use ice water in the dough to prevent it from overheating as you process it. You will need a Dutch oven that holds at least 6 quarts.

1 For the filling Place potatoes and 1 tablespoon salt in large saucepan and add water to cover by 1 inch. Bring to boil, then reduce heat to maintain simmer and cook until potatoes are tender and paring knife can be inserted into potatoes with little resistance, 12 to 15 minutes. Drain potatoes and set aside to cool slightly.

2 Heat oil in 12-inch nonstick skillet over medium-high heat until shimmering. Add fennel seeds, cumin seeds, mustard seeds, fenugreek, turmeric, and pepper flakes and cook until fragrant, about 10 seconds. Stir in onion and salt and cook until onion is softened, 5 to 7 minutes. Stir in garlic and ginger and cook until fragrant, about 30 seconds. Stir in potatoes and cook until beginning to brown around edges, 5 to 7 minutes. Stir in peas.

3 Transfer mixture to bowl; let cool; then refrigerate until completely cool, about 1 hour. Stir in cilantro and lemon juice and season with salt and pepper to taste.

4 For the dough Pulse flour and salt in food processor until combined, about 4 pulses. Drizzle oil and yogurt over flour mixture and process until mixture resembles coarse cornmeal, about 5 seconds. With processor running, slowly add ¼ cup ice water until dough forms ball. If dough doesn't come together, add remaining 2 tablespoons ice water, 1 tablespoon at a time, with processor running, until dough ball forms. Dough should feel very soft and malleable.

5   Transfer dough to floured counter and knead by hand until slightly firm, about 2 minutes. Wrap dough in plastic wrap and let rest for at least 20 minutes.

6   Divide dough into 12 equal pieces. Working with one piece of dough at a time, roll dough into 5-inch rounds; when not working with them, keep dough pieces covered with plastic wrap greased with oil spray. Cut each dough round in half to form 24 half-moons.

7   Moisten straight side of one half-moon with your wet finger, then fold in half. Press to seal seam on straight side only and crimp with fork to secure; leave rounded edge open and unsealed. Pick up piece of dough and hold gently in your cupped hand, with open, unsealed edge facing up; gently open dough into cone shape. Fill dough cone with 2 tablespoons filling and pack filling in tightly, leaving ¼-inch rim at top. Moisten inside rim of cone with your wet finger and pinch top edges together to seal. Lay samosa on flat surface and crimp sealed edge with fork to secure. Repeat with remaining half-moons and remaining filling.

8   Adjust oven rack to middle position and heat oven to 200 degrees. Line rimmed baking sheet with several layers of paper towels. Heat 3 quarts oil in large Dutch oven over medium-high heat to 375 degrees. Add 8 samosas and fry until golden brown and bubbly, 2½ to 3 minutes, adjusting burner, if necessary, to maintain oil temperature of 375 degrees. Using spider skimmer or slotted spoon, transfer samosas to prepared sheet and keep warm in oven. Return oil to 375 degrees and repeat with remaining samosas in 2 batches. Serve.

Head Start

Make filling up to 2 days ahead (reserving cilantro and lemon juice to stir in just before shaping samosas) and refrigerate until needed. Make dough through step 5 up to 1 day ahead and refrigerate until needed.

Finish Line

Serve samosas with Cilantro-Mint Chutney (page 18).

Perfect Pair

Crispy Lentil and Herb Salad (page 198) and Stir-Fried En Choy with Garlic (page 220) provide complementary proteins and leafy greens for a well-rounded small plate offering.

stuffed tomatoes with couscous and spinach

6 large vine-ripened tomatoes (8 to 10 ounces each)

1 tablespoon sugar

½ teaspoon table salt, plus salt for salting tomatoes

4½ tablespoons extra-virgin olive oil, divided

¼ cup panko bread crumbs

3 ounces Gruyère cheese, shredded (¾ cup), divided

1 onion, halved and sliced thin

2 garlic cloves, minced

⅛ teaspoon red pepper flakes

8 ounces (8 cups) baby spinach, chopped coarse

1 cup couscous

½ teaspoon grated lemon zest

1 tablespoon red wine vinegar

WHY THIS RECIPE WORKS A stuffed tomato is a substantial offering, a mini meal on a plate. Baking concentrates the tomatoes' flavor, softens their texture (making them easier to eat), and helps meld the tomato case with the stuffing. To remove excess liquid before baking, we salt the tomatoes and include a bit of sugar. We drain the tomato pulp to extract the tomato juice and use that to plump the couscous, which absorbs some of the tomato juices and stays moist while the tomatoes bake. To bolster the stuffing's flavor, we add onion and garlic, baby spinach, lemon zest, and red pepper flakes, while nutty Gruyère adds cohesiveness. A toasted panko topping crowns the tomatoes with crunch. Choose large tomatoes, about 3 inches in diameter.

1 Adjust oven rack to middle position and heat oven to 375 degrees. Cut top ½ inch off stem end of tomatoes and set aside. Using melon baller, scoop out tomato pulp and transfer to fine-mesh strainer set over bowl. Press on pulp with wooden spoon to extract juice; set aside juice and discard pulp. (You should have about ⅔ cup tomato juice; if not, add water as needed to equal ⅔ cup.)

2 Combine sugar and 1 tablespoon salt in bowl. Sprinkle each tomato cavity with 1 teaspoon sugar mixture, then turn tomatoes upside down on plate to drain for 30 minutes.

3 Meanwhile, combine 1½ teaspoons oil and panko in 10-inch skillet and toast over medium-high heat, stirring frequently, until golden brown, about 3 minutes. Transfer to bowl and let cool for 10 minutes. Stir in ¼ cup Gruyère and set aside.

4 Heat 2 tablespoons oil in now-empty skillet over medium heat until shimmering. Add onion and ½ teaspoon salt and cook until softened, 5 to 7 minutes. Stir in garlic and pepper flakes and cook until fragrant, about 30 seconds. Add spinach, 1 handful at a time, and cook until wilted, about 3 minutes. Stir in couscous, lemon zest, and reserved tomato juice. Cover, remove from heat, and let sit until couscous has absorbed liquid, about 7 minutes. Transfer couscous mixture to bowl and stir in remaining ½ cup Gruyère. Season with salt and pepper to taste.

5 Coat bottom of 13 by 9-inch baking dish with remaining 2 tablespoons oil. Blot tomato cavities dry with paper towels and season with salt and pepper. Pack tomatoes with couscous mixture, about ½ cup per tomato, mounding excess. Top each stuffed tomato with 1 heaping tablespoon panko mixture. Place tomatoes in prepared baking dish. Season reserved tops with salt and pepper and place in empty spaces in dish.

6 Bake, uncovered, until tomatoes have softened but still hold their shape, about 20 minutes. Using slotted spoon, transfer tomatoes and tops to serving platter. Whisk vinegar into oil remaining in dish, then drizzle over tomatoes. Place tops on tomatoes and serve.

Variation

Stuffed Tomatoes with Capers and Pine Nuts
Substitute shredded mozzarella for Gruyère. Stir 2 tablespoons rinsed capers and 2 tablespoons toasted pine nuts into cooked couscous mixture with mozzarella in step 4.

Finish Line

To serve, arrange tomatoes on a bed of Bibb lettuce or garnish platter with parsley.

Perfect Pair

Serve with Pinchos Morunos or Pigs in Blankets (page 46), Pimento Cheese Spread (page 87), or Blue Cheese and Chive Popovers with Blue Cheese Butter (page 328).

braised eggplant with soy, garlic, and ginger

1½ cups water

¼ cup Shaoxing wine or dry sherry

2 tablespoons soy sauce

4 teaspoons sugar

2 teaspoons doubanjiang

1 teaspoon cornstarch

2 (8- to 10-ounce) globe or Italian eggplants

1 tablespoon vegetable oil

1 garlic clove, minced

1 teaspoon grated fresh ginger

½ teaspoon toasted sesame oil

2 scallions, sliced thin on bias

Perfect Pair

Dakgangjeon (page 299) or Chile Marinated Pork Belly (page 313) are hearty choices that complement this braise's flavors.

WHY THIS RECIPE WORKS The meltingly tender, creamy texture of braised eggplant surrounded by a flavorful sauce makes for a luxurious small plate. For easy-to-eat pieces, we cut the eggplant into slim wedges, each with some skin attached to keep it from falling apart during cooking. Once the eggplant is tender, we reduce the flavorful braising liquid to create the sauce. Large globe and Italian eggplants disintegrate when braised, so do not substitute a single 1- to 1¼-pound eggplant here. You can substitute 1 to 1¼ pounds of long, slim Chinese or Japanese eggplants if they are available; cut them as directed. Doubanjiang or Asian broad bean chili paste is also known as toban djan.

1 Whisk water, Shaoxing wine, soy sauce, sugar, doubanjiang, and cornstarch in medium bowl until sugar is dissolved. Trim ½ inch from top and bottom of one eggplant. Halve eggplant crosswise. Cut each half lengthwise into 2 pieces. Cut each piece into ¾-inch-thick wedges. Repeat with remaining eggplant.

2 Heat vegetable oil in 12-inch nonstick skillet over medium heat until shimmering. Add garlic and ginger and cook, stirring constantly, until fragrant, about 30 seconds. Spread eggplant evenly in skillet (pieces will not form single layer). Pour rice wine mixture over eggplant. Increase heat to high and bring to boil. Reduce heat to maintain gentle boil. Cover and cook until eggplant is soft and has decreased in volume enough to form single layer on bottom of skillet, about 15 minutes, gently shaking skillet to settle eggplant halfway through cooking (some pieces will remain opaque).

3 Uncover and continue to cook, swirling skillet occasionally, until liquid is thickened and reduced to just a few tablespoons, 12 to 14 minutes longer. Transfer to platter, drizzle with sesame oil, sprinkle with scallions, and serve.

Variation

Braised Eggplant with Paprika, Coriander, and Yogurt
Omit Shaoxing wine, soy sauce, sugar, chili paste, cornstarch, and fresh ginger. Cook garlic for 30 seconds then add 1 tablespoon tomato paste, 2 teaspoons paprika, 1 teaspoon table salt, 1 teaspoon ground coriander, ½ teaspoon sugar, ½ teaspoon ground cumin, ½ teaspoon ground cinnamon, and ½ teaspoon ground nutmeg, and spread eggplant into skillet. Pour 2¾ cup water over eggplant. Substitute ⅓ cup plain whole-milk yogurt for sesame oil and 2 tablespoons minced fresh cilantro for scallions.

skillet-roasted brussels sprouts with chorizo and manchego

5 ounces Spanish-style chorizo sausage, quartered lengthwise and sliced crosswise ¼ inch thick

¼ cup extra-virgin olive oil

4 garlic cloves, sliced thin

2 pounds brussels sprouts, trimmed and quartered through stem end

1½ teaspoons smoked paprika

1½ teaspoons table salt

¾ teaspoon pepper

1 tablespoon sherry vinegar

2 teaspoons honey

2 ounces Manchego cheese, shredded (½ cup)

WHY THIS RECIPE WORKS The combination of brussels sprouts, cheese, and sausage has it all, and the ingredients unite to make a hearty and superflavorful small plate. The caramelized sprouts and chorizo are tossed with sherry vinegar and floral honey for a balanced sweet-and-sour element, and a final flourish of nutty Manchego takes the dish over the top. Look for brussels sprouts that are similar in size, with small, tight heads that are no more than 1½ inches in diameter. Cut very small brussels sprouts in half rather than quartering them.

1 Combine chorizo, oil, and garlic in 12-inch nonstick skillet. Cook over medium heat until oil is bright red and garlic is just beginning to brown, about 6 minutes. Off heat, using slotted spoon, transfer chorizo and garlic to bowl; set aside.

2 Add brussels sprouts, paprika, salt, and pepper to oil in skillet and stir to combine. Cover and cook over medium-high heat, stirring occasionally, until brussels sprouts are bright green and starting to brown, 5 to 7 minutes.

3 Uncover and continue to cook, stirring occasionally, until brussels sprouts are well browned in spots and tender, 5 to 7 minutes longer. Off heat, stir in vinegar, honey, and chorizo mixture. Transfer to serving platter, sprinkle with Manchego, and serve.

Head Start

Cut brussels sprouts up to 1 day ahead and refrigerate in airtight container until needed.

Perfect Pair

For a tantalizing blend of flavors, serve sprouts with Patatas Bravas (page 210) and Shrimp Rémoulade (page 267).

butternut squash steaks with honey-nut topping

¼ cup extra-virgin olive oil, divided

2 teaspoons sugar

2 teaspoons ground cumin

1 teaspoon garlic powder

1 teaspoon table salt

½ teaspoon ground dried Aleppo pepper

½ teaspoon ground coriander

½ teaspoon ground cinnamon

½ teaspoon pepper

2 (3-pound) butternut squashes

2 tablespoons chopped toasted pistachios

1 tablespoon sesame seeds, toasted

2 tablespoons honey

1 tablespoon torn fresh mint

1 recipe Yogurt–Tahini Sauce (page 17)

Lime wedges

WHY THIS RECIPE WORKS Butternut squash's dense texture gives it a meaty bite that's satisfying, even in a small portion, and its mild flavor can handle a liberal coating of bold seasonings (think cinnamon, coriander, and Aleppo pepper), much like a beef steak. As we do with meat, we use a reverse-searing method, first cooking slabs from the necks of butternut squash through in the oven and then browning and crisping them in a skillet. To serve as a small plate, we halve each steak, sprinkle it with toasted pistachios and sesame seeds for nuttiness and crunch, and dollop it with a tangy yogurt sauce. A drizzle of honey brings all the flavors together, ensuring that every forkful has a balance of sweet, spicy, and savory.

1 Adjust oven rack to middle position and heat oven to 450 degrees. Combine 3 tablespoons oil, sugar, cumin, garlic powder, salt, Aleppo pepper, coriander, cinnamon, and pepper; set aside.

2 Working with 1 squash at a time, cut crosswise into 2 pieces at base of neck; reserve bulb for another use. Peel away skin and fibrous threads just below skin (squash should be completely orange, with no white flesh), then carefully cut each piece in half lengthwise. Cut one ¾-inch-thick slab lengthwise from each half. (You should have four steaks; reserve remaining squash for another use.)

3 Place steaks on wire rack set on rimmed baking sheet and brush evenly with spice mixture. Flip steaks and brush second side with spice mixture. Roast until nearly tender and knife inserted into steaks meets with slight resistance, 15 to 20 minutes; remove from oven.

4 Heat remaining 1 tablespoon oil in 12-inch nonstick skillet over medium-high heat until just smoking. Carefully place steaks in skillet and cook, without moving, until well browned and crisp on first side, about 3 minutes. Flip steaks and continue to cook until well browned and crisp on second side, about 3 minutes. Cut steaks in half and transfer to serving platter.

5 Sprinkle steaks with pistachios and sesame seeds. Microwave honey until fluid, about 10 seconds, then drizzle evenly over steaks. Sprinkle with mint and serve with yogurt sauce and lime wedges.

Finish Line

For a flavor twist, try Pistachio Dukkah (page 20) on squash instead of sesame seeds and pistachios.

Perfect Pair

Serve with Patatas Bravas (page 210) or Marinated Zucchini (page 208).

loaded sweet potato wedges with tempeh

2 pounds sweet potatoes, unpeeled, cut lengthwise into 2-inch-wide wedges

5 tablespoons extra-virgin olive oil, divided

¾ teaspoon table salt, divided

8 ounces tempeh, crumbled into pea-size pieces

1 teaspoon ground cumin

1 teaspoon ground coriander

1 teaspoon smoked paprika

⅛ teaspoon ground cinnamon

4 ounces cherry tomatoes, halved

4 radishes, trimmed and sliced thin

1 jalapeño, sliced into thin rings

¾ cup chopped fresh cilantro

3 scallions, sliced thin

Plain yogurt

Lime wedges

WHY THIS RECIPE WORKS Sturdy caramelized wedges of roasted sweet potatoes make an excellent bottom layer for a hearty plant-based small plate. Next up, ground tempeh, browned with a generous amount of spices, brings complementary flavor and contrasting texture. Sweet cherry tomatoes, crisp radishes, spicy jalapeño, and fresh cilantro add more vegetables, more flavor, and more color.

1 Adjust oven rack to middle position and heat oven to 450 degrees. Line rimmed baking sheet with aluminum foil and spray with vegetable oil spray. Toss potatoes, 1 tablespoon oil, and ½ teaspoon salt together in bowl, then arrange potato wedges, cut sides down, in single layer on prepared sheet. Roast until tender and sides in contact with sheet are well browned, about 30 minutes.

2 Meanwhile, heat remaining ¼ cup oil in 12-inch skillet over medium heat until shimmering. Add tempeh, cumin, coriander, paprika, cinnamon, and remaining ¼ teaspoon salt and cook until well browned, 8 to 12 minutes, stirring often; set aside until ready to serve.

3 Transfer sweet potatoes to platter or individual serving plates and top with tempeh, cherry tomatoes, radishes, jalapeño, cilantro, and scallion. Serve with yogurt and lime wedges.

Head Start
Make crumbled tempeh topping up to 2 hours ahead. To maintain texture, hold at room temperature until serving time.

Finish Line
Serve yogurt and lime wedges. For an extra pop of color and acidic bite, garnish with Quick Pickled Red Onion (page 19).

Perfect Pair
Serve with Gochujang and Cheddar Pinwheels (page 321) or Kombdi, Jira Ghalun (page 304).

spiralized sweet potatoes with crispy shallots, pistachios, and urfa

⅓ cup extra-virgin olive oil

2 shallots, sliced thin

2 pounds sweet potatoes, peeled

¾ teaspoon table salt, divided

2 teaspoons Urfa pepper, divided

1 teaspoon grated lemon zest plus 2 tablespoons juice

1 teaspoon honey

¼ cup shelled pistachios, toasted and chopped coarse

2 tablespoons chopped fresh tarragon

WHY THIS RECIPE WORKS This swirly salad is a star on the plate, as delightful to look at as it is to eat. Spicy, smoky, slightly sweet Urfa pepper gives earthy sweet potatoes a kick. We add more depth by incorporating crispy shallots and brighten everything with a lemon vinaigrette. Spiralizing the sweet potatoes creates a beautiful-looking dish that comes together quickly. Tossing the sweet potatoes in shallot oil from the crispy shallots before roasting adds more flavor. Finishing the sweet potatoes with tarragon and toasted pistachios contributes delicate fresh licorice flavor and sweet crunch. Use sweet potatoes that are at least 2 inches in diameter at their widest point.

1 Adjust oven racks to upper-middle and lower-middle positions and heat oven to 450 degrees. Microwave oil and shallots in bowl for 5 minutes. Stir and continue to microwave in 2-minute increments until beginning to brown, 2 to 6 minutes. Stir and microwave in 30-second increments until golden brown, 30 seconds to 2 minutes. Using slotted spoon, transfer shallots to paper towel–lined plate; season with salt to taste. Let shallots drain for at least 5 minutes, reserving shallot oil; set shallots and oil aside, separately.

2 Square off potatoes by cutting ¼-inch-thick slices from each of their two short sides. Using spiralizer, cut sweet potatoes into ¼-inch-thick noodles; cut noodles into 12-inch lengths. Toss potato noodles with 2 tablespoons reserved shallot oil and ½ teaspoon salt and spread in single layer over two rimmed baking sheets. Roast until potatoes are just tender, 12 to 14 minutes, switching and rotating sheets halfway through baking. Transfer potatoes to serving platter.

3 Whisk 1 teaspoon urfa, lemon zest and juice, honey, and remaining ¼ teaspoon salt together in bowl. Whisking constantly, slowly drizzle in 1 tablespoon reserved shallot oil until emulsified. Drizzle vinaigrette over potatoes. Sprinkle with reserved crispy shallots, pistachios, tarragon, and remaining 1 teaspoon urfa. Serve.

Head Start

Make crispy shallots up to 1 month ahead; store in airtight container at room temperature until needed. Refrigerate shallot oil for up to 1 month.

Perfect Pair

Serve with Espinacas con Garbanzos (page 256) or Red Lentil Kibbeh (page 287).

pressure-cooker winter squash with halloumi and brussels sprouts

3 tablespoons extra-virgin olive oil, divided

2 tablespoons lemon juice

2 garlic cloves, minced, divided

⅛ teaspoon plus ½ teaspoon table salt, divided

8 ounces brussels sprouts, trimmed, halved, and sliced very thin

1 (8-ounce) block halloumi cheese, sliced crosswise into ¾-inch-thick slabs

4 scallions, white parts minced, green parts sliced thin on bias, divided

½ teaspoon ground cardamom

¼ teaspoon ground cumin

⅛ teaspoon cayenne pepper

2 pounds butternut squash, peeled, seeded, and cut into 1-inch pieces (5 cups)

½ cup chicken or vegetable broth

2 teaspoons honey

¼ cup dried cherries

2 tablespoons roasted pepitas

WHY THIS RECIPE WORKS This eminently shareable small plate pairs crispy slices of halloumi with shaved brussels sprouts and a warmly spiced mash of butternut squash. Cubes of raw squash are transformed into meltingly tender chunks when cooked under pressure, and we quickly coax the pieces into a smooth puree with a masher. A lemony brussels sprouts salad provides acidity to offset the squash's sweetness and adds some crunch against its silky texture. A drizzle of honey accentuates the salty cheese, and chewy dried cherries and roasted pepitas bring textural contrast. Use brussels sprouts no bigger than golf balls, as larger ones are often tough and woody. This recipe will work only in an electric pressure cooker.

1 Whisk 1 tablespoon oil, lemon juice, ¼ teaspoon garlic, and ⅛ teaspoon salt together in large bowl. Add brussels sprouts and toss to coat; let sit until ready to serve.

2 Using highest sauté or browning function, heat remaining 2 tablespoons oil in electric pressure cooker until shimmering. Arrange halloumi around edges of pot and cook until browned, about 3 minutes per side; transfer to plate. Add scallion whites to fat left in pot and cook until softened, about 2 minutes. Stir in remaining garlic, —cardamom, cumin, and cayenne and cook until fragrant, about 30 seconds. Stir in squash, broth, and remaining ½ teaspoon salt. Lock lid in place and close pressure release valve. Select high pressure cook function and cook for 6 minutes.

3 Turn off pressure cooker and quick-release pressure. Carefully remove lid, allowing steam to escape away from you. Using highest sauté or browning function, continue to cook squash mixture, stirring occasionally, until liquid is almost completely evaporated, about 5 minutes. Turn off pressure cooker. Using potato masher, mash squash until mostly smooth. Season with salt and pepper to taste.

4 Spread portion of squash over bottom of individual serving plates. Top with brussels sprouts and halloumi. Drizzle with honey and sprinkle with cherries, pepitas, and scallion greens. Serve.

Head Start

Marinate brussels sprouts for up to 4 hours before continuing with recipe.

Perfect Pair

Savory, aromatic Keftedes (page 280) or Sizzling Beef Lettuce Wraps (page 309) stand up to this dish's bold, layered flavors.

proteins

espinacas con garbanzos

1 loaf crusty bread, divided

2 (15-ounce) cans chickpeas (1 can drained, 1 can undrained)

1½ cups chicken broth

6 tablespoons extra-virgin olive oil, divided

6 garlic cloves, minced

1 tablespoon smoked paprika

1 teaspoon ground cumin

¼ teaspoon table salt

⅛ teaspoon ground cinnamon

⅛ teaspoon cayenne pepper

1 small pinch saffron

2 small plum tomatoes, halved lengthwise, flesh shredded on large holes of box grater and skins discarded

4 teaspoons sherry vinegar, plus extra for seasoning

10 ounces frozen chopped spinach, thawed and squeezed dry

WHY THIS RECIPE WORKS A traditional tapa in Seville, espinacas con garbanzos ("spinach with chickpeas") is a saucy and substantive (but not too heavy) part of a larger spread. Briefly simmering convenient canned chickpeas in chicken broth and chickpea canning liquid infuses them with savory flavor. A picada (a paste of garlic and bread cooked in plenty of olive oil) thickens the sauce. Smoked paprika and Moorish spices such as cumin, cinnamon, and saffron imbue the picada with heady aromas. Thawed frozen chopped spinach disperses beautifully throughout the dish and requires no additional prep. For a vegan version, substitute vegetable broth or water for the chicken broth. If using chickpeas that you've cooked from dried, use 3⅓ cups of cooked chickpeas and ⅔ cup of the cooking liquid. Use a fruity, spicy, high-quality olive oil here. Red wine vinegar can be substituted for the sherry vinegar.

1 Cut 1½-ounce piece from loaf of bread (thickness will vary depending on size of loaf) and tear into 1-inch pieces. Process in food processor until finely ground (you should have ¾ cup crumbs). Combine chickpeas and broth in large saucepan and bring to boil over high heat. Adjust heat to maintain simmer and cook until level of liquid is just below top layer of chickpeas, about 10 minutes.

2 While chickpeas cook, heat ¼ cup oil in 10-inch nonstick or carbon-steel skillet over medium heat until just shimmering. Add bread crumbs and cook, stirring frequently, until deep golden brown, 3 to 4 minutes. Add garlic, paprika, cumin, salt, cinnamon, cayenne, and saffron and cook until fragrant, 30 seconds. Stir in tomatoes and vinegar; remove from heat.

3 Stir bread mixture and spinach into chickpeas. Continue to simmer, stirring occasionally, until mixture is thick and stew-like, 5 to 10 minutes longer. Off heat, stir in remaining 2 tablespoons oil. Cover and let stand for 5 minutes. Season with salt and extra vinegar to taste. Transfer to serving bowl and serve with remaining bread.

Head Start

Refrigerate espinacas con garbanzos in airtight container for up to 3 days. Reheat gently over low heat before serving.

Perfect Pair

Serve with Saganaki (page 143), Moroccan-Style Carrot Salad (page 159), or Pajeon (page 54).

Serves 8 | **Active Time** 55 minutes
Total Time 55 minutes

caramel tofu

21 ounces firm tofu, cut into ¾-inch cubes

½ teaspoon table salt

1¼ teaspoons pepper, divided

1¾ cups water, divided

⅓ cup sugar

6 tablespoons vegetable oil, divided

5 garlic cloves, minced

1 onion, halved and sliced thin

3 tablespoons fish sauce

2 teaspoons plus ½ cup cornstarch, divided

½ cup fresh cilantro leaves

¼ cup dry-roasted peanuts, chopped

3 scallions, green parts only, sliced thin on bias

Finish Line

Set out a small bowl of toothpicks next to serving platter for guests to use to pick up tofu.

Perfect Pair

Serve with Fennel, Orange, and Olive Salad (page 165), Spinach Squares (page 56), or Gochujang and Cheddar Pinwheels (page 321).

WHY THIS RECIPE WORKS This surprisingly savory Vietnamese recipe will have even tofu skeptics coming back for another bite. We toss cubes of tofu with cornstarch, lightly pan-fry them, and serve them with a traditional salty-sweet caramel sauce. To achieve the tricky balance of sweet and savory in our sauce, we keep the caramel base simple with water and sugar and then add a healthy dose of garlic, fish sauce, and pepper. An onion gives the sauce more depth. Chopped peanuts and a sprinkling of cilantro and scallions provide textural contrast and a fresh finish. You can substitute extra-firm tofu for the firm tofu in this recipe. The caramel can go from amber-colored to burnt quickly after the garlic is added, so it's important to have the measured water at the ready to stop the caramelization. For a vegan version, use vegan fish sauce substitute instead of the fish sauce.

1 Spread tofu over paper towel–lined baking sheet, let drain for 20 minutes, then gently press dry with paper towels. Sprinkle with salt and ¼ teaspoon pepper.

2 Meanwhile, pour ¼ cup water into medium saucepan, then sprinkle sugar evenly over top. Cook over medium heat, gently swirling pan occasionally (do not stir), until sugar melts and mixture turns color of maple syrup, 7 to 10 minutes.

3 Stir in 3 tablespoons oil and garlic and cook until fragrant, about 30 seconds. Off heat, slowly whisk in remaining 1½ cups water (sauce will sizzle). Stir in onion, fish sauce, 2 teaspoons cornstarch, and remaining 1 teaspoon pepper. Return pan to medium-low heat and simmer vigorously until onion is softened and sauce has thickened, 10 to 15 minutes. Remove from heat and cover to keep warm.

4 Spread remaining ½ cup cornstarch in shallow dish. Working with several tofu pieces at a time, coat thoroughly with cornstarch, pressing gently to adhere; transfer to plate.

5 Heat remaining 3 tablespoons oil in 12-inch nonstick skillet over high heat until just smoking. Add tofu and cook, turning as needed, until all sides are crispy and well browned, 10 to 15 minutes; transfer to paper towel–lined plate to drain. Transfer tofu to platter, drizzle with sauce, and sprinkle with cilantro, peanuts, and scallions. Serve.

gambas a la plancha

¼ cup table salt for brining

¼ cup sugar for brining

2 pounds extra-large (10 to 15 per pound) unpeeled head-on shrimp

2 tablespoons extra-virgin olive oil

2 large cloves garlic, minced to paste

2 teaspoons lemon juice, plus 1 lemon, halved

1 teaspoon smoked paprika

¼ teaspoon cayenne pepper

Head Start

Refrigerate shrimp in marinade, covered, for up to 1 hour.

Finish Line

Serve shrimp on a platter alongside a bowl of Red Pepper Mayonnaise (page 17) for dipping and encourage guests to eat with their hands.

Perfect Pair

Serve with Cajun-Spiced Popcorn (page 31) or grilled polenta (see page 52). Use hot plancha to quickly sear other small bites such as Blistered Shishito Peppers (page 25).

WHY THIS RECIPE WORKS This iconic tapas dish is supremely satis-fying and elemental—a simple food that you eat with your hands, hot off the grill. Employing a plancha (a broad griddle that can be placed over grill grates) gives the shrimp the woodsiness of grilling while preventing their flavorful juices from being lost through the grate. The shrimp are traditionally served with their heads on so that after gently twisting apart the head and body, the head can be sucked to extract every last bit of flavor. Brining the shrimp before grilling makes them especially plump and juicy. A lemony garlic paste adheres perfectly to the shrimps' shells. Extra-large, unpeeled head-off shrimp may be substituted in this recipe.

1 Dissolve salt and sugar in 2 quarts cold water in large container. Submerge shrimp in brine, cover, and refrigerate for 15 minutes. Drain shrimp. Using kitchen shears or sharp paring knife, cut through shrimp shells and devein if desired.

2 Combine oil, garlic, lemon juice, paprika, and cayenne in large bowl. Add shrimp and toss to coat.

3A **For a charcoal grill** Open bottom vent completely. Light large chimney starter filled with charcoal briquettes (6 quarts). When top coals are partially covered with ash, pour evenly over grill. Set cooking grate in place, center plancha on grill, cover, and open lid vent completely. Heat plancha until hot, about 5 minutes.

3B **For a gas grill** Turn all burners to high, center plancha on grill, cover, and heat plancha until hot, about 15 minutes. Leave all burners on high.

4 Cook half of shrimp in even layer until shells are bright pink and just beginning to char and shrimp are opaque throughout, 2 to 6 minutes, turning halfway through cooking. Transfer shrimp to platter and repeat with remaining shrimp. Meanwhile, cook lemon halves cut side down on open space of plancha until well charred, 2 to 4 minutes; set aside for serving. Serve shrimp warm or at room temperature with lemon.

gambas al ajillo

16 garlic cloves, peeled, divided

 2 pounds large tail-on shrimp
(26 to 30 per pound),
peeled and deveined

½ cup plus 2 tablespoons
extra-virgin olive oil, divided

½ teaspoon table salt

 1 (2-inch) piece mild dried
chile, such as New Mexican,
roughly broken

 1 bay leaf

 1 tablespoon sherry vinegar

 1 tablespoon chopped
fresh parsley

Finish Line

To serve shrimp as a Nibble,
set out small bowls of toothpicks
near serving platter for picking
up individual shrimp.

Perfect Pair

Serve with Spanish Tortilla (page
148), Skillet-Roasted Broccoli
with Parmesan and Black Pepper
Topping (page 225), or Bruschetta
with Whipped Feta and Roasted
Red Pepper Topping (page 331).

WHY THIS RECIPE WORKS Shrimp sizzling in a pool of olive oil
perfumed with the heady aroma of garlic are a much-beloved tapas-
menu staple. In our version, we opt for larger shrimp than you'd likely
find at a restaurant, so we have less prep work to do and each bite
is more substantial. Marinating the shrimp in garlic-infused oil before
cooking them ensures that bold garlic flavor pierces every morsel.
And rather than submerging the shrimp in hot oil to cook them
(which would leave us with far more flavored oil than even a large
party of guests could reasonably finish off), we reduce the amount
of oil to just a little over ½ cup and flip the shrimp for even cooking.
We prefer the slightly sweet flavor of dried chile in this recipe, but if
it is unavailable, ½ teaspoon of sweet paprika can be substituted.

1   Mince 4 garlic cloves and toss with shrimp, ¼ cup oil, and salt
in medium bowl. Let shrimp marinate at room temperature for
30 minutes.

2   Meanwhile, using flat side of chef's knife, smash 4 garlic cloves. Heat
smashed garlic with remaining 6 tablespoons oil in 12-inch skillet over
medium-low heat, stirring occasionally, until garlic is light golden
brown, 4 to 7 minutes. Remove skillet from heat and let oil cool to
room temperature. Using slotted spoon, remove smashed garlic
from skillet and discard.

3   Slice remaining 8 garlic cloves thin. Return skillet to low heat and
add sliced garlic, chile, and bay leaf. Cook, stirring occasionally, until
garlic is tender but not browned, 4 to 7 minutes. (If garlic has not
begun to sizzle after 3 minutes, increase heat to medium-low.)
Increase heat to medium-low; add half of shrimp with marinade to
skillet and spread into single layer. Cook shrimp, undisturbed, until
oil starts to gently bubble, about 2 minutes. Using tongs, flip shrimp
and continue to cook until cooked through, about 3 minutes longer.
Using slotted spoon, transfer shrimp to serving platter. Repeat with
remaining shrimp and marinade. Increase heat to high and add vinegar and parsley to oil in skillet. Cook, stirring constantly, until oil is
bubbling vigorously, 15 to 20 seconds. Pour oil mixture over shrimp.
Serve immediately.

pan-seared shrimp with pistachios, cumin, and parsley

1½ pounds extra-large shrimp (21 to 25 per pound), peeled, deveined, and tails removed

1 teaspoon kosher salt, divided

1 garlic clove, minced

1 teaspoon ground cumin

1 teaspoon paprika

⅛ teaspoon cayenne pepper

2 tablespoons extra-virgin olive oil, divided

⅛ teaspoon sugar

¼ cup chopped fresh cilantro leaves and tender stems

¼ cup chopped fresh parsley leaves and tender stems

1 tablespoon lemon juice

¼ cup shelled pistachios, toasted and chopped coarse

Perfect Pair

Serve with Butternut Squash Steaks with Honey-Nut Topping (page 246) or whole-grain salad (see pages 192–195).

WHY THIS RECIPE WORKS These tender, spice-coated shrimp are so packed with palate-pleasing flavor and textural variation that they don't need fancy plating or sauces: Each one is a satisfying bite on its own. To achieve that elusive combination of deep browning on the outside and snappy, succulent meat on the inside, we start by briefly salting the shrimp so that they retain moisture even as they're seared over high heat. Starting the shrimp in a cold skillet heats them gradually, so they don't buckle and thus brown uniformly. Once the shrimp are spotty brown and pink at the edges on the first side, we remove them from the heat and quickly turn each one, letting residual heat gently cook them the rest of the way. A potent seasoning mixture of garlic, cumin, paprika, and cayenne comes together in the same skillet used to cook the shrimp.

1 Toss shrimp and ½ teaspoon salt together in bowl; set aside for 15 to 30 minutes.

2 Meanwhile, combine garlic, cumin, paprika, cayenne, and remaining ½ teaspoon salt in small bowl.

3 Pat shrimp dry with paper towels. Add 1 tablespoon oil and sugar to bowl with shrimp and toss to coat. Add shrimp to cold 12-inch non-stick skillet in single layer and cook over high heat until undersides of shrimp are spotty brown and edges turn pink, 3 to 4 minutes. Remove skillet from heat. Working quickly, use tongs to flip each shrimp; let stand until second side is opaque, about 2 minutes. Transfer shrimp to platter.

4 Add remaining 1 tablespoon oil to now-empty skillet. Add spice mixture and cook over medium heat until fragrant, about 30 seconds. Off heat, return shrimp to skillet. Add cilantro, parsley, and lemon juice and toss to combine. Transfer to platter, sprinkle with pistachios, and serve.

easy chilled shrimp

Sweet bite-size shrimp are a party food staple, and chilled shrimp may just be a host's best friend, since unlike many other dishes, they don't have to be prepared at the very last minute. These simple recipes are sure to be a hit.

cóctel de camarón

Serves 8
Active Time 35 minutes
Total Time 35 minutes, plus 30 minutes chilling

Look for Clamato juice next to the tomato juice in the grocery store. If you can't find Clamato juice, substitute a combination of 1½ cups V8 juice, ½ cup water, and 1 teaspoon sugar. You can refrigerate the tomato-shrimp mixture for up to 1 day before garnishing with avocado and cilantro and serving.

1½ pounds medium shrimp (41 to 50 per pound), peeled, deveined, and tails removed

¼ cup chopped fresh cilantro, stems reserved

1 teaspoon black peppercorns

1 tablespoon sugar

1 teaspoon table salt

3 tomatoes, cored and cut into ½-inch pieces

1 cucumber, peeled, halved lengthwise, seeded, and cut into ½-inch pieces

1 small red onion, chopped fine

2 cups Clamato juice

½ cup ketchup

2 tablespoons lime juice, plus lime wedges for serving

1 tablespoon hot sauce

1 avocado, halved, pitted, and cut into ½-inch pieces

1 Combine shrimp, 3 cups water, cilantro stems, peppercorns, sugar, and salt in large saucepan. Place saucepan over medium heat and cook, stirring occasionally, until shrimp are pink and firm to touch, 8 to 10 minutes (water should be just bubbling around edge of saucepan and register 165 degrees). Remove saucepan from heat, cover, and let shrimp sit in cooking liquid for 2 minutes.

2 Meanwhile, fill large bowl halfway with ice and water. Drain shrimp in colander; discard cilantro stems and spices. Immediately transfer shrimp

to ice bath to stop cooking and chill thoroughly, about 3 minutes. Remove shrimp from ice bath and thoroughly pat dry with paper towels.

3 Combine tomatoes, cucumber, onion, Clamato juice, ketchup, lime juice, and hot sauce in serving bowl. Stir in shrimp, cover, and refrigerate for at least 30 minutes. Stir in avocado and chopped cilantro and season with salt and pepper to taste. Serve with lime wedges.

shrimp rémoulade

Serves 8
Active Time 35 minutes
Total Time 35 minutes, plus 1 hour chilling

You can refrigerate the rémoulade for up to 1 day before serving.

1½ pounds jumbo shrimp (16 to 20 per pound), peeled, deveined, and tails removed

¼ teaspoon table salt, plus salt for cooking shrimp

⅔ cup mayonnaise

¼ cup finely chopped celery

¼ cup finely chopped green bell pepper

3 tablespoons minced cornichons

2 scallions, sliced thin

1 tablespoon lemon juice

1½ teaspoons prepared horseradish, drained

1 teaspoon spicy brown mustard

1 teaspoon ketchup

1 garlic clove, minced

½ teaspoon paprika

½ teaspoon Worcestershire sauce

¼ teaspoon pepper

⅛ teaspoon cayenne pepper

½ head Bibb lettuce (4 ounces), leaves separated and torn

Lemon wedges

Hot sauce

1 Combine 3 cups cold water, shrimp, and 1½ teaspoons salt in large saucepan. Set pot over medium-high heat and cook, stirring occasionally, until water registers 170 degrees and shrimp are just beginning to turn pink, 5 to 7 minutes.

2 Remove from heat, cover, and let sit until shrimp are completely pink and firm, about 5 minutes. Drain shrimp in colander. Rinse shrimp under cold water, then pat dry with paper towels. Transfer shrimp to large bowl and refrigerate until ready to use.

3 Combine mayonnaise, celery, bell pepper, cornichons, scallions, lemon juice, horseradish, mustard, ketchup, garlic, paprika, Worcestershire sauce, ¼ teaspoon table salt, pepper, and cayenne in bowl.

4 Fold sauce into shrimp until combined. Season with salt and pepper to taste. Cover and refrigerate until flavors meld, at least 1 hour. Serve over lettuce with lemon wedges and hot sauce.

Perfect Pair

To take full advantage of these chilled shrimp dishes' make-ahead potential, serve them with dishes that require last-minute preparation such as Sausage-and-Cheddar Stuffed Mushrooms (page 216) or Southern Corn Fritters (page 212). Alternatively, serve them with simple dishes like bruschetta (see page 330) or Brown Rice Salad with Fennel, Mushrooms, and Walnuts (page 190) and use that extra time to relax.

tuna poke

1 pound skinless yellowfin tuna, cut into ¾-inch cubes

¼ cup thinly sliced sweet onion, halved and sliced through root end

⅓ cup finely chopped salted dry-roasted macadamia nuts

3 scallions, white and green parts separated and sliced thin on bias

3 tablespoons soy sauce

2 tablespoons vegetable oil

2 teaspoons toasted sesame oil

2 teaspoons grated fresh ginger

1 garlic clove, minced

¾ teaspoon red pepper flakes

Furikake (optional)

WHY THIS RECIPE WORKS A good Hawaiian-style poke is great on its own, but can also be used to round out a spread of raw and chilled seafood (think oysters and shrimp cocktail) or as an accompaniment to crispy fried dishes. Using good-quality fresh fish is key; taking inspiration from ahi shoyu poke, here we use yellowfin tuna. Macadamia nuts and the Japanese spice blend furikake stand in for the kukui nuts and seaweed in traditional Hawaiian versions. The raw tuna should appear moist and shiny, feel firm to the touch (the flesh should spring right back when pressed), and smell clean, not fishy. Tell your fishmonger that you plan to serve the fish raw and inquire about its freshness. Try to have the fishmonger slice tuna steaks to order that have little to no connective tissue, since it can be unpleasantly chewy when eaten raw. Vidalia, Maui, or Walla Walla sweet onions will all work here. If you can't find sweet onions, you can substitute a yellow onion by soaking the thinly sliced onion in ice water for 20 minutes and then draining and patting it dry. Furikake is a Japanese seasoning blend that comes in many styles. We recommend using a blend containing dried seaweed (nori and/or kombu), bonito flakes, and sesame seeds. Look for it at an Asian market, in the Asian section of the grocery store, or online.

Gently combine tuna, onion, macadamia nuts, scallion whites, soy sauce, vegetable oil, sesame oil, ginger, garlic, and pepper flakes in large bowl using rubber spatula. Season with salt to taste. Sprinkle with furikake, if using, and scallion greens, and serve.

Head Start

Refrigerate poke for up to 1 day.

Perfect Pair

Serve with popcorn (see page 30), Molletes (page 333), or Habanero and Mango Guacamole (page 92) and Patatas Bravas (page 210).

peruvian ceviche with radishes and orange

1 pound skinless red snapper fillets, ½ inch thick

3½ teaspoons kosher salt, divided

¾ cup lime juice (6 limes)

3 tablespoons extra-virgin olive oil, divided

1 tablespoon ají amarillo chile paste

2 garlic cloves, peeled

3 oranges

8 ounces radishes, trimmed, halved, and sliced thin

¼ cup coarsely chopped fresh cilantro

1 cup corn nuts

1 cup lightly salted popcorn

WHY THIS RECIPE WORKS Ceviche, the Latin American dish in which pieces of raw fish are "cooked" in an acidic marinade until the flesh firms and turns opaque, is a lively summer go-to that allows fresh seafood to shine. To create a flavorful yet balanced liquid and sauce, we make what's known as a leche de tigre ("tiger's milk") by blending lime juice, ají amarillo chile paste, garlic, extra-virgin olive oil, and a small amount of fish for body. We then soak thinly sliced and briefly salted red snapper in the leche for 30 to 40 minutes until just opaque and slightly firm. To complete the dish, we add sweet oranges; crisp, peppery radishes; and chopped cilantro. Ají amarillo chile paste can be found in the Latin section of grocery stores; if you can't find it, you can substitute one stemmed and seeded habanero chile. You can substitute halibut or black sea bass for the red snapper if desired.

1 Using sharp knife, cut snapper lengthwise into ½-inch-wide strips. Slice each strip crosswise ⅛ inch thick. Set aside ⅓ cup (2½ ounces) fish pieces. Toss remaining fish with 1 teaspoon salt and refrigerate for at least 10 minutes or up to 30 minutes.

2 Meanwhile, process reserved fish pieces, remaining 2½ teaspoons salt, lime juice, 2 tablespoons oil, chile paste, and garlic in blender until smooth, 30 to 60 seconds. Strain leche de tigre through fine-mesh strainer set over large bowl, pressing on solids to extract as much liquid as possible; discard solids.

3 Cut away peel and pith from oranges. Holding fruit over bowl, use paring knife to slice between membranes to release segments. Cut orange segments into ¼-inch pieces. Add oranges, salted fish, and radishes to bowl with sauce and toss to combine. Refrigerate for 30 to 40 minutes (for more-opaque fish, refrigerate for 45 minutes to 1 hour).

4 Add cilantro to ceviche and toss to combine. Portion ceviche into individual bowls and drizzle with remaining 1 tablespoon oil. Serve, passing corn nuts and popcorn separately.

Head Start

Refrigerate leche de tigre for up to 1 day; whisk to recombine before using.

Finish Line

Serve corn nuts and popcorn in small bowls alongside ceviche to allow guests to customize their portions with crunchy garnishes.

Perfect Pair

Serve with Chili-Lime Spiced Nuts (page 33), Beet Muhammara (page 103), or Avocado, Tomato, and Bell Pepper Arepas (page 351).

crab croquettes

Croquettes

- **4** tablespoons unsalted butter
- **½** cup finely chopped onion
- **½** cup finely chopped green bell pepper
- **3** garlic cloves, minced
- **1¼** teaspoons table salt
- **1** cup all-purpose flour, divided
- **1½** cups whole milk
- **8** ounces lump crabmeat, picked over for shells
- **3** scallions, sliced thin
- **1** teaspoon Tabasco sauce
- **1** teaspoon Tony Chachere's Original Creole Seasoning, plus extra for sprinkling
- **½** teaspoon pepper
- **2** large eggs
- **2** cups panko bread crumbs
- **1½** quarts vegetable oil for frying

Dipping Sauce

- **½** cup mayonnaise
- **2** teaspoons Tabasco sauce
- **½** teaspoon Worcestershire sauce

WHY THIS RECIPE WORKS We set out to create a home version of fried crab croquettes in the same crunchy-creamy Spanish style of Louisiana's bayou country. A superthick béchamel—seasoned with onion, bell pepper, garlic, scallions, spicy Creole seasoning, and vinegary Tabasco hot sauce—binds everything together. After mixing flaked crab into the béchamel, we refrigerate the mixture for 3 hours to firm it up before shaping it into croquettes. For an exterior that cracks between your teeth to reveal a soft, creamy interior, we bread the croquettes before deep-frying them in hot oil. If you can find and afford fresh crabmeat, the recipe results will be better. However, refrigerated canned crabmeat, often found at the supermarket fish counter, is the next best thing.

1 **For the croquettes** Melt butter in large saucepan over medium heat. Add onion, bell pepper, garlic, and salt and cook until vegetables are softened, about 5 minutes.

2 Stir in ½ cup flour until no dry flour remains; cook for 1 minute, stirring often. Slowly whisk in milk; continue to whisk 1 minute longer to ensure no lumps of flour remain. Cook until bubbles begin to break surface and mixture is thickened to consistency of paste, 1 to 2 minutes.

3 Off heat, stir in crabmeat, scallions, Tabasco, Creole seasoning, and pepper until well combined. Transfer to 8-inch square baking dish and refrigerate, uncovered, until fully chilled and firm, about 3 hours.

4 **For the dipping sauce** Whisk mayonnaise, Tabasco, and Worcestershire together in bowl; refrigerate until ready to serve.

5 Place remaining ½ cup flour in shallow dish, beat eggs together in second shallow dish, and place panko in third shallow dish. Divide croquette mixture into 18 heaping 2-tablespoon portions (about 1½ ounces each) and place on rimmed baking sheet. Roll portions between your hands to make balls, then shape into 2-inch-long ovals.

6 Working with few croquettes at a time, dredge lightly in flour, shaking off excess; roll in beaten egg, allowing excess to drip off; and coat with panko. Return to sheet.

7 Line large plate with triple layer of paper towels. Heat oil in large Dutch oven over medium-high heat to 375 degrees. Place 9 croquettes in oil and fry until golden brown, about 2 minutes per side. Transfer to prepared plate. Return oil to 375 degrees and repeat with remaining 9 croquettes. Sprinkle lightly with extra Creole seasoning and serve with dipping sauce.

Head Start

Refrigerate crab mixture, prepared through step 3 and covered with plastic wrap, for up to 12 hours. Refrigerate shaped, uncooked croquettes, covered with plastic, for up to 3 hours before frying.

Perfect Pair

Serve with Tomato Salad (page 154) or Caprese Skewers (page 34).

Serves 8 to 10 | Active Time 40 minutes
Total Time 55 minutes

fritto misto di mare

12 ounces shell-on medium-large shrimp (31 to 40 per pound)

3 quarts vegetable oil for frying

½ cup all-purpose flour

¼ cup cornstarch

12 ounces squid, bodies sliced crosswise into ½-inch-thick rings, tentacles left whole

12 ounces skinless sole or flounder fillets, ¼ to ½ inch thick, halved lengthwise, and cut on bias into 1-inch strips

Lemon wedges

Perfect Pair

Serve with Olives all'Ascolana (page 36) and Pinto Bean, Ancho, and Beef Salad (page 204) or Baguette with Radishes, Butter, and Herbs (page 327).

WHY THIS RECIPE WORKS Fritto misto di mare, a mix of fried seafood commonly including red mullet, squid or cuttlefish, and shrimp, can be found throughout Italy. Our version calls for frying the seafood in batches to prevent the oil temperature from dropping excessively. Adding cornstarch to the mix keeps the first batch crispy while we fry the second. For the fish, easy-to-find, mild-tasting sole or flounder fillets are thin enough to cook through in the time it takes the coating to adequately brown. The shrimp are fried and eaten shell and all, as the shell fries up crispy. To ensure that the shells do fry up crispy, avoid using shrimp that are overly large or jumbo. We prefer 31- to 40-count shrimp here, but 26- to 30-count may be substituted. Use a Dutch oven that holds 6 quarts or more. Trim any squid tentacles longer than 3 inches.

1 Adjust oven rack to middle position and heat oven to 225 degrees. Using kitchen shears or sharp paring knife, cut through shrimp shells and devein (do not remove shell). Pat shrimp dry with paper towels. Set wire rack in rimmed baking sheet and line with triple layer of paper towels. Add oil to large Dutch oven until it measures about 2 inches deep and heat over medium-high heat to 400 degrees. Whisk flour and cornstarch in large bowl until combined; set aside.

2 Carefully add shrimp to oil and cook, stirring occasionally, until lightly browned, about 3 minutes. Adjust burner as necessary to maintain oil temperature between 350 and 375 degrees. Using spider skimmer or slotted spoon, transfer shrimp to prepared rack. Season with salt and transfer to oven.

3 Return oil to 400 degrees. Pat squid dry with paper towels. Dredge squid in flour mixture, shaking off excess, and carefully add to oil. Cook, stirring as needed to prevent sticking, until squid is crisp and pale golden brown, about 2 minutes. Transfer to rack with shrimp. Season with salt and return to oven.

4 Return oil to 400 degrees. Pat sole dry with paper towels. Dredge sole in flour mixture, shaking off excess, and carefully add to oil. Cook, stirring as needed to prevent sticking, until sole is crisp and pale golden brown, about 3 minutes. Transfer to rack with shrimp and squid. Season with salt and let drain briefly. Once drained, serve immediately with lemon wedges.

albóndigas en salsa de almendras

¼ cup slivered almonds

2 slices hearty white sandwich bread, torn into 1-inch pieces, divided

3 tablespoons extra-virgin olive oil, divided

5 tablespoons fresh parsley (3 tablespoons minced, 2 tablespoons chopped)

4 garlic cloves, minced, divided

1 large egg

2 tablespoons water

1 teaspoon table salt

½ teaspoon pepper

1 pound ground pork

½ cup finely chopped onion

½ teaspoon paprika

1 cup chicken broth

½ cup dry white wine

¼ teaspoon saffron threads, crumbled

1 teaspoon sherry vinegar

WHY THIS RECIPE WORKS These tender, bite-size meatballs cloaked in a rich almond-based sauce frequently appear on tapas menus in Spain. To streamline the process of making them at home, we mix the ingredients in a food processor and skip the browning, simmering the mini meatballs in a mixture of white wine, chicken broth, and softened onion flavored with paprika and saffron. For the picada, which thickens and flavors the sauce, we pan-fry finely ground blanched almonds and bread and then mix in minced garlic and parsley before stirring the picada into the sauce. A splash of sherry vinegar and a sprinkling of fresh parsley at the end add brightness. Sometimes fully cooked ground pork retains a slightly pink hue; trust your thermometer.

1 Process almonds in food processor until finely ground, about 20 seconds. Add half of bread and process until bread is finely ground, about 15 seconds. Transfer almond-bread mixture to 12-inch nonstick skillet. Add 2 tablespoons oil and cook over medium heat, stirring often, until mixture is golden brown, 3 to 5 minutes. Transfer to bowl. Stir in minced parsley and half of garlic and set picada aside. Wipe skillet clean with paper towels.

2 Process remaining bread in now-empty processor until finely ground, about 15 seconds. Add egg, water, 1 tablespoon chopped parsley, salt, pepper, and remaining garlic and process until smooth paste forms, about 20 seconds, scraping down sides of bowl as necessary. Add pork and pulse until combined, about 5 pulses.

3 Remove processor blade. Using your moistened hands, form generous 1 tablespoon pork mixture into 1-inch round meatball and transfer to plate; repeat with remaining pork mixture to form about 24 meatballs.

4 Heat remaining 1 tablespoon oil in now-empty skillet over medium heat until shimmering. Add onion and cook, stirring occasionally, until softened, 4 to 6 minutes. Add paprika and cook until fragrant, about 30 seconds. Add broth and wine and bring to simmer. Stir in

saffron. Add meatballs and adjust heat to maintain simmer. Cover and cook until meatballs register 160 degrees, 6 to 8 minutes, flipping meatballs once.

5 Stir in picada and continue to cook, uncovered, until sauce has thickened slightly, 1 to 2 minutes longer. Off heat, stir in vinegar. Season with salt and pepper to taste. Transfer to platter, sprinkle with remaining 1 tablespoon parsley, and serve.

Variation

Plant-Based Albóndigas

Omit egg. Reduce salt to ½ teaspoon and substitute 12 ounces ground plant-based meat for ground pork and vegetable broth for chicken broth. Break meat into small pieces before adding to food processor. Chill meatballs for at least 15 minutes before cooking.

Head Start

Refrigerate shaped meatballs for up to 1 day before proceeding with step 4.

Finish Line

Set small bowl of toothpicks for picking up meatballs next to serving platter.

Perfect Pair

Serve with Baked Goat Cheese (page 139) or Citrus and Radicchio Salad with Dates and Smoked Almonds (page 166).

pork and ricotta meatballs

Meatballs

- 4 slices hearty white sandwich bread, crusts removed, torn into small pieces
- 8 ounces (1 cup) whole-milk ricotta cheese
- 2 pounds ground pork
- 1 ounce Parmesan cheese, grated (½ cup), plus extra for serving
- ½ cup chopped fresh parsley
- 2 large eggs
- 2 shallots, minced
- 4 garlic cloves, minced
- 1 tablespoon table salt
- 1½ teaspoons pepper
- 1 teaspoon grated lemon zest

Sauce

- ¼ cup extra-virgin olive oil
- 10 garlic cloves, smashed and peeled
- 1 teaspoon red pepper flakes
- 2 (28-ounce) cans crushed tomatoes
- 1 teaspoon table salt
- 2 tablespoons chopped fresh basil

WHY THIS RECIPE WORKS Adding a ricotta cheese is an old trick for producing extra-tender meatballs; here, the combination of sweet, mild ground pork and creamy ricotta makes for moist, delicate, comforting meatballs that will keep guests coming back for more. Roasting the meatballs allows the circulating hot air to produce even, all-around browning. We then simmer the meatballs in an easy marinara sauce, where they pick up extra flavor while simultaneously finishing cooking through. It takes about 10 minutes of occasional mashing with a fork for the ricotta to fully wet the bread enough for the panade to achieve the desired paste consistency. Use a greased ¼-cup dry measuring cup or equal-size portion scoop to divvy up the meatballs.

1 **For the meatballs** Adjust oven rack to lower-middle position and heat oven to 450 degrees. Set wire rack in aluminum foil–lined rimmed baking sheet and spray evenly with vegetable oil spray. Combine bread and ricotta in large bowl and let sit, mashing occasionally with fork, until smooth paste forms, about 10 minutes.

2 Add pork, Parmesan, parsley, eggs, shallots, garlic, salt, pepper, and lemon zest to bread mixture and mix with your hands until thoroughly combined. Divide meat mixture into 24 portions (about ¼ cup each) and place on platter. Roll meat between your moistened hands to form meatballs and space evenly on prepared wire rack. Roast meatballs until browned, 30 to 35 minutes, rotating sheet halfway through roasting. Remove from oven and reduce oven temperature to 300 degrees.

3 **For the sauce** Meanwhile, combine oil and garlic in Dutch oven set over low heat and cook until garlic is soft and golden on all sides, 12 to 14 minutes, stirring occasionally. Add pepper flakes and cook until fragrant, about 30 seconds. Stir in tomatoes and salt. Cover, with lid slightly ajar, and bring to simmer over medium-high heat. Reduce heat to medium-low and simmer until sauce has thickened slightly, about 30 minutes. Season with salt and pepper to taste.

4 Nestle meatballs into sauce, cover, and transfer pot to oven. Bake until meatballs are tender and sauce has thickened, about 30 minutes. Transfer meatballs and sauce to serving platter. Sprinkle with basil and serve, passing extra Parmesan separately.

Head Start

Refrigerate shaped, uncooked meatballs, covered with plastic wrap, for up to 1 day before roasting.

Finish Line

Serve meatballs on several small platters scattered throughout your entertaining space to encourage guests to graze.

Perfect Pair

Serve with Apple-Fennel Rémoulade (page 162) or Roasted Carrots and Shallots with Chermoula (page 229).

keftedes

20 square saltines

½ cup milk

½ cup chopped fresh mint or dill, plus extra for sprinkling

6 scallions, minced

2 tablespoons dried oregano

5 garlic cloves, minced

1 tablespoon grated lemon zest

2 teaspoons ground cumin

2 teaspoons ground coriander

1½ teaspoons pepper

1¼ teaspoons table salt

2 pounds ground lamb

1 recipe Yogurt-Tahini Sauce (page 17)

WHY THIS RECIPE WORKS This Greek dish—which gives lamb its rightful turn in meatballs—can be found on many restaurant menus. We wanted to make our own version with tender, juicy ground lamb; lemony brightness; and bold yet balanced seasoning from garlic, spices, and herbs. We chose crushed saltine crackers and milk as a panade to keep the meatballs tender and juicy. Lemon zest and a hefty dose of minced garlic add punch and pungency, and citrusy coriander and earthy cumin provide complexity. Aromatic mint and scallions, as well as dried oregano with its slight licorice undertones, provide the best herb mix. We roast the meatballs and then serve them cocktail-style with a smooth and creamy tahini and yogurt dip. The zippy flavor and cooling nature of the sauce is the perfect finish for these rich, spiced, sophisticated meatballs, as is a refreshing garnish of complementary fresh mint.

1 Adjust oven rack to upper-middle position and heat oven to 450 degrees. Set wire rack in aluminum foil–lined rimmed baking sheet.

2 Place saltines in large zipper-lock bag, seal bag, and crush fine with rolling pin (you should end up with 1 scant cup crushed saltines). Combine saltines and milk in large bowl, mashing with rubber spatula until paste forms, about 1 minute.

3 Add chopped mint, scallions, oregano, garlic, lemon zest, cumin, coriander, pepper, and salt to saltine mixture and mash until thoroughly combined. Add lamb and mix with your hands until thoroughly combined.

4 Divide mixture into 40 portions (1 heaping tablespoon each). Roll portions between your wet hands to form 1½-inch meatballs and evenly space on prepared wire rack. Roast until meatballs are lightly browned, about 20 minutes.

5 Using tongs, transfer meatballs to serving platter. Serve with sauce and sprinkle with mint leaves.

Head Start

Refrigerate shaped, uncooked meatballs, covered with plastic wrap, for up to 1 day before roasting.

Finish Line

For a composed small plate presentation, smear a small amount of sauce on individual plates and top with meatballs.

Perfect Pair

Serve with Butternut Squash and Apple Fattoush (page 185) or a roasted or grilled vegetable such as zucchini, or Skillet Roasted Brussels Sprouts with Chorizo and Manchego Cheese (page 245).

lamb rib chops with mint-rosemary relish

Relish

½ cup minced fresh mint

5 tablespoons extra-virgin olive oil

2 teaspoons minced fresh rosemary

2 teaspoons red wine vinegar

1 garlic clove, minced

⅛ teaspoon red pepper flakes

Lamb

8 (5- to 6-ounce) lamb rib chops, 1¼ to 1½ inches thick, trimmed

½ teaspoon table salt

½ teaspoon pepper

2 tablespoons vegetable oil

Perfect Pair

Serve with Brown Rice Salad with Fennel, Mushrooms, and Walnuts (page 190), Fingerling Potato Salad with Sun-Dried Tomato Dressing (page 186), or Marinated Eggplant with Capers and Mint (page 209).

WHY THIS RECIPE WORKS The refined appearance and flavor of lamb chops make them a popular cut to serve when entertaining guests, and their small size means that they can easily be served alongside other small plates without dominating the meal. The intense heat of a pre-heated cast-iron skillet produces a rich crust on the lamb while melting away its abundant fat. Searing the chops quickly on both sides over medium-high heat and then gently finishing them over lower heat yields lamb chops with crispy crusts and juicy interiors. We season the chops simply, with just salt and pepper; to add flavor and complement the lamb we create a quick olive oil–based mint and rosemary relish. The bold combination of mint and rosemary, along with garlic, spicy red pepper flakes, and tart red wine vinegar, is the perfect pairing for the lamb.

1 Adjust oven rack to middle position, place 12-inch cast-iron skillet on rack, and heat oven to 500 degrees.

2 **For the relish** While oven heats, combine all ingredients in serving bowl. Season with salt and pepper to taste; set aside for serving.

3 **For the lamb** Pat chops dry with paper towels and sprinkle with salt and pepper. When oven reaches 500 degrees, remove skillet from oven using pot holders and place over medium-high heat; turn off oven. Being careful of hot skillet handle, add oil and heat until just smoking. Cook chops, without moving them, until lightly browned on first side, about 2 minutes. Flip chops and cook until lightly browned on second side, about 2 minutes.

4 Flip chops, reduce heat to medium-low, and cook until well browned and meat registers 120 to 125 degrees (for medium-rare), 3 to 5 minutes, flipping chops halfway through cooking. Transfer chops to serving platter, tent with aluminum foil, and let rest for 5 to 10 minutes. Serve with relish.

chickpea cakes

2 (15-ounce) cans chickpeas, drained, with 6 ounces (¾ cup) aquafaba reserved

6 tablespoons extra-virgin olive oil, divided

1 teaspoon ground coriander

⅛ teaspoon cayenne pepper

⅛ teaspoon table salt

1 cup panko bread crumbs

2 scallions, sliced thin

3 tablespoons minced fresh cilantro

1 shallot, minced

Lemon wedges

Head Start

Refrigerate uncooked cakes, wrapped in plastic wrap, for up to 1 day.

Perfect Pair

Serve patties with a yogurt sauce (see pages 17–18) or atop one of the layerable salads on pages 154–155. Or serve alongside Braised Eggplant with Paprika, Coriander, and Yogurt (page 243) or Pink Pickled Turnips (page 77).

WHY THIS RECIPE WORKS Tender canned chickpeas, blended with plenty of seasonings and aromatics and pan-fried until crispy and deep golden brown, make flavorful patties that can be served as an appealing small plate alongside (or on top of) a light salad. Pulsing the chickpeas in the food processor until they're coarsely ground results in a mixture that holds its shape once pressed into patties but still retains some texture. To bind the patties, we stir in aquafaba (the liquid from the can of chickpeas) along with panko bread crumbs, and for richness we add olive oil. A combination of coriander, cayenne, scallions, and cilantro ensures that these patties are ultraflavorful. Avoid overmixing the chickpea mixture in step 1 or the cakes will have a mealy texture.

1 Pulse chickpeas in food processor until coarsely ground, about 8 pulses. Whisk reserved aquafaba, 2 tablespoons oil, coriander, cayenne, and salt together in medium bowl. Gently stir in chickpeas, panko, scallions, cilantro, and shallot until combined. Divide chickpea mixture into 6 equal portions. Using your lightly moistened hands, firmly pack each portion into ¾-inch-thick cake.

2 Adjust oven rack to middle position and heat oven to 200 degrees. Heat 2 tablespoons oil in 12-inch nonstick skillet over medium heat until shimmering. Place 3 cakes in skillet and cook until deep golden brown and crispy on first side, 4 to 5 minutes. Using 2 spatulas, gently flip cakes and cook until browned and crispy on second side, 4 to 5 minutes.

3 Transfer cakes to wire rack set in rimmed baking sheet and place in oven to keep warm. Wipe out skillet with paper towels and repeat with remaining 2 tablespoons oil and remaining 3 patties. Serve with lemon wedges.

red lentil kibbeh

3 tablespoons extra-virgin olive oil, divided

1 onion, chopped fine

1 red bell pepper, stemmed, seeded, and chopped fine

1 teaspoon table salt

2 tablespoons harissa

2 tablespoons tomato paste

½ teaspoon cayenne pepper (optional)

1 cup medium-grind bulgur

4 cups water

¾ cup dried red lentils, picked over and rinsed

½ cup chopped fresh parsley

2 tablespoons lemon juice

1 head Bibb lettuce (8 ounces), leaves separated

½ cup plain yogurt

Lemon wedges

WHY THIS RECIPE WORKS Kibbeh is a popular Middle Eastern dish made from bulgur, minced onions, varying spices, and, typically, ground meat. During Lent, however, lentils are often used in lieu of meat, making this dish a flavor-packed vegetarian option, perfect for spooning into lettuce cups and eating with your hands. Starting with quick-cooking red lentils, we enhance their flavor and their vibrant hue with the additions of tomato paste, for sweetness and umami, and harissa, a smoky, spicy chili paste. We give the bulgur (which we use to bulk up the filling) a head start before adding the lentils to the same saucepan to allow both components to finish cooking at the same time. To balance the deep flavors from the aromatics and pastes, we stir in lemon juice and fresh parsley at the end. The spiciness of store-bought harissa can vary greatly by brand; if your harissa is spicy, omit the cayenne. For a vegan version, use plant-based yogurt.

1 Heat 1 tablespoon oil in large saucepan over medium heat until shimmering. Add onion, bell pepper, and salt and cook until softened, about 5 minutes. Stir in harissa, tomato paste, and cayenne, if using, and cook, stirring frequently, until fragrant, about 1 minute.

2 Stir in bulgur and water and bring to simmer. Reduce heat to low, cover, and simmer gently until bulgur is barely tender, about 8 minutes. Stir in lentils, cover, and continue to cook, stirring occasionally, until lentils and bulgur are tender, 8 to 10 minutes.

3 Off heat, lay clean dish towel underneath lid and let mixture sit for 10 minutes. Stir in 1 tablespoon oil, parsley, and lemon juice and stir vigorously until mixture is cohesive. Season with salt and pepper to taste. Transfer to platter and drizzle with remaining 1 tablespoon oil. Spoon kibbeh into lettuce leaves and drizzle with yogurt. Serve with lemon wedges.

Perfect Pair

Serve as part of meze platter with Whipped Feta and Roasted Red Pepper Dip (page 88), Baba Ghanoush (page 106) or hummus (see pages 74–75), and spiced roasted chickpeas (see page 31).

seared tempeh with tomato jam

1 pound tomatoes, cored and cut into ½-inch pieces

2 tablespoons honey

½ cup plus 2 tablespoons red wine vinegar, divided

7 garlic cloves, minced, divided

1 tablespoon grated fresh ginger

1 teaspoon ras el hanout

1 anchovy fillet, rinsed, patted dry, and minced (optional)

½ teaspoon ground dried Aleppo pepper, divided

1 pound tempeh

¼ cup water

1 teaspoon dried oregano

½ teaspoon table salt

3 tablespoons extra-virgin olive oil

2 tablespoons chopped fresh cilantro

WHY THIS RECIPE WORKS Protein-rich tempeh has a distinct nutty, savory taste all on its own, but this fermented vegetarian protein is also a champ at absorbing added flavors, making it the perfect candidate for the plant-based "steak" treatment. Marinating the tempeh in a seasoned vinegar-and-water base infuses it with flavor. Patting the marinated tempeh dry and pan-searing it creates a delectably crispy edge and a tender interior texture. The tempeh's earthy flavor is well balanced by bright, sweet, meaty tomato jam that gets additional depth from an optional anchovy and warm spice from fresh ginger and ras el hanout. Freshness comes at the end in a sprinkling of fresh cilantro. For a vegetarian version, omit the anchovy.

1 Combine tomatoes; honey; 6 tablespoons vinegar; half of garlic; ginger; ras el hanout; anchovy, if using; and ¼ teaspoon Aleppo pepper in 12-inch nonstick skillet. Bring to boil over medium-high heat, then reduce to simmer and cook, stirring often, until tomatoes have broken down and begun to thicken, 15 to 20 minutes.

2 Mash jam with potato masher to even consistency. Continue to cook until mixture has thickened and darkened in color, 5 to 10 minutes. Let jam cool completely, about 1 hour. Season with salt and pepper to taste; set aside.

3 Cut each block of tempeh into 4 even pieces, then halve each piece into approximately ¼-inch-thick slabs. Whisk water, oregano, salt, remaining ¼ cup vinegar, remaining garlic, and remaining ¼ teaspoon Aleppo pepper together in bowl. Transfer marinade to 1-gallon zipper-lock bag. Add tempeh, press out air, seal, and toss gently to coat. Refrigerate tempeh for at least 1 hour, flipping bag occasionally.

4 Remove tempeh from marinade and pat dry with paper towels. Heat oil in 12-inch nonstick skillet over medium heat until shimmering. Add 8 pieces tempeh and cook until golden brown on first side, 2 to 4 minutes. Flip tempeh, reduce heat to medium-low, and continue to cook until golden brown on second side, 2 to 4 minutes. Transfer to serving platter and tent with aluminum foil to keep warm. Repeat with remaining tempeh. Serve tempeh steaks with tomato jam, sprinkling individual portions with cilantro.

Head Start

Refrigerate tomato jam for up to 4 days; let come to room temperature before serving. Refrigerate tempeh in marinade for up to 1 day.

Perfect Pair

Serve with Roasted King Trumpet Mushrooms (page 219), Stir-Fried En Choy with Garlic (page 220), or Skillet-Roasted Broccoli with Sesame and Orange Topping (page 224).

tempeh with sambal sauce

12 ounces Fresno chiles, stemmed, seeded, and chopped coarse

1 small onion, chopped coarse

5 garlic cloves, peeled

2 teaspoons shrimp paste

½ teaspoon table salt

1 cup vegetable oil for frying

1 pound tempeh, cut into ½-inch pieces

½ cup water

2 tablespoons kecap manis

1½ cups fresh lemon basil, Thai basil, or Italian basil leaves

Perfect Pair

Serve with Pai Huang Gua (page 156), Marinated Manchego (page 127), or Braised Eggplant with Soy, Garlic, and Ginger (page 242).

WHY THIS RECIPE WORKS Nutty, protein-packed tempeh is often served as the foundation of a main dish, but cut into small pieces that can be picked up with a toothpick and draped with a flavorful sauce, it's also right at home as a small plate. Here the tempeh is coated in a spicy-rich sambal sauce made with ground red chile peppers fried in oil to deepen its flavor. Last-minute additions of kecap manis (an Indonesian soy sauce with a viscous consistency and sweet, molasses-like flavor) and aromatic Thai lemon basil add dimension. Lemon basil is traditional in Indonesia, but Thai and Italian basil are excellent substitutes. If shrimp paste is unavailable, substitute 2 anchovy fillets minced to a paste. (Or, for a vegetarian version, omit the shrimp paste.) It's worth seeking out kecap manis; if you can't find it, you can substitute a combination of 1½ tablespoons dark brown sugar and 1 teaspoon soy sauce. You will need a 12-inch nonstick skillet or a 14-inch flat-bottomed wok for this recipe.

1 Process chiles, onion, garlic, shrimp paste, and salt in food processor until finely chopped, about 30 seconds, scraping down sides of bowl as needed; transfer to bowl.

2 Adjust oven rack to middle position and heat oven to 200 degrees. Set wire rack in rimmed baking sheet and line rack with triple layer of paper towels. Heat oil in 12-inch nonstick skillet or 14-inch flat-bottomed wok over medium-high heat to 375 degrees. Carefully add half of tempeh to hot oil and increase heat to high. Cook, turning as needed, until golden brown, 3 to 5 minutes. Adjust burner, if necessary, to maintain oil temperature between 350 and 375 degrees. Off heat, transfer tempeh to prepared rack and keep warm in oven. Return oil to 375 degrees over medium-high heat and repeat with remaining tempeh; transfer to rack.

3 Carefully pour off all but 2 tablespoons oil from pan. Add chile mixture to oil left in pan and cook over medium-high heat, tossing slowly but constantly, until darkened in color and completely dry, 7 to 10 minutes. Off heat, stir in water and kecap manis until combined. Add tempeh and basil and toss until well coated. Serve.

shrimp tostadas with coconut and pineapple slaw

½ cup canned coconut milk

1 teaspoon grated lime zest plus 1 tablespoon juice

1 teaspoon table salt, divided

⅛ teaspoon cayenne pepper

2½ cups (7 ounces) shredded coleslaw mix

1 cup ¼-inch pineapple pieces

1 jalapeño chile, stemmed, seeded, and minced

2 ripe avocados, halved and pitted

1 cup vegetable oil for frying

8 (6-inch) corn tortillas

1 pound large shrimp (26 to 30 per pound), peeled, deveined, and tails removed

Perfect Pair

Serve with Sikil P'ak (page 112), Esquites (page 177), or Gajarachi Koshimbir (page 160).

WHY THIS RECIPE WORKS Coconut milk spiked with lime zest acts both as a dressing for pineapple coleslaw and as a sauce for sautéed shrimp in these quick, crisp-crunchy tostadas. Mashed avocado contributes creaminess and richness to the refreshing combination of slaw and shrimp. And as for the shrimp themselves, we simmer them in cayenne- and lime zest–spiked coconut milk, so they absorb sweetness and spice as they cook through. We like to garnish these tostadas with fresh cilantro leaves and serve them with hot sauce.

1 Combine coconut milk, lime zest, ¾ teaspoon salt, and cayenne in bowl. Reserve ¼ cup coconut milk mixture. Stir lime juice into remaining coconut milk mixture. Add coleslaw mix, pineapple, and jalapeño and toss to combine. Season with salt to taste; set aside. Mash avocados and remaining ¼ teaspoon salt with fork in separate bowl; set aside.

2 Heat oil in medium saucepan over medium heat to 350 degrees. Using fork, poke each tortilla 3 or 4 times. Fry 1 tortilla until crisp and lightly browned, 1 to 2 minutes, flipping tortilla halfway through frying. Transfer to paper towel–lined plate and let drain, then season with salt to taste. Repeat with remaining tortillas.

3 Pat shrimp dry with paper towels. Combine shrimp and reserved coconut milk mixture in 12-inch nonstick skillet. Cook over medium-high heat, stirring occasionally, until shrimp are pink and cooked through, about 5 minutes; transfer to plate. Spread avocado evenly on tostada shells. Divide slaw and shrimp evenly among tostadas. Serve.

pan-seared scallops with asparagus-citrus salad

Salad

2 tablespoons extra-virgin olive oil, divided

12 ounces asparagus, trimmed

6 scallions, trimmed

¼ teaspoon table salt

⅛ teaspoon pepper

1 red grapefruit

1 orange, plus 2 teaspoons grated orange zest

½ cup torn fresh mint, basil, parsley, and/or tarragon

Scallops

1½ pounds large sea scallops, tendons removed

½ teaspoon table salt

¼ teaspoon pepper

2 tablespoons vegetable oil, divided

2 tablespoons unsalted butter, divided

WHY THIS RECIPE WORKS To get beautifully browned scallops on a home stovetop, we heat the oil until it just starts to smoke and cook the scallops in batches to avoid crowding. Basting the scallops with butter adds richness and further aids the scallops in achieving a deep golden-brown crust. To give this small plate a stunning presentation, we serve the scallops atop a colorful bed of salad. We recommend buying "dry" scallops, which don't have chemical additives and taste better than "wet." Dry scallops will look ivory or pinkish; wet scallops are bright white.

1 **For the salad** Heat 2 teaspoons oil in 12-inch nonstick skillet over medium-high heat until shimmering. Add asparagus, scallions, salt, and pepper and cook until asparagus is crisp-tender and vegetables are lightly charred, about 5 minutes. Transfer vegetables to cutting board and let cool. Wipe skillet clean with paper towels.

2 Cut away peel and pith from grapefruit and orange. Cut each citrus fruit through stem end into 8 wedges, then cut wedges crosswise into ½-inch-thick pieces. Add citrus pieces to large bowl. Cut asparagus into 2-inch lengths and cut scallions into ½-inch pieces. Add vegetables, mint, orange zest, and remaining 4 teaspoons oil to bowl with citrus and toss gently to combine. Season with salt and pepper to taste.

3 **For the scallops** Place scallops on rimmed baking sheet lined with clean dish towel. Top with second clean dish towel and press gently on scallops to dry. Let scallops sit between towels at room temperature for 10 minutes.

4 Sprinkle scallops with salt and pepper. Heat 1 tablespoon oil in now-empty skillet over medium-high heat until just smoking. Add half of scallops in single layer, flat side down, and cook until well browned, 1½ to 2 minutes.

5 Add 1 tablespoon butter to skillet. Using tongs, flip scallops. Continue to cook, using large spoon to baste scallops with melted butter (tilt skillet so butter runs to 1 side), until sides of scallops are firm and centers are opaque, 30 to 90 seconds (remove smaller scallops as they finish cooking).

6 Transfer scallops to platter and tent with aluminum foil. Wipe out skillet with paper towels and repeat with remaining 1 tablespoon oil, remaining scallops, and remaining 1 tablespoon butter.

7 Serve salad on individual plates, topped with scallops.

Variation

Pan-Seared Scallops with Mango-Cucumber Salad

Omit salad ingredients and skip steps 1 and 2. While scallops dry, whisk 5 teaspoons extra-virgin olive oil, 2 teaspoons grated fresh ginger, 1 teaspoon honey, ½ teaspoon ground turmeric, ½ teaspoon ground coriander, and ¼ teaspoon table salt together in medium bowl. Microwave until fragrant, about 30 seconds; let cool slightly. Whisk in 1 teaspoon grated lime zest, 1 tablespoon lime juice, 1 thinly sliced shallot, and 1 thinly sliced Thai chile. Add 1 English cucumber, shaved into ribbons; 1 peeled, pitted, and thinly sliced mango; ¼ cup fresh cilantro leaves; and 2 tablespoons roasted pepitas to bowl with dressing and toss gently to combine. Season salad with salt and pepper to taste and serve with scallops.

Finish Line

For a neat presentation, spear scallops on small wooden skewers before placing them atop individual portions of salad.

Perfect Pair

Serve with Chile-Marinated Pork Belly (page 313), topped naan (page 334), or Kataifi-Wrapped Feta with Tomatoes and Artichokes (page 357).

sung choy bao

Chicken

- 1 pound boneless, skinless chicken thighs, trimmed and cut into 1-inch pieces
- 2 teaspoons Shaoxing wine or dry sherry
- 2 teaspoons soy sauce
- 2 teaspoons toasted sesame oil
- 2 teaspoons cornstarch

Sauce

- 3 tablespoons oyster sauce
- 1 tablespoon Shaoxing wine or dry sherry
- 2 teaspoons soy sauce
- 2 teaspoons toasted sesame oil
- ½ teaspoon sugar
- ¼ teaspoon red pepper flakes

Stir-Fry

- 2 tablespoons vegetable oil
- 2 celery ribs, cut into ¼-inch pieces
- 6 ounces shiitake mushrooms, stemmed and sliced thin
- ½ cup water chestnuts, cut into ¼-inch pieces
- 2 scallions, white parts minced, green parts sliced thin
- 2 garlic cloves, minced
- 1 head Bibb lettuce (8 ounces), washed and dried, leaves separated and left whole

  Hoisin sauce

WHY THIS RECIPE WORKS Cantonese sung choy bao, a savory-spicy stir-fry served up in lettuce cups, is a terrific option for a light dinner or as the centerpiece of a small plates spread. To yield tender, juicy chicken lightly coated in a flavorful sauce, we start with chicken thighs and marinate them in soy sauce and Shaoxing wine. We then coat the chicken in a cornstarch slurry to help it retain moisture and prevent the meat from drying out once cooked, a process known as velveting. Spooning the saucy chicken into crisp lettuce leaves makes for a fun handheld eating experience.

1 **For the chicken** Place chicken pieces on large plate in single layer. Freeze meat until firm and starting to harden around edges, about 20 minutes.

2 Whisk Shaoxing wine, soy sauce, oil, and cornstarch together in bowl. Pulse half of meat in food processor until coarsely chopped into ¼- to ⅛-inch pieces, about 10 pulses. Transfer meat to bowl with rice wine mixture and repeat with remaining chunks. Toss chicken to coat and refrigerate for 15 minutes.

3 **For the sauce** Whisk all ingredients together in bowl; set aside.

4 **For the stir-fry** Heat 1 tablespoon oil in 12-inch nonstick skillet over high heat until smoking. Add chicken and cook, stirring constantly, until opaque, 3 to 4 minutes. Transfer to bowl and wipe out skillet.

5 Heat remaining 1 tablespoon oil in now-empty skillet over high heat until smoking. Add celery and mushrooms; cook, stirring constantly, until mushrooms have reduced in size by half and celery is crisp-tender, 3 to 4 minutes. Add water chestnuts, scallion whites, and garlic; cook, stirring constantly, until fragrant, about 1 minute. Whisk sauce to recombine. Return chicken to skillet; add sauce and toss to combine. Spoon into lettuce leaves and sprinkle with scallion greens. Serve, passing hoisin sauce separately.

Finish Line

You can also serve filling, sauce, and scallion greens in separate bowls, with lettuce leaves so guests can assemble wraps themselves.

Perfect Pair

Serve with Blistered Shishito Peppers (page 25), Soy-Marinated Eggs (page 131), or sweet potato salad (see page 188).

dakgangjeong

1 tablespoon toasted
  sesame oil

1 teaspoon garlic, minced
  to paste

1 teaspoon grated
  fresh ginger

1¾ cups water, divided

3 tablespoons sugar

2–3 tablespoons gochujang

1 tablespoon soy sauce

2 quarts vegetable oil for
  frying

1 cup all-purpose flour

3 tablespoons cornstarch

3 pounds chicken wings,
  cut at joints, wing tips
  discarded

Perfect Pair

Serve wings with Herbed Aïoli
(page 16), Cajun Pickled Okra
(page 80) and Moroccan-Style
Carrot Salad (page 159).

WHY THIS RECIPE WORKS A thin, crispy exterior and a spicy-sweet-salty sauce are the hallmarks of dakgangjeong, Korean fried chicken. The biggest challenge, though, is preventing the sauce from destroying the crust. We dunk the chicken (here, we use wings, although traditionally dakgangjeong can be made with a whole cut-up chicken) in a loose batter of flour, cornstarch, and water, and for an extra-crispy coating that can withstand a wet sauce, we double-fry the wings. The Korean chile paste known as gochujang gives our sauce the proper spicy, fermented notes. A rasp-style grater makes quick work of turning the garlic into a paste. Tailor the heat level of your wings by adjusting the amount of gochujang. Use a Dutch oven that holds 6 quarts or more.

1 Combine sesame oil, garlic, and ginger in large bowl and microwave until mixture is bubbly and fragrant but not browned, 40 to 60 seconds. Whisk in ¼ cup water, sugar, gochujang, and soy sauce until smooth and set aside.

2 Heat oil in large Dutch oven over medium-high heat to 350 degrees. While oil heats, whisk flour, cornstarch, and remaining 1½ cups water in second large bowl until smooth. Set wire rack in rimmed baking sheet and set aside.

3 Place half of wings in batter and stir to coat. Using tongs, remove wings from batter one at a time, allowing any excess batter to drip back into bowl, and add to hot oil. Increase heat to high and cook, stirring occasionally to prevent wings from sticking, until coating is light golden and beginning to crisp, about 7 minutes. (Oil temperature will drop sharply after adding chicken.) Transfer wings to prepared rack. Return oil to 350 degrees and repeat with remaining wings. Reduce heat to medium and let second batch of chicken rest for 5 minutes.

4 Return oil to 375 degrees. Carefully return all chicken to oil and cook, stirring occasionally, until exterior is deep golden brown and very crispy, about 7 minutes. Transfer to rack and let stand for 2 minutes. Add chicken to reserved sauce and toss until coated. Return chicken to rack and let stand for 2 minutes to allow surface to set. Transfer to platter and serve.

pretzel-crusted chicken fingers with honey mustard

6 ounces thin pretzel sticks

½ cup all-purpose flour

2 large eggs

2 tablespoons plus ½ cup Dijon mustard, divided

3 tablespoons honey

1½ pounds chicken tenderloins, trimmed

6 tablespoons vegetable oil, divided

Perfect Pair

Serve with Buffalo Chicken Dip (page 115), Butternut Squash Steaks with Honey-Nut Topping (page 246), or Apple-Fennel Rémoulade (page 162).

WHY THIS RECIPE WORKS Chicken fingers don't have to be relegated to the kids' table. Chicken tenderloins cook quickly, and there is no faster sauce than honey mustard, making these tenders perfect as the anchor of a casual small plates meal. We set out to create a quick recipe for chicken tenders that remain juicy on the inside and crunchy on the outside. To make the crispy coating, we blitz thin pretzel sticks in the food processor to yield finely ground crumbs that stick to the tenders easily during the coating process. Shallow frying the chicken in just a few tablespoons of oil crisps them right up, and the classic honey-mustard sauce comes together in seconds for a dish that's dippable to the last bite.

1 Process pretzels in food processor until finely ground, about 20 seconds (you should have about 1½ cups crumbs); transfer to shallow dish. Spread flour in second shallow dish. Beat eggs and 2 tablespoons mustard in third shallow dish. Whisk remaining ½ cup mustard with honey in bowl and set aside.

2 Pat chicken dry with paper towels and season with salt and pepper. Dredge chicken in flour, dip in egg mixture, then coat with pretzel crumbs, pressing gently to adhere.

3 Heat 3 tablespoons oil in 12-inch nonstick skillet over medium-high heat until shimmering. Cook half of tenderloins until golden brown and cooked through, about 5 minutes per side, adjusting heat if crust begins to burn. Transfer to paper towel–lined plate, discard oil, and wipe out skillet with paper towels. Repeat with remaining 3 tablespoons oil and remaining tenderloins. Serve tenderloins with honey mustard.

chicken satay

¼ cup soy sauce

¼ cup vegetable oil

¼ cup packed dark brown sugar

¼ cup minced fresh cilantro

4 scallions, sliced thin

3 tablespoons ketchup

2 garlic cloves, minced

1 teaspoon hot sauce

2 pounds boneless, skinless chicken breasts, trimmed and sliced diagonally into ¼-inch-thick strips

30 (6-inch) wooden skewers

1 recipe Spicy Peanut Dipping Sauce (page 15)

WHY THIS RECIPE WORKS Cloaked in a sweet-spicy marinade and broiled until lightly caramelized on the edges but still juicy, these mini skewers are the perfect pick-up-and-nibble-as-you-mingle party fare. They're also a great all-seasons option, as, unlike most skewered meats, which are typically cooked on the grill, these are cooked in under 10 minutes beneath the intense, direct heat of the broiler. A marinade containing brown sugar, soy sauce, ketchup, and hot sauce guarantees full-flavored meat, and a peanut dipping sauce echoes the flavors in the marinade for a bright finish. Covering the exposed ends of the skewers with aluminum foil protects them from burning. You can freeze the chicken for 30 minutes to make it easier to slice into strips. You will need thirty 6-inch wooden skewers for this recipe.

1 Combine soy sauce, oil, sugar, cilantro, scallions, ketchup, garlic, and hot sauce in medium bowl; add chicken and toss to combine. Cover and refrigerate for at least 30 minutes. Weave chicken onto skewers.

2 Adjust oven rack 6 inches from broiler element and heat broiler. Set wire rack in aluminum foil–lined rimmed baking sheet. Lay skewers on prepared rack and cover skewer ends with foil. Broil until fully cooked, about 8 minutes, flipping skewers halfway through broiling. Serve with peanut sauce.

Perfect Pair

Serve skewers on Herb Salad (page 155). For something a little heartier, serve with sweet potato salad (see page 188).

kombdi, jira ghalun

3⅓ cups water, divided

¼ cup plain whole-milk yogurt, plus extra for serving

8 garlic cloves, smashed and peeled

1 (2-inch) piece ginger, peeled and chopped coarse

1½ tablespoons paprika

1 tablespoon table salt, divided

½–1½ teaspoons cayenne pepper

2 tomatoes, cored and chopped coarse

2¾ pounds boneless, skinless chicken breasts, cut into 1- to 2-inch pieces

3 tablespoons cumin seeds

¼ cup vegetable oil

1 large onion, chopped fine

½ cup fresh cilantro leaves

WHY THIS RECIPE WORKS Kombdi, Jira Ghalun (cumin-scented chicken) is a simple, aromatic dish from Maharashtra, a state on India's west coast. The chicken is marinated in tangy yogurt before being cooked; the cumin is added just before serving so that its smokiness adds fresh top notes to both the chicken and the sauce. Here we opt to use quick-cooking chicken breasts cut into pieces so that the tender morsels can be eaten in just a bite or two. You can substitute 2 tablespoons of Indian red chile powder for the paprika and cayenne, if desired. We strongly recommend toasting and grinding your own whole cumin seeds for this recipe, but you can substitute 7 teaspoons of ground cumin, if desired. If using ground cumin, toast it in an 8-inch skillet over medium heat until fragrant, about 1½ minutes.

1 Process ⅓ cup water, yogurt, garlic, ginger, paprika, 2 teaspoons salt, and cayenne in blender until smooth, about 2 minutes, scraping down sides of blender jar as needed. Transfer yogurt marinade to bowl.

2 Process tomatoes in now-empty blender until coarsely pureed, about 5 seconds. Transfer to second bowl.

3 Add chicken to bowl with yogurt marinade and toss to coat, rubbing marinade into chicken. Cover and refrigerate for at least 1 hour.

4 Heat cumin seeds in 8-inch skillet over medium heat, stirring frequently, until fragrant, about 3 minutes. Transfer to spice grinder or mortar and pestle and grind to powder; set aside.

5 Heat oil in large Dutch oven over medium-high heat until just smoking. Add onion and remaining 1 teaspoon salt and cook until onion is softened, 5 to 7 minutes. Add tomatoes, increase heat to high, and cook until mixture darkens slightly and begins to stick to bottom of pot, 5 to 7 minutes.

6 Add chicken, along with any marinade left in bowl, and remaining 3 cups water and bring to boil. Cover; reduce heat to medium-low; and simmer, stirring occasionally, until chicken registers 160 degrees, 18 to 25 minutes.

7 Using tongs, transfer chicken to large plate. Increase heat to high and cook sauce, uncovered and stirring occasionally, until thickened and reduced to about 2¾ cups, 12 to 15 minutes. Stir cumin into sauce. Add chicken back to pot and stir to coat with sauce. Serve, sprinkled with cilantro and passing extra yogurt separately.

Head Start

Cover and refrigerate tomatoes and chicken in marinade separately for up to 1 day.

Perfect Pair

Serve with Quick Pickled Red Onion (page 19), Samosas (page 238), or Herb Salad (page 155).

spicy chicken flautas

2 avocados, halved, pitted, and chopped coarse

½ cup sour cream

6 tablespoons water, divided

5 tablespoons lime juice (3 limes), divided

¼ cup minced fresh cilantro, divided

1 tablespoon vegetable oil

1 onion, chopped fine

2 jalapeño chiles, stemmed, seeded, and minced

1 tablespoon chili powder

2 garlic cloves, minced

½ teaspoon table salt

¼ teaspoon pepper

¼ teaspoon dried oregano

⅛ teaspoon cayenne pepper

1 (8-ounce) can tomato sauce

2 pounds boneless, skinless chicken breasts, trimmed

2 tablespoons all-purpose flour

12 (8-inch) flour tortillas

1 cup vegetable oil for frying

WHY THIS RECIPE WORKS Take a soft flour tortilla, roll it around a savory, spicy filling (here, tender shredded chicken), and fry it until crispy and golden brown, and you have a flauta (Spanish for "flute"). We cook the chicken directly in the spiced tomato sauce to keep it succulently juicy before shredding it, stirring it back into the sauce, and using it to fill 8-inch flour tortillas. Cutting off one-third of the tortillas ensures that the proportion of filling to crispy exterior is just right; "gluing" the edge of the tortillas down with a flour-water paste keeps the flautas from spilling their filling everywhere during frying. A creamy avocado sauce is the perfect accompaniment for these oh-so-dunkable bites.

1 Mash avocados, sour cream, 2 tablespoons water, 3 tablespoons lime juice, and 2 tablespoons cilantro in bowl with potato masher (or fork) until smooth. Season with salt and pepper to taste; set avocado sauce aside for serving.

2 Heat 1 tablespoon oil in 12-inch nonstick skillet over medium heat until shimmering. Add onion and cook until softened, about 5 minutes. Stir in jalapeños, chili powder, garlic, salt, pepper, oregano, and cayenne and cook until fragrant, about 30 seconds. Stir in tomato sauce and bring to simmer. Nestle chicken into sauce. Reduce heat to medium-low, cover, and cook until chicken registers 160 degrees, 10 to 15 minutes, flipping chicken halfway through cooking.

3 Transfer chicken to cutting board, let cool slightly, then shred into bite-size pieces using 2 forks. Stir chicken, remaining 2 tablespoons cilantro, and remaining 2 tablespoons lime juice into sauce.

4 Line rimmed baking sheet with parchment paper. Whisk flour and remaining 2 tablespoons water together in bowl. Cut off bottom third of each tortilla (discard or reserve for another use). Wrap tortillas in damp dish towel and microwave until warm and pliable, about 1 minute.

5 Lay 6 warm tortillas on clean counter with trimmed edge facing you. Mound half of chicken filling alongside trimmed edges. Working with 1 tortilla at a time, roll trimmed edge of tortilla up over filling, then pull back on tortilla to tighten it around filling. Brush remaining

exposed tortilla with flour paste, then roll it up tightly around filling.
Press on edges firmly to seal; transfer to prepared baking sheet, seam
side down. Repeat with remaining 6 tortillas and remaining filling.

6 Adjust oven rack to middle position and heat oven to 200 degrees.
Line plate with several layers of paper towels. Set wire rack in second
rimmed baking sheet. Heat 1 cup oil in clean 12-inch nonstick skillet
over medium-high heat to 325 degrees. Place 6 flautas, seam side
down, in oil and fry, turning as needed, until golden brown on all
sides, 3 to 5 minutes. Adjust burner, if necessary, to maintain oil temperature between 300 and 325 degrees. Transfer flautas to prepared
plate, let drain briefly, then transfer to wire rack and keep warm in
oven. Return oil to 325 degrees and repeat with remaining flautas.
Serve with avocado sauce.

Head Start

Refrigerate formed flautas,
covered with damp dish towel
and wrapped in plastic wrap,
for up to 1 day before frying.

Perfect Pair

Serve with Parmesan–Black
Pepper Cheese Straws (page 29),
Pineapple-Watermelon Salsa
(page 14), or stuffed mushrooms
(see pages 216-217).

sizzling beef lettuce wraps

1 English cucumber, halved and sliced thin

¼ cup seasoned rice vinegar

¼ cup mayonnaise

2 tablespoons sriracha

3 tablespoons soy sauce

2 tablespoons packed brown sugar

4 garlic cloves, minced

1 tablespoon toasted sesame oil

1½ pounds 85 percent lean ground beef

1 head Bibb, green leaf, or red leaf lettuce (8 ounces), leaves separated

WHY THIS RECIPE WORKS This lighter take on ground beef tacos uses farm-fresh lettuce leaves to hold a satisfying filling. We love to serve these little bundles at warm summertime gatherings, as the crisp cucumber is the perfect cooling counterpoint to the rich beef and spicy sauce. To punch up the filling, we take inspiration from the sweet and savory flavor of Korean barbecue. We toss browned ground beef with a quickly made umami-filled barbecue sauce of soy sauce, brown sugar, garlic, and toasted sesame oil. Quickly pickled cucumber adds a refreshing crunchy topping, and a superquick sriracha mayonnaise adds a touch of heat.

1 Combine cucumber and vinegar in bowl; set aside. Combine mayonnaise and sriracha in second bowl; set aside. Combine soy sauce, sugar, garlic, and oil in third bowl.

2 Cook beef in 12-inch nonstick skillet over high heat until any juices have evaporated and beef begins to fry in its own fat, 8 to 10 minutes. Add soy sauce mixture to skillet and cook until nearly evaporated, about 2 minutes. To serve, fill lettuce leaves with beef mixture and top with pickled cucumbers and sriracha mayonnaise.

Finish Line

For a fun presentation, serve filling, pickles, and sauce in separate bowls alongside lettuce leaves and allow guests to assemble wraps themselves.

Perfect Pair

Serve with Loaded Sweet Potato Wedges with Tempeh (page 249) or Gougères (page 324).

pinchos morunos

3 tablespoons table salt for brining

2 pounds boneless country-style pork ribs, trimmed

¼ cup vegetable oil

2 tablespoons lemon juice, plus lemon wedges for serving

6 garlic cloves, minced

1 tablespoon grated fresh ginger

2 teaspoons minced fresh oregano, divided

2 teaspoons smoked paprika

1 teaspoon ground coriander

1 teaspoon table salt

½ teaspoon ground cumin

½ teaspoon pepper

¼ teaspoon cayenne pepper

Perfect Pair

Serve with Whipped Feta Dip (page 88), Gambas a la Plancha (page 260), or Grilled Polenta with Charred Scallion and Gorgonzola Topping (page 52) as well as a hydrating pitcher of lemonade (see page 382).

WHY THIS RECIPE WORKS A common sight on many a tapas menu, pinchos morunos is easy to make at home. We like country-style ribs for their convenience and their ability to remain juicy and tender when grilled in 1-inch chunks. To increase the pork's juiciness, we brine it for 30 minutes before cutting it into cubes and coating it with a robust spice paste that includes garlic, lemon, ginger, coriander, smoked paprika, and fresh oregano. Because country-style ribs contain a mix of lighter loin meat and darker shoulder meat, we keep the light meat and dark meat on separate skewers to ensure that the light meat doesn't overcook and the dark meat isn't chewy. You will need four or five 12-inch metal skewers for this recipe.

1 Dissolve 3 tablespoons salt in 1½ quarts cold water in large container. Submerge ribs in brine and let stand at room temperature for 30 minutes. Meanwhile, whisk oil, lemon juice, garlic, ginger, 1 teaspoon oregano, paprika, coriander, remaining 1 teaspoon salt, cumin, pepper, and cayenne in small bowl until combined.

2 Remove pork from brine and pat dry with paper towels. Cut ribs into 1-inch chunks; place dark meat and light meat in separate bowls. Divide spice paste proportionately between bowls and toss to coat. Thread light and dark meat onto separate skewers (do not crowd pieces). Place dark-meat kebabs on left side of rimmed baking sheet and light-meat kebabs on right side.

3A **For a charcoal grill** Open bottom vent completely. Light large chimney starter filled with charcoal briquettes (6 quarts). When top coals are partially covered with ash, pour evenly over half of grill. Set cooking grate in place, cover, and open lid vent completely. Heat grill until hot, about 5 minutes.

3B **For a gas grill** Turn all burners to high, cover, and heat grill until hot, about 15 minutes. Leave primary burner on high and turn off other burner(s).

4   Clean and oil cooking grate. Place dark meat on hotter side of grill and cook for 6 minutes. Flip dark meat and add light meat to hotter side of grill. Cook for 4 minutes, then flip all kebabs. Continue to cook, flipping kebabs every 4 minutes, until dark meat is well charred and registers 155 degrees and light meat is lightly charred and registers 140 degrees, 4 to 8 minutes longer. Transfer to serving platter, tent with aluminum foil, and let rest for 5 minutes. Remove pork from skewers, toss to combine, sprinkle with remaining 1 teaspoon oregano, and serve, passing lemon wedges separately.

chile-marinated pork belly

1½ pounds center-cut fresh pork belly, 1½ inches thick, skin removed

1 tablespoon plus ¼ cup water, divided

¼ teaspoon baking soda

1 tablespoon soy sauce

6 scallions, white parts chopped, green parts cut into 1½-inch pieces

3 tablespoons gochujang paste

2 tablespoons gochugaru

2 tablespoons sugar

3 garlic cloves, peeled

1 (1-inch) piece ginger, peeled and sliced into ¼-inch-thick rounds

2 teaspoons vegetable oil, plus extra as needed

2 teaspoons sesame seeds, toasted

Finish Line

Top pork with Quick Pickled Cucumber and Bean Sprouts (page 20).

Perfect Pair

Serve with Honeydew Salad with Peanuts and Lime (page 173) or Lop Cheung Bao (page 352).

WHY THIS RECIPE WORKS Bokkeum is a generalized Korean term for dishes that are stir-fried over high heat. Jeyuk (pork) bokkeum offers a great balance of sweet and spicy meatiness. To start, we soak thinly sliced pork belly in a baking soda solution to tenderize the meat and keep it moist. We toss the pork in a simple soy sauce marinade and then cook it quickly in batches over high heat. For the sauce, we combine scallion whites with gochujang and gochugaru (Korean red pepper flakes) for heat. Boneless country-style pork ribs can be substituted for the pork belly, if desired. You will need a 12-inch nonstick skillet or a 14-inch flat-bottomed wok for this recipe.

1 Cut pork into 2-inch-wide strips and place on large plate; freeze until firm, about 30 minutes. Slice strips crosswise ⅛ inch thick. Combine 1 tablespoon water and baking soda in medium bowl. Add pork and toss to coat; let sit for 5 minutes. Add soy sauce and toss to coat.

2 Process scallion whites, remaining ¼ cup water, gochujang paste, gochugaru, sugar, garlic, and ginger in food processor until smooth, about 1 minute, scraping down sides of bowl as needed; set aside.

3 Heat oil in 12-inch nonstick skillet or 14-inch flat-bottomed wok over medium-high heat until just smoking. Add half of pork and increase heat to high. Cook, tossing pork slowly but constantly, until no longer pink, 2 to 6 minutes; using slotted spoon, transfer pork to clean bowl. Pour off all but 2 teaspoons fat. (If necessary, add extra oil to equal 2 teaspoons.) Repeat with remaining pork.

4 Return first batch of pork and any accumulated juices to pan. Add reserved sauce and scallion greens and cook, tossing constantly, until sauce is slightly thickened and darkens in color, about 2 minutes. Sprinkle with sesame seeds and serve.

chinese barbecue spareribs

1 (6-inch) piece fresh ginger, peeled and sliced thin

8 garlic cloves, smashed and peeled

1 cup honey

¾ cup hoisin sauce

¾ cup soy sauce

½ cup water

½ cup Shaoxing wine or dry sherry

2 teaspoons five-spice powder

1 teaspoon ground white pepper

1 teaspoon red food coloring (optional)

2 (2½- to 3-pound) racks St. Louis–style spareribs, trimmed and cut into individual ribs

2 tablespoons toasted sesame oil

Head Start

Prepare ribs through step 2. Refrigerate ribs and defatted cooking liquid separately for up to 1 day before continuing with step 3.

Perfect Pair

Serve with Easy Egg Rolls (page 62), Gobi Manchurian (page 234), or Roasted Carrots and Shallots with Chermoula (page 229).

WHY THIS RECIPE WORKS Chinese barbecue ribs are usually marinated for several hours and then slow-roasted and basted repeatedly to build up a thick crust. We skip both of those time-consuming steps and instead braise the ribs—cut into individual pieces to speed cooking and create more surface area—in a highly seasoned liquid, which helps the flavor penetrate the meat thoroughly and quickly. Then we strain, defat, and reduce the braising liquid to make a full-bodied glaze in which we toss the ribs before roasting them on a rack in a hot oven to color and crisp their exteriors. It's not necessary to remove the membrane on the bone side of the ribs. These ribs are chewier than American-style ribs; if you prefer them more tender, cook them for an additional 15 minutes in step 1. You can serve the first batch immediately or tent them with foil to keep them warm.

1 Pulse ginger and garlic in food processor until finely chopped, 10 to 12 pulses, scraping down sides of bowl as needed. Transfer ginger-garlic mixture to Dutch oven. Add honey, hoisin, soy sauce, water, Shaoxing wine, five-spice powder, pepper, and food coloring, if using, and whisk until combined. Add ribs and stir to coat (ribs will not be fully submerged). Bring to simmer over high heat, then reduce heat to low, cover, and cook for 1¼ hours, stirring occasionally.

2 Adjust oven rack to middle position and heat oven to 425 degrees. Using tongs, transfer ribs to large bowl. Strain braising liquid through fine-mesh strainer set over large container, pressing on solids to extract as much liquid as possible; discard solids. Let cooking liquid settle for 10 minutes. Using wide, shallow spoon, skim fat from surface and discard.

3 Return braising liquid to pot and add oil. Bring to boil over high heat and cook until syrupy and reduced to 2½ cups, 16 to 20 minutes.

4 Set wire rack in aluminum foil–lined rimmed baking sheet and pour ½ cup water into sheet. Transfer half of ribs to pot with braising liquid and toss to coat. Arrange ribs bone side up on prepared rack, letting excess glaze drip off. Roast until edges of ribs start to caramelize, 5 to 7 minutes. Flip ribs and continue to roast until second side starts to caramelize, 5 to 7 minutes longer. Transfer ribs to serving platter; repeat process with remaining ribs. Serve.

arrosticini

2 pounds boneless lamb shoulder roast, trimmed and cut into ½-inch pieces

1½ teaspoons kosher salt

1 teaspoon pepper

3 tablespoons extra-virgin olive oil

WHY THIS RECIPE WORKS Originally eaten by Italian shepherds as a quick and portable meal, today these grilled lamb skewers are a popular street food. The lamb (or mutton) is cut into tiny cubes, cooked over a blazing-hot fire, and eaten directly off the skewers. To prevent the small pieces of meat from overcooking, we pack them tightly onto the skewers. Using a half-grill fire setup produces concentrated heat that browns the meat in minutes and bastes it in its own fat until tender. Straight off the grill, the skewers are so flavorful that they need no further embellishment to stand out in a crowd of small plates. You can substitute 2½ pounds lamb shoulder chops (blade or round bone) for the lamb shoulder. You will need twelve 12-inch metal skewers for this recipe.

Perfect Pair

Serve these skewers with Baba Ghanoush (page 106) or Shaved Zucchini Salad with Pepitas (page 155) and a refreshing pitcher of Sangria for a Crowd (page 392).

1 Pat lamb dry with paper towels and sprinkle with salt and pepper. Tightly thread lamb onto twelve 12-inch metal skewers, leaving top 3 inches of each skewer exposed. Brush skewered meat with oil.

2A **For a charcoal grill** Open bottom vent completely. Light large chimney starter filled with charcoal briquettes (6 quarts). When top coals are partially covered with ash, pour evenly over half of grill. Set cooking grate in place, cover, and open lid vent completely. Heat grill until hot, about 5 minutes.

2B **For a gas grill** Turn all burners to high, cover, and heat grill until hot, about 15 minutes. Leave all burners on high.

3 Clean and oil cooking grate. Place skewers on hotter side of grill, and cook (covered if using gas), turning frequently, until well browned on all sides, 5 to 7 minutes. Serve.

breads, dumplings, and savory pastries

put puff pastry to work

Store-bought puff pastry makes it easy to create these impressive nibbles. Cheesy richness and heat play against the flaky layers of laminated dough. Before you start baking, check out Puff Pastry Know-How (page 3___)

easy cheese straws

Serves 6 to 8 (makes 14 straws)
Active Time 15 minutes
Total Time 25 minutes

  1 (9½ by 9-inch) sheet puff pastry, thawed
  2 ounces Parmesan cheese, grated (1 cup)
  ¼ teaspoon table salt
  ⅛ teaspoon pepper

Adjust oven racks to upper-middle and lower-middle positions and heat oven to 425 degrees. Roll pastry into 10½-inch square on lightly floured counter. Sprinkle puff pastry with Parmesan, salt, and pepper and press lightly to adhere. Cut dough into fourteen ¾-inch-wide strips. Gently twist each strip several times and transfer to 2 parchment paper–lined baking sheets. Bake until fully puffed and golden, about 10 minutes. Let cool before serving. (Straws can be stored in an airtight container for up to 3 days.)

gochujang and cheddar pinwheels

Serves 8 to 10 (makes 18 pinwheels)
Active Time 20 minutes
Total Time 40 minutes, plus 1 hour chilling

  1 (9½ by 9-inch) sheet puff pastry, thawed
  2 tablespoons gochujang paste
  2 ounces sharp cheddar cheese, shredded (½ cup)
  3 tablespoons minced fresh chives, divided
  1 tablespoon sesame seeds
  1 large egg beaten with 1 teaspoon water

1 Dust counter lightly with flour. Unfold puff pastry and roll into 10-inch square. Spread gochujang evenly over entire surface of pastry, leaving ½-inch border along top edge. Sprinkle evenly with cheddar, 2 tablespoons chives, and sesame seeds. Gently roll rolling pin over toppings to press into pastry.

2 Starting at edge of pastry closest to you, roll into tight log and pinch seam to seal. Wrap in plastic wrap and refrigerate until firm, about 1 hour. (Rolled pastry log can be refrigerated for up to 2 days before slicing and baking.)

3 Adjust oven rack to middle position and heat oven to 400 degrees. Line rimmed baking sheet with parchment paper and set inside second rimmed baking sheet. Using sharp serrated or slicing knife, trim ends of log, then slice into ½-inch-thick rounds (you should have 18 rounds). Space them about 1 inch apart on prepared sheet.

4 Brush pastries with egg wash and bake until golden brown and crispy, 14 to 16 minutes, rotating sheet halfway through baking. Transfer pinwheels to wire rack, sprinkle with remaining 1 tablespoon chives, and let cool for 5 minutes. Serve warm or at room temperature.

Perfect Pair

Serve with Tomato Salad (page 154) or Grilled Prosciutto-Wrapped Asparagus (page 230).

Puff Pastry Know-How

Thaw in the Fridge
Thaw puff pastry on the counter for 30 minutes to 1 hour if your kitchen is cool. Your safest bet is to thaw it in the fridge for 24 hours. That way, the pastry defrosts slowly, and there's no risk of it overheating.

Avoid Rolling Over the Edges
When rolling puff pastry, try to avoid rolling over the edges of the sheet too much. Flattening the edges can inhibit the "puff" during baking.

Use a Sharp Knife
A sharp knife edge will make clean, precise cuts that preserve the layers rather than pinch them together.

Chill Before Baking
After you've shaped and cut your puff pastry, it is a good idea to chill the dough for 15 to 30 minutes before baking to firm it up and help it retain flakiness.

OK to Refreeze
If you thaw more puff pastry than you need, simply pop the leftovers back in the freezer. We've found that there is little difference between dough frozen once and dough frozen twice; all-butter pastry won't rise quite as high after a double freeze as pastry made with shortening will, but the effect is minimal.

blini

½ **cup (2½ ounces) all-purpose flour**

½ **cup (2½ ounces) buckwheat flour**

1 **tablespoon sugar**

½ **teaspoon table salt**

½ **teaspoon baking powder**

¼ **teaspoon baking soda**

¾ **cup buttermilk**

½ **cup whole milk**

1 **large egg**

4 **tablespoons unsalted butter, melted and cooled, divided**

Head Start

Freeze blini for up to 1 week. Thaw frozen blini in refrigerator for 24 hours, then spread out on baking sheet and warm in 350-degree oven for about 5 minutes before serving.

Perfect Pair

Top with sour cream or crème frâiche. Add smoked salmon or trout and garnishes like capers, chopped chives, or red onion. Or go all out and serve blini with caviar. Add Apple-Fennel Rémoulade (page 166) or Seared Tempeh with Tomato Jam (page 288).

WHY THIS RECIPE WORKS These mini buckwheat pancakes are usually topped with a variety of luxurious and flavorful elements, making them a versatile addition to a small plates spread. Blini come in all sizes, from plate-size versions that get rolled up around the fillings and are eaten with a knife and fork to finger-food versions such as this silver dollar–size one known as oladi. While many blini are yeasted and gain a certain tanginess from the fermenting of the yeasted dough, this recipe is leavened with baking powder and baking soda, making it much quicker to prepare. Buttermilk adds tanginess to the batter to compensate for the lack of yeast. Since buckwheat flour contains no gluten, incorporating some all-purpose flour helps give structure and sturdiness.

1 Adjust oven rack to middle position and heat oven to 200 degrees. Line rimmed baking sheet with aluminum foil, top with wire rack, and spray rack with vegetable oil spray; set aside.

2 Whisk all-purpose flour, buckwheat flour, sugar, salt, baking powder, and baking soda together in medium bowl. In separate bowl, whisk buttermilk, milk, egg, and 2 tablespoons melted butter together. Whisk buttermilk mixture into flour mixture until just combined (do not overmix).

3 Using pastry brush, brush bottom and sides of 12-inch nonstick skillet very lightly with some of remaining melted butter; heat skillet over medium heat. When butter stops sizzling, add batter in spots to skillet using 1 scant tablespoon batter per pancake (6 to 8 pancakes will fit at a time). Cook until large bubbles begin to appear on surface of pancakes, 1½ to 2 minutes. Flip pancakes and cook until golden on second side, about 1½ minutes longer.

4 Transfer pancakes to prepared rack and keep warm, uncovered, in oven. Repeat with remaining butter and remaining batter. Let cool slightly before topping and serving. (Blini can be frozen to for up to 1 week; let them cool completely, wrap them in plastic wrap, and freeze.)

gougères

2 large eggs plus 1 large white

¼ teaspoon table salt

½ cup water

2 tablespoons unsalted butter, cut into 4 pieces

Pinch cayenne pepper

½ cup (2½ ounces) all-purpose flour

4 ounces Gruyère cheese, shredded (1 cup)

WHY THIS RECIPE WORKS The airy French cheese puffs, known as gougères, have huge appeal. These two-bite puffs look impressive and can be made ahead and frozen. Gougères begin with a pâte à choux or choux pastry. An extra egg white improves crispness and provides more water, which turns to steam and helps the gougères puff even more. Most gougères lack cheese flavor, but we pack in a full cup of Gruyère. Look for a Gruyère that has been aged for about one year. Doubled baking sheets prevent the undersides of the puffs from overbrowning. Alternatively, loosely roll up an 18 by 12-inch piece of aluminum foil, unroll it, and set it on a rimmed baking sheet. Cover the foil with a sheet of parchment paper and proceed with the recipe. In step 4, the dough can be piped using a pastry bag fitted with a ½-inch plain tip.

1 Adjust oven rack to upper-middle position and heat oven to 425 degrees. Line rimmed baking sheet with parchment paper and nest it in second rimmed baking sheet. In 2-cup liquid measuring cup, beat eggs, egg white, and salt until well combined. (You should have about ½ cup egg mixture; discard excess.) Set aside.

2 Heat water, butter, and cayenne in small saucepan over medium heat. When mixture begins to simmer, reduce heat to low and immediately stir in flour using wooden spoon. Cook, stirring constantly, using smearing motion, until mixture is very thick, forms ball, and pulls away from sides of pan, about 30 seconds.

3 Immediately transfer mixture to food processor and process with feed tube open for 5 seconds to cool slightly. With processor running, gradually add reserved egg mixture in steady stream, then scrape down sides of bowl and add Gruyère. Process until paste is very glossy and flecked with coarse cornmeal–size pieces of cheese, 30 to 40 seconds. (If not using immediately, transfer paste to bowl, press sheet of greased parchment directly on surface, and store at room temperature for up to 2 hours.)

4 Scoop 1 level tablespoon of dough. Using second small spoon, scrape dough onto prepared sheet into 1½-inch-wide, 1-inch-tall mound. Repeat, spacing mounds 1 to 1¼ inches apart. (You should have 24 mounds.) Using back of spoon lightly coated with vegetable oil spray, smooth away any creases and large peaks on each mound.

5 Bake until gougères are puffed and upper two-thirds of each are light golden brown (bottom third will still be pale), 14 to 20 minutes. Turn off oven; leave gougères in oven until uniformly golden brown, 10 to 15 minutes (do not open oven for at least 8 minutes). Transfer gougères to wire rack and let cool for 15 minutes. Serve warm.

Head Start

Store gougères in an airtight container at room temperature for up to 1 day. Alternatively, freeze gougères in zipper-lock bag for up to 1 month. Recrisp in 300-degree oven for 5 to 8 minutes or, if frozen, for 8 to 10 minutes.

Perfect Pair

A classic served with a champagne cocktail (page 391). Albóndigas en Salsa de Almendras (page 276) are also a tasty accompaniment.

baguette with radishes, butter, and herbs

10 tablespoons unsalted butter, softened

6 tablespoons minced fresh chives, divided

¼ teaspoon table salt

¼ teaspoon pepper

1 teaspoon lemon juice

1 teaspoon extra-virgin olive oil

1 cup coarsely chopped fresh parsley

1 (18-inch) baguette, halved lengthwise

8 ounces radishes, trimmed and sliced thin

Flake sea salt

Perfect Pair

Add Stir–Fried En Choy with Garlic (page 220), Pretzel-Crusted Chicken Fingers with Honey Mustard (page 300), and lemonade (see pages 382–383) for a satisfying spread.

WHY THIS RECIPE WORKS Crusty baguette, radishes, and butter are a time-tested combination and supereasy to put together. We halve a baguette lengthwise and lay down just enough butter to coat both halves. Leaving the baguette whole allows room for more radishes on the bread and makes an impressive presentation. We shingle thinly sliced radishes all over in a fish-scale pattern. Easter egg and watermelon radishes are especially pretty. Use a mandoline to slice radishes. To complement the pepperiness of the radishes, we top the baguette with a parsley salad for visual contrast and welcome brightness, and to finish, a generous sprinkle of sea salt. The success of this recipe depends on high-quality ingredients, including fresh baguette, European-style butter, and in-season radishes.

1 Combine butter, ¼ cup chives, salt, and pepper in bowl. Whisk remaining 2 tablespoons chives, lemon juice, and oil in second bowl. Add parsley and toss to coat. Season parsley salad with salt and pepper to taste.

2 Spread butter mixture over cut sides of baguette. Shingle radishes evenly over butter and top with parsley salad. Season with flake sea salt to taste.

3 Cut baguette crosswise into 12 pieces. Serve.

blue cheese and chive popovers with blue cheese butter

Blue Cheese Butter

- 8 tablespoons unsalted butter, softened
- 2 ounces blue cheese, crumbled (½ cup)
- ¼ cup minced fresh chives

Popovers

- 1¼ cups (6¾ ounces) bread flour
- 3 tablespoons minced fresh chives
- 1½ teaspoons dry mustard
- ¾ teaspoon table salt

  Pinch cayenne pepper
- 1½ cups 2 percent low-fat milk, heated to 110 to 120 degrees
- 3 large eggs
- 2 ounces blue cheese, crumbled (½ cup)

WHY THIS RECIPE WORKS These rich popovers are easy to make, and they are a flavorful light bite that can accompany a variety of small plates. What makes them magical is how they turn out so crisp and browned on the outside, with inner walls that are lush, custardy, and oh-so-cheesy. The cheese and chives in the batter are echoed in the butter poured over the baked popovers. Do not open the oven during the first 30 minutes of baking. This recipe works best in a 6-cup popover pan, but you can substitute a 12-cup muffin tin, distributing the batter evenly among all 12 cups. Start checking the smaller popovers after 25 minutes.

1 **For the blue cheese butter** Whip butter with fork until light and fluffy. Mix in blue cheese and chives and season with salt and pepper to taste. Cover with plastic wrap and let rest to blend flavors, about 10 minutes (or roll into log and refrigerate for up to 4 days).

2 **For the popovers** Adjust oven rack to middle position and heat oven to 400 degrees. Lightly spray cups of popover pan with vegetable oil spray. Using paper towel, wipe out cups, leaving thin film of oil on bottom and sides.

3 Whisk together flour, chives, dry mustard, salt, and cayenne in 8-cup liquid measuring cup or medium bowl. Add milk and eggs and whisk until mostly smooth (some small lumps are OK). Whisk in blue cheese. Distribute batter evenly among prepared cups in popover pan. Bake until popovers are lofty and deep golden brown all over, 40 to 45 minutes. Serve hot, passing blue cheese butter alongside.

Head Start

Store popovers in zipper-lock bag at room temperature for up to 2 days; reheat directly on middle rack of 300-degree oven for 5 minutes. Freeze butter for up to 2 months. Leftover butter can be refrigerated in an airtight container for up to 4 days.

Perfect Pair

Serve with Skillet Roasted Brussels Sprouts with Chorizo and Manchego (page 245) or Honeydew Salad with Peanuts and Lime (page 173).

bruschetta

Bruschetta make a great small plate and are supereasy to put together. They are infinitely customizable and combine the heartiness of bread with fresh toppings such as pesto, vegetables, and cheese.

toasts for bruschetta

1 loaf country bread, ends discarded, sliced crosswise into ¾-inch-thick pieces

½ garlic clove, peeled

Extra-virgin olive oil, for brushing

Adjust oven rack 4 inches from broiler element and heat broiler. Place bread on aluminum foil–lined baking sheet. Broil until bread is deep golden on both sides, 1 to 2 minutes per side. Lightly rub 1 side of each slice with garlic and brush with oil. Season with salt to taste.

bruschetta with artichoke hearts and basil

Serves 8 to 10
Active Time 15 minutes
Total Time 15 minutes

You can substitute 6 ounces frozen artichoke hearts, thawed and patted dry, for jarred.

1 cup jarred whole baby artichoke hearts packed in water, rinsed and patted dry

3 tablespoons chopped fresh basil, divided

½ ounce Parmesan cheese, grated (¼ cup), divided

2 tablespoons extra-virgin olive oil, plus extra for drizzling

2 teaspoons lemon juice

¼ teaspoon table salt

¼ teaspoon pepper

1 recipe Toasts for Bruschetta

Pulse artichoke hearts, 2 tablespoons basil, 3 tablespoons Parmesan, oil, lemon juice, salt, and pepper in food processor until coarsely ground, 6 to 8 pulses, scraping down sides of bowl as needed; season with salt and pepper to taste. Spread artichoke mixture evenly over toasted bread and sprinkle with remaining 1 tablespoon basil and remaining 1 tablespoon Parmesan. Drizzle with extra oil to taste. Serve.

bruschetta with arugula pesto and goat cheese topping

Serves 8 to 10
Active Time 15 minutes
Total Time 15 minutes

5 ounces (5 cups) baby arugula

¼ cup extra-virgin olive oil, plus extra for drizzling

¼ cup pine nuts, toasted

1 tablespoon minced shallot

1 teaspoon grated lemon zest plus 1 teaspoon juice

½ teaspoon table salt

¼ teaspoon pepper

2 ounces goat cheese, crumbled (½ cup)

1 recipe Toasts for Bruschetta (page 330)

Pulse arugula, oil, pine nuts, shallot, lemon zest and juice, salt, and pepper in food processor until mostly smooth, about 8 pulses, scraping down sides of bowl as needed. Spread arugula mixture evenly on toasted bread, top with goat cheese, and drizzle with extra oil to taste. Serve.

Variation

Bruschetta with Whipped Feta and Roasted Red Pepper Topping

24 ounces jarred roasted peppers, rinsed and cut into ½ inch pieces

2 tablespoons red wine vinegar

2 tablespoons sugar

1 garlic clove, minced

¼ teaspoon red pepper flakes

¼ teaspoon table salt

8 ounces feta cheese, crumbled

2 tablespoons extra-virgin olive oil, plus extra for drizzling

2 teaspoons lemon juice

¼ teaspoon pepper

1 recipe Toasts for Bruschetta (page 330)

Mix roasted peppers, vinegar, sugar, garlic, pepper flakes, and salt in medium bowl; set aside. Process feta, oil, lemon juice, and pepper in food processor until smooth, about 10 seconds, scraping down bowl once during processing. Spread feta mixture evenly on toasted bread, top with pepper mixture, and drizzle with extra oil to taste. Serve.

More Bruschetta Ideas

Try laying out the components for everyone to make their own bruschetta. Here are some of our favorite combinations to try.

- Tapenade + roasted tomatoes + flake sea salt
- Ricotta cheese + caramelized onions + artichoke hearts + olive oil drizzle
- Avocado + flaked salmon + capers + olive oil drizzle
- Boursin + roast beef + parsley
- Blue cheese + thinly sliced steak + arugula + olive oil drizzle
- Ricotta cheese + sliced peaches + balsamic drizzle
- Brie + fresh figs + honey drizzle

molletes

3 tomatoes, cored and chopped

¼ teaspoon table salt

½ cup finely chopped onion

½ cup fresh cilantro leaves

1 jalapeño chile, stemmed, seeded, and minced

1 garlic clove, minced

2 tablespoons lime juice

1 (16-inch) loaf French or Italian bread

4 tablespoons unsalted butter, softened

1 cup refried beans

8 ounces mild cheddar cheese, shredded (2 cups)

Head Start

Store pico de gallo, covered, at room temperature for up to 4 hours.

Perfect Pair

Serve with other topped breads such as Naan with Fig Jam, Blue Cheese, and Prosciutto (page 334) and Bruschetta with Arugula Pesto and Goat Cheese Topping (page 331).

WHY THIS RECIPE WORKS In Mexico, molletes are a popular snack or appetizer. They are a simple combination of toasted bread, refried beans, melted cheese, and fresh salsa. They are often made with individual bolillo rolls, but a standard loaf of French bread works well and is easier to handle. We remove some of the interior crumb so that the bread cradles the beans and cheese, helping the molletes hold together. As for the cheese, Chihuahua, a good melting cheese, is commonly used, but mild cheddar also works. To build our molletes, we first butter and toast the hollowed-out bread and then spread it with refried beans and a generous handful of cheese. Once the cheese is just melted, we top the loaves with fresh homemade pico de gallo. The salsa provides the perfect contrast to the rich cheese and creamy beans. To make sure it doesn't make the bread soggy, we eliminate excess moisture by salting the chopped tomatoes and letting them drain. We like French or Italian bread here; avoid using rustic loaves with thick crusts. Any type of refried beans will work well. If you can find Chihuahua cheese, substitute it for the cheddar.

1 Toss tomatoes with ¼ teaspoon salt in colander and let drain for 30 minutes. While tomatoes drain, layer onion, cilantro, jalapeño, and garlic on top. Shake colander to drain and discard excess tomato juice. Transfer mixture to bowl, stir in lime juice, and season with salt and pepper to taste.

2 Adjust oven rack to middle position and heat oven to 400 degrees. Line baking sheet with aluminum foil. Slice bread in half horizontally, then remove all but ¼ inch of interior crumb; reserve removed crumb for another use. Spread butter evenly inside hollowed bread and place cut side up on prepared sheet. Bake until lightly toasted and browned, about 8 minutes.

3 Let bread cool slightly. Spread refried beans evenly inside toasted bread and top with cheese. Bake until cheese is just melted, 5 to 7 minutes. Transfer bread to cutting board, top with salsa, and slice crosswise into 2-inch pieces. Serve warm.

naan with ricotta, sun-dried tomatoes, and olive tapenade

¼ cup extra-virgin olive oil, divided

2 (8-inch) naan breads

4 ounces (½ cup) whole-milk ricotta cheese

½ ounce Parmesan cheese, grated (¼ cup)

1½ teaspoons lemon juice

1 garlic clove, minced

¼ teaspoon table salt

⅛ teaspoon pepper

3 tablespoons oil-packed sun-dried tomatoes, rinsed, patted dry, and chopped fine

3 tablespoons finely chopped pitted kalamata olives

1½ tablespoons pine nuts

1 scallion, sliced thin

WHY THIS RECIPE WORKS Naan, a traditional north Indian flatbread, serves as a convenient prebaked crust on which to build a variety of quick and savory toppings. Here we use the concentrated flavors of salty kalamata olives against a backdrop of sun-dried tomatoes and crunchy pine nuts. To add richness and to hold everything together, we mix ricotta with Parmesan, garlic, and lemon juice and spread the mixture over the naan. The toppings need only a brief stint in the oven to warm through, so we brush the baking sheet with olive oil and bake the naan on the lowest rack in a 500-degree oven to help it crisp up during the short baking time. We recommend using either whole-milk or part-skim ricotta; do not use fat-free ricotta here.

1 Adjust oven rack to lowest position and heat oven to 500 degrees. Brush baking sheet with 1 tablespoon oil and arrange naan on sheet. Combine ricotta, Parmesan, 1 tablespoon oil, lemon juice, garlic, salt, and pepper in bowl. In separate bowl, combine tomatoes, olives, pine nuts, and remaining 2 tablespoons oil.

2 Spread ricotta mixture evenly over each naan, leaving ½-inch border around edge. Scatter tomato-olive mixture evenly over top. Bake until naan are golden brown around edges, 8 to 10 minutes, rotating baking sheet halfway through baking. Sprinkle with scallion, cut into wedges, and serve.

Variations

Naan with Roasted Red Peppers, Feta, and Olives
Omit ricotta cheese, Parmesan cheese, lemon juice, garlic, sun-dried tomatoes, pine nuts, and scallion. Process ½ cup jarred roasted red peppers, rinsed and patted dry, and 2 tablespoons oil in food processor, scraping down sides of processor bowl as needed until smooth, about 30 seconds. Season with salt and pepper to taste. Spread red pepper puree evenly over naan, leaving ½-inch border around edge. Scatter 2 ounces (½ cup) crumbled feta cheese and olives evenly over top. Bake as directed in step 2 above. Sprinkle with 2 tablespoons fresh parsley leaves before serving.

Naan with Fig Jam, Blue Cheese, and Prosciutto

Omit ricotta cheese, Parmesan cheese, lemon juice, garlic, sun-dried tomatoes, olives, pine nuts, and scallion. Whisk ¼ cup fig jam with 1 teaspoon water in bowl to loosen, then spread evenly over naan, leaving ½-inch border around edge. Sprinkle with ⅛ teaspoon salt and ⅛ teaspoon pepper, 2 ounces (½ cup) crumbled blue cheese, 2 ounces thinly sliced prosciutto cut into 1-inch strips, and ¼ teaspoon fresh thyme. Bake as directed in step 2.

Naan with Artichokes, Pesto, and Goat Cheese

Omit ricotta cheese, Parmesan cheese, lemon juice, garlic, salt, pepper, sun-dried tomatoes, olives, pine nuts, and scallion. Combine 3 ounces (¾ cup) crumbled goat cheese, ½ cup store-bought or homemade basil pesto, and 1 tablespoon water in bowl. Spread goat cheese mixture evenly over naan, leaving ½-inch border around edge. Scatter ½ cup marinated artichoke hearts, drained and patted dry, evenly over top. Bake as directed in step 2 . Sprinkle with 1 tablespoon fresh parsley leaves before serving.

Perfect Pair

Serve with Texas Caviar (page 196), Gajarachi Koshimbir (page 160), Fresh Fig Salad (page 174), or Pineapple–Roasted Red Pepper Salsa (page 14).

grilled onion, pear, and prosciutto flatbread

1 pound pizza dough, room temperature, split into 2 pieces

1 red onion, sliced into ½-inch-thick rounds

2 ripe but firm Bartlett or Bosc pears, peeled, halved, and cored

5 tablespoons extra-virgin olive oil, divided

½ teaspoon table salt

¼ teaspoon pepper

6 ounces firm Brie cheese, sliced thin

4 ounces thinly sliced prosciutto

2 teaspoons minced fresh thyme

Honey for drizzling

WHY THIS RECIPE WORKS Topped with a vegetable, fruit, and cheese, store-bought pizza dough is transformed into an elegant flatbread. The direct heat of the grill mellows the onion's bite and enhances the natural sweetness of the pears. They're united on top of the lightly charred flatbreads by slices of rich Brie. Once the cheese is softened, the flatbreads are ready to serve, topped with ribbons of pink prosciutto and a drizzle of honey. We love the convenience of using ready-made pizza dough from the local pizzeria or supermarket. Make sure to flour the counter generously so the dough doesn't stick as you work with it. You will need two 12-inch metal skewers for this recipe. For the best flavor and texture, serve the grilled flatbread as soon as possible.

1 Cover dough pieces loosely with plastic wrap and set aside. Push toothpick horizontally through each onion round to keep rings intact while grilling. Brush onion and pear halves with 1 tablespoon oil and sprinkle with salt and pepper; set aside.

2 Line rimmed baking sheet with parchment paper and dust liberally with flour. Working with one piece of dough at a time on lightly floured counter, press and roll to form 12-inch by 8-inch rectangle. Transfer dough to prepared sheet, reshaping as needed, sprinkle with flour, and top with second sheet of parchment. Dust second sheet of parchment liberally with flour and repeat with remaining dough, stacking dough rectangle on floured parchment.

3A **For a charcoal grill** Open bottom vent completely. Light large chimney starter filled with charcoal briquettes (6 quarts). When top coals are partially covered with ash, pour evenly over grill. Set cooking grate in place, cover, and open lid vent completely. Heat grill until hot, about 5 minutes.

3B **For a gas grill** Turn all burners to high, cover, and heat grill until hot, about 15 minutes. Leave all burners on high.

4 Clean and oil cooking grate. Grill pear halves, cut side down, and onion (covered if using gas) until tender and charred, 8 minutes

for pears and 18 to 22 minutes for onions, turning as needed. Transfer onions and pears to cutting board as they finish cooking. Remove onions from skewers and discard any charred outer rings. Chop onions and slice pears thin; set aside.

5 Brush top of each dough rectangle with 1 tablespoon oil. Grill dough rectangles oiled sides down until undersides are spotty brown and top is covered with bubbles, 2 to 3 minutes (pop any large bubbles that form). Brush top of each rectangle with 1 tablespoon oil, then flip. Layer flatbreads with Brie, pear, and onion. Cover and grill until second side of flatbreads is spotty brown and cheese is melted, 3 to 5 minutes. Transfer to cutting board.

6 Top flatbreads with prosciutto. Cut into wedges and serve.

Variation

Grilled Butternut Squash, Apple, and Goat Cheese Flatbread
Omit prosciutto and thyme. Substitute 1 pound butternut squash, peeled, halved lengthwise, seeded, and sliced crosswise ½ inch thick, for onion; do not thread on skewer. Substitute 1 Granny Smith apple, peeled, halved, and cored, for pears. Substitute crumbled goat cheese for Brie and maple syrup for honey. Sprinkle flatbreads with ground sumac before serving.

Head Start

Refrigerate grilled, cooled, and cut vegetables and fruit for up to 1 day. Let come to room temperature before topping on flatbreads on grill to finish.

Finish Line

Sprinkle flatbreads with 2 teaspoons minced fresh thyme and drizzle with honey.

Perfect Pair

Serve when you are grilling Chicken Satay (page 303), Pinchos Morunos (page 310), or Arrosticini (page 330).

Serves 6 to 8 (makes 24 empanadas) | **Active Time** 40 minutes
Total Time 1 hour, plus 35 minutes resting

easy mini chicken empanadas

Empanadas

- 1 (6- to 8-ounce) boneless, skinless chicken breast, trimmed
- 1 tablespoon vegetable oil
- 4 ounces sharp cheddar cheese, shredded (1 cup)
- ½ cup pitted green olives, chopped fine
- ¼ cup minced fresh cilantro
- 2 teaspoons lime juice
- 1 teaspoon minced canned chipotle chile in adobo sauce
- 2 packages store-bought pie dough

Salsa

- 1 small onion, quartered
- 1 green bell pepper, stemmed, seeded, and quartered
- 1 jalapeño chile, stemmed, seeded, and minced
- 2 tablespoons fresh cilantro leaves
- ½ teaspoon table salt
- 2 tomatoes, cored and chopped coarse
- ⅓ cup white wine vinegar
- 3 tablespoons extra-virgin olive oil

WHY THIS RECIPE WORKS Empanadas are perfectly suited for small plates sharing, especially this bite-size version that streamlines the process by using store-bought pie dough. The empanadas can be assembled ahead of time and baked just before serving. The filling requires no cooking other than the chicken. The remaining ingredients—sharp cheddar cheese, lime juice, cilantro, chipotle, and green olives—don't require a lot of coaxing either. For a finishing touch, we use the food processor to create a vibrant salsa that comes together in minutes. To make this dish spicier, reserve the jalapeño seeds and add them with the jalapeño.

1 **For the empanadas** Adjust oven rack to middle position and heat oven to 425 degrees. Pat chicken dry with paper towels and season with salt and pepper. Heat oil in 12-inch nonstick skillet over medium-high heat until just smoking. Add chicken and cook until browned on one side, about 3 minutes. Flip chicken over, add ½ cup water, and cover. Reduce heat to medium and continue to cook until thickest part of breast registers 160 degrees, 5 to 7 minutes longer. Transfer chicken to cutting board. When cool enough to handle, shred chicken into bite-size pieces.

2 Combine shredded chicken, cheddar, olives, cilantro, lime juice, and chipotle in bowl. Season with salt and pepper to taste. Cover bowl with plastic wrap and refrigerate until needed.

3 Line rimmed baking sheet with parchment paper. Using 3½-inch round cutter, cut circles out of dough rounds (6 circles per round); discard scraps.

4 Working with half of dough circles at a time, place 2 teaspoons empanada filling in center of each. Moisten edges of dough circles with water, then fold dough over filling into half-moon shape. Pinch edges to seal, then crimp with fork to secure. Arrange empanadas on prepared sheet.

5 **For the salsa** Pulse onion, bell pepper, jalapeño, cilantro, and salt in food processor until minced, about 10 pulses, scraping down sides of bowl as needed. Add tomatoes and pulse until chopped, about 2 pulses. Transfer to serving bowl and stir in vinegar and oil. Let salsa sit at room temperature until flavors meld, at least 30 minutes.

6 Bake empanadas until golden, 23 to 28 minutes, rotating sheet halfway through baking. Let cool for 5 minutes, then serve with salsa.

Head Start

Refrigerate filling for up to 1 day and salsa for up to 2 days. Alternatively, freeze empanadas on baking sheet until firm, then transfer to zipper-lock bag and freeze for up to 1 month. Do not thaw empanadas before cooking.

Perfect Pair

Serve with Sweet Potato Salad with Cumin, Smoked Paprika, and Almonds (page 188) or Fried Green Tomatoes (page 215).

lamb fatayer

Dough

- 3 cups (16½ ounces) bread flour
- 2 teaspoons sugar
- ½ teaspoon instant or rapid-rise yeast
- 1⅓ cups ice water
- 3 tablespoons extra-virgin olive oil, divided
- 1½ teaspoons table salt

Filling

- 1 tablespoon extra-virgin olive oil
- 1 pound ground lamb
- 1 onion, chopped fine
- 3 garlic cloves, minced
- 1 teaspoon table salt
- ¼ teaspoon ground cinnamon
- ¼ teaspoon ground nutmeg
- ¼ teaspoon pepper
- ⅛ teaspoon cayenne pepper
- ⅓ cup pine nuts, toasted
- 2 tablespoons tahini
- 1 tablespoon pomegranate molasses

WHY THIS RECIPE WORKS Fatayer are crispy triangular hand pies beloved throughout the Middle East but especially in Lebanon, where they originated. These individual little pockets can be filled with a wide assortment of greens, meat, or labneh, and are often served on a meze platter. The crust is made with a cold-fermented yeasted dough; giving it a long rest in the refrigerator lets it develop better flavor and structure, resulting in a crisp outer crust that maintains a slight chewiness. This method ensures that the fatayer holds its shape well during baking—which is necessary to contain the luscious filling of lamb sautéed with onion, garlic, traditional warm spices, and a pinch of cayenne. Toasted pine nuts are a classic addition and enrich the filling with pops of texture. Tahini and pomegranate molasses add delicious complexity while helping bind everything together. To ensure that the fatayer seal completely, be sure to tightly pinch the seams. It is important to use ice water in the dough to prevent it from overheating in the food processor.

1 For the dough Pulse flour, sugar, and yeast in food processor until combined, about 5 pulses. With processor running, slowly add ice water and process until dough is just combined and no dry flour remains, about 10 seconds. Let dough rest for 10 minutes.

2 Add 1 tablespoon oil and salt to dough and process until dough forms satiny, sticky ball that clears sides of bowl, 30 to 60 seconds. Transfer dough to lightly oiled counter and knead by hand to form smooth, round ball, about 30 seconds. Place dough seam side down in lightly greased large bowl or container, cover tightly with plastic wrap, and refrigerate for at least 24 hours or up to 3 days.

3 For the filling Heat oil in 12-inch nonstick skillet over medium heat until shimmering. Add lamb and onion and cook, stirring occasionally, until lamb is no longer pink and onion is lightly browned, 10 to 12 minutes. Stir in garlic, salt, cinnamon, nutmeg, pepper, and cayenne and cook until fragrant, about 30 seconds. Off heat, stir in pine nuts, tahini, and pomegranate molasses. Transfer to bowl and let cool completely, about 30 minutes.

4 Press down on dough to deflate. Transfer dough to clean counter and divide into 24 equal portions (about 1¼ ounces each). Working with 1 dough portion at a time and keeping remaining dough portions covered with plastic wrap, cup dough with your palm and roll against counter into smooth, tight ball. Space dough balls 1 inch apart on counter. Spray plastic wrap with vegetable oil spray. Cover dough balls loosely with greased plastic, and let rest for 1½ hours.

5 Adjust oven rack to middle position and heat oven to 450 degrees. Line 2 rimmed baking sheets with parchment paper. Working with 1 dough ball at a time, generously coat with flour and place on well-floured counter (keeping remaining balls covered). Press and roll into 4-inch circle, then place 1 tablespoon lamb filling in center of circle. Grasping edges of dough at 4 and 8 o'clock, lift dough around filling and pinch tightly to seal. Grasp top of dough (12 o'clock) and lift around filling to meet at center seam, pinching tightly to seal. Pinch edges of dough where they meet to seal seam (dough should be rough triangle shape). Transfer to prepared sheet, evenly spacing 12 fatayer over each prepared sheet.

6 Brush fatayer with remaining 2 tablespoons oil. Bake, 1 sheet at a time, until deep golden brown, 12 to 15 minutes. Transfer fatayer to wire rack and let cool for 15 minutes. Serve warm or at room temperature.

Head Start

Refrigerate filling for up to 1 day.

Finish Line

Serve with Yogurt-Tahini Sauce (page 17) and Pink Pickled Turnips (page 77) for meze flavors.

Perfect Pair

Homemade Labneh (page 91) makes a terrific pairing as does Roasted Asparagus with Mustard–Dill Hollandaise (page 226). The hollandaise can also be used for dipping the fatayer.

cabbage and mushroom dumplings

3 cups minced napa cabbage leaves

½ teaspoon table salt, divided

8 ounces white mushrooms, trimmed and quartered

2 teaspoons plus 2 tablespoons vegetable oil, divided

4 scallions, minced

2 large egg whites, lightly beaten

4 teaspoons soy sauce

1 teaspoon grated fresh ginger

1 garlic clove, minced

⅛ teaspoon pepper

24 (3½-inch) round gyoza wrappers

1 cup water, divided, plus extra for brushing

WHY THIS RECIPE WORKS A pan-fried dumpling is the perfect choice for a small plate: One bite is tantalizing, two bites are heavenly, and the third satisfies. For a hearty vegetarian filling, we combine cabbage and mushrooms. To remove excess moisture, we salt and drain the cabbage and chop and sauté the mushrooms. Combining the ingredients and chilling the mixture prevents it from leaking out when we fill and cook the dumplings. To prevent the filling from becoming tough during cooking, we add egg whites. We arrange the dumplings in a cold, lightly oiled skillet before turning on the burner, then add water to the skillet and steam them until tender. As the dumplings cook, the egg whites puff up almost like a soufflé, making the otherwise compact filling light and tender. We remove the lid and cook the dumplings uncovered until they develop a nice, flavorful crust. You will need a 12-inch skillet with a tight-fitting lid for this recipe. You can substitute wonton wrappers for the gyoza wrappers; wonton wrappers are smaller, so they will yield about 40 dumplings and you may need to reduce their steaming time slightly.

1 Toss cabbage with ¼ teaspoon salt in colander and let drain for 20 minutes; press gently to squeeze out excess moisture.

2 Meanwhile, pulse mushrooms in food processor until finely chopped, about 15 pulses. Heat 2 teaspoons oil in 12-inch nonstick skillet over medium-high heat until shimmering. Add mushrooms and remaining ¼ teaspoon salt, and cook until liquid has evaporated and mushrooms clump and are starting to brown, 5 to 7 minutes. Transfer to large bowl and let cool for 15 minutes.

3 Stir drained cabbage, scallions, egg whites, soy sauce, ginger, garlic, and pepper into mushrooms. Cover and refrigerate until chilled, at least 30 minutes.

4 Working with 4 wrappers at a time (cover others with damp paper towel), brush edges of wrappers with water and place scant tablespoon of filling in center. Fold wrapper in half and pinch dumpling closed, pressing out any air pockets. Place dumpling on one side

and gently flatten bottom. Transfer to baking sheet and cover with damp dish towel.

5 Brush 1 tablespoon oil over bottom of 12-inch nonstick skillet and arrange half of dumplings in skillet, flat side facing down (they may overlap). Cook over medium heat, without moving them, until golden brown on bottom, 3 to 4 minutes.

6 Reduce heat to low, add ½ cup water, and cover. Cook until most of water is absorbed and wrappers are slightly translucent, 8 to 10 minutes. Uncover, increase heat to medium, and cook, without stirring dumplings, until bottoms are well browned and crisp, 1 to 2 minutes; transfer to paper towel–lined plate.

7 Wipe out now-empty skillet with paper towels and repeat with remaining oil, dumplings, and water. Serve.

Head Start

Refrigerate dumplings for up to 1 day. Alternatively, freeze until solid, about 3 hours. Transfer to zipper-lock bag and freeze for up to 1 month. Do not thaw dumplings before cooking.

Finish Line

Serve with Scallion Dipping Sauce (page 18) or Spicy Peanut Dipping Sauce (page 15).

Perfect Pair

Also good served with Som Tam (page 181) or Tempeh with Sambal Sauce (page 291).

pork and cabbage dumplings

Filling

½ head napa cabbage, cored and chopped fine (6 cups)

¾ teaspoon table salt

12 ounces ground pork

4 scallions, minced

1 large egg, lightly beaten

4 teaspoons soy sauce

1½ teaspoons grated fresh ginger

1 garlic clove, minced

⅛ teaspoon pepper

Dumplings

24 round gyoza wrappers

4 teaspoons vegetable oil, divided

1 cup water, divided, plus extra for brushing

WHY THIS RECIPE WORKS These soft and savory dumplings are filled with tender ground pork and crunchy cabbage, and spiked with a pleasing hit of garlic, ginger, and soy sauce. We use ready-made wrappers and lighten the filling by increasing the amount of cabbage, after getting rid of its excess moisture. We also add a lightly beaten egg whites for airiness. To keep the filling in place and the wrapper from puffing up and away from the meat during cooking, we fold each filled wrapper into a half-moon, pinch the middle closed, then carefully press out any air while sealing the edges. You will need a 12-inch skillet with a tight-fitting lid for this recipe. You can substitute wonton wrappers for the gyoza wrappers; wonton wrappers are smaller, so they will yield about 40 dumplings and you may need to reduce their steaming time slightly.

1 **For the filling** Toss cabbage with salt in colander set over bowl and let stand until cabbage begins to wilt, about 20 minutes. Press cabbage gently with rubber spatula to squeeze out any excess moisture, then transfer to medium bowl. Add pork, scallions, egg, soy sauce, ginger, garlic, and pepper and mix thoroughly to combine. Cover with plastic wrap and refrigerate until mixture is cold, at least 30 minutes or up to 24 hours.

2 **For the dumplings** Working with 4 wrappers at a time (keep remaining wrappers covered with plastic wrap), place wrappers flat on counter. Spoon 1 slightly rounded tablespoon filling in center of each wrapper. Using pastry brush or your fingertip, moisten edge of wrapper with water. Fold each wrapper in half; starting in center and working toward outside edges, pinch edges together firmly to seal, pressing out any air pockets. Position each dumpling on its side and gently flatten, pressing down on seam to make sure it lies flat against counter. Transfer dumplings to baking sheet and repeat with remaining wrappers and filling.

3 Line large plate with double layer of paper towels. Brush 2 teaspoons oil over bottom of 12-inch nonstick skillet and arrange half of dumplings in skillet, flat side down (overlapping just slightly if necessary). Place skillet over medium-high heat and cook dumplings, without moving them, until golden brown on bottom, about 5 minutes.

4 Reduce heat to low, add ½ cup water, and cover immediately. Continue to cook, covered, until most of water is absorbed and wrappers are slightly translucent, about 10 minutes. Uncover skillet, increase heat to medium-high, and continue to cook, without stirring, until dumpling bottoms are well browned and crisp, 3 to 4 minutes more. Slide dumplings onto paper towel–lined plate, browned side facing down, and let drain briefly. Transfer dumplings to serving platter. Wipe out now-empty skillet with paper towels and repeat with remaining dumplings, oil, and water. Serve.

Head Start

Refrigerate dumplings for up to 1 day. Alternatively, freeze until solid, about 3 hours. Transfer to zipper-lock bag and freeze for up to 1 month. Do not thaw dumplings before cooking.

Finish Line

Serve with Scallion Dipping Sauce (page 18) or Spicy Peanut Dipping Sauce (page 15).

Perfect Pair

Serve with Cannellini Bean and Edamame Dip with Tarragon (page 99).

shu mai

2 tablespoons soy sauce

½ teaspoon unflavored gelatin

1 pound boneless country-style pork ribs, cut into 1-inch pieces

8 ounces shrimp, peeled, tails removed, halved lengthwise

¼ cup chopped water chestnuts

4 dried shiitake mushroom caps (about ¾ ounce), soaked in hot water for 30 minutes, squeezed dry, and chopped fine

2 tablespoons cornstarch

2 tablespoons minced fresh cilantro

1 tablespoon toasted sesame oil

1 tablespoon Shaoxing wine or dry sherry

1 tablespoon rice vinegar

2 teaspoons sugar

2 teaspoons grated fresh ginger

½ teaspoon table salt

½ teaspoon pepper

1 (1-pound) package 5½-inch square egg roll wrappers

¼ cup finely grated carrot (optional)

Sichuan Chili Oil (page 19)

WHY THIS RECIPE WORKS These intensely flavorful, open-faced Chinese steamed dumplings boast a tender, thin skin and a moist filling of pork and shrimp, water chestnuts, shiitake mushrooms, cilantro, and ginger. To ensure the proper texture, we chop the pork (boneless country-style ribs) in a food processor, grinding half to a fine consistency and keeping the other half coarse. To prevent the meat from drying out during steaming, we add a little powdered gelatin dissolved in soy sauce. We chop the shrimp in the food processor as well. For the wrappers, we use egg roll wrappers cut into 3-inch rounds. Use any size shrimp except popcorn shrimp; there's no need to halve shrimp smaller than 26 to 30 per pound. You will need a bamboo steamer for this recipe.

1 Combine soy sauce and gelatin in small bowl. Set aside to allow gelatin to bloom, about 5 minutes.

2 Meanwhile, place half of pork in food processor and pulse until coarsely ground into ⅛-inch pieces, about 10 pulses; transfer to large bowl. Add shrimp and remaining pork to food processor and pulse until coarsely chopped into ¼-inch pieces, about 5 pulses. Add to more finely ground pork. Stir in soy sauce mixture, water chestnuts, mushrooms, cornstarch, cilantro, sesame oil, Shaoxing wine, vinegar, sugar, ginger, salt, and pepper.

3 Divide egg roll wrappers into 3 stacks. Using 3-inch biscuit cutter, cut two 3-inch rounds from each stack. Cover with moist paper towels to prevent drying.

4 Working with 6 rounds at a time, brush edges of each round lightly with water. Place heaping tablespoon of filling in center of each round. Form dumplings by pinching opposing sides of wrapper with your fingers until you have 8 equidistant pinches. Gather up sides of dumpling and squeeze gently to create "waist." Hold dumpling in your hand and gently but firmly pack down filling with butter knife. Transfer to parchment paper–lined baking sheet, cover with damp dish towel, and repeat with remaining wrappers and filling. Top center of each dumpling with pinch of grated carrot, if using.

5 Cut piece of parchment paper slightly smaller than diameter of steamer basket and place in basket. Poke about 20 small holes in parchment and lightly coat with vegetable oil spray. Place batches of dumplings on parchment, making sure they are not touching. Set steamer over simmering water and cook, covered, until no longer pink, 8 to 10 minutes. Repeat with remaining dumplings. Serve immediately with chili oil.

Head Start

Freeze Shu Mai in an airtight container for up to 3 months; cook from frozen, increasing cooking time in step 5 to 13 to 15 minutes.

Perfect Pair

Add Pink Pickled Turnips (page 77) or Sikil P'ak (page 112).

potato-cheddar pierogi

Filling

- 1 pound russet potatoes, peeled and sliced ½ inch thick
- ½ teaspoon table salt, plus salt for cooking potatoes
- 4 ounces sharp cheddar cheese, shredded (1 cup)
- 2 tablespoons unsalted butter
- ½ teaspoon pepper

Dough

- 2½ cups (13¾ ounces) bread flour
- 1 teaspoon baking powder
- ½ teaspoon table salt, plus salt for cooking pierogi
- 1 cup sour cream
- 1 large egg plus 1 large yolk

Topping

- 4 tablespoons unsalted butter
- 1 large onion, chopped fine
- ½ teaspoon table salt

WHY THIS RECIPE WORKS These Polish dumplings, which combine potatoes and cheese tucked into a tender dough, make a hearty bite. We combine boiled russet potatoes, shredded cheddar cheese, and butter in a stand mixer. The heat from the potatoes melts the butter and cheese for an even consistency. We create a pliable, rollable dough using higher-protein bread flour, sour cream, and egg and stamp out rounds with a biscuit cutter. The filling is sealed in by pinching the edges together before boiling the pierogi. A caramelized onion topping mixed with the dumplings gives a traditional sweet-savory finish. When rolling the dough in step 4, be sure not to dust the top surface with too much flour, as that will prevent the edges from forming a tight seal when pinched.

1 **For the filling** Combine potatoes and 1 tablespoon salt in large saucepan and cover with water by 1 inch. Bring to boil over medium-high heat; reduce heat to medium and cook at vigorous simmer until potatoes are very tender, about 15 minutes.

2 Drain potatoes in colander. While still hot, combine potatoes, cheddar, butter, pepper, and salt in bowl of stand mixer. Fit mixer with paddle and mix on medium speed until potatoes are smooth and all ingredients are fully combined, about 1 minute. Transfer filling to 8-inch square baking dish and refrigerate until fully chilled, about 30 minutes.

3 **For the dough** Whisk flour, baking powder, and salt together in clean bowl of stand mixer. Add sour cream, egg, and egg yolk. Fit mixer with dough hook and knead on medium-high speed for 8 minutes (dough will be smooth and elastic). Transfer dough to floured bowl, cover with plastic, and refrigerate for at least 30 minutes until ready to assemble.

4 Line rimmed baking sheet with parchment paper and dust with flour. Roll dough on lightly floured counter into 18-inch circle, about ⅛ inch thick. Using 3-inch biscuit cutter, cut 20 to 24 circles from dough. Place 1 tablespoon chilled filling in center of each dough round. Fold dough over filling to create half-moon shape and pinch edges firmly to seal. Transfer to prepared sheet.

5 Gather dough scraps and reroll to ⅛-inch thickness. Cut 6 to
   10 more circles from dough and repeat with remaining filling. (It
   may be necessary to reroll dough once more to yield 30 pierogi.)

6 **For the topping** Melt butter in 12-inch skillet over medium-low heat.
   Add onion and salt and cook until onion is caramelized, 15 to 20 minutes. Remove skillet from heat and set aside.

7 Bring 4 quarts water to boil in Dutch oven. Add 1 tablespoon salt and
   half of pierogi to boiling water and cook until tender, about 5 minutes. Using spider skimmer or slotted spoon, remove pierogi from
   water and transfer to skillet with caramelized onion. Return water to
   boil, cook remaining pierogi, and transfer to skillet with first batch.

8 Add 2 tablespoons cooking water to pierogi in skillet. Cook over
   medium-low heat, stirring gently, until onion mixture is warmed
   through and adhered to pierogi. Transfer to platter and serve.

Head Start

Refrigerate filling in a baking dish
for up to 1 day. Freeze uncooked
pierogi on a baking sheet for
3 hours, then transfer to a zipper-
lock bag and keep frozen for up
to 1 month. Cook from frozen,
increasing boiling time in step
7 to about 7 minutes.

Perfect Pair

Serve with a tomato salad (see
pages 154 and 170) or Keftedes
(page 280).

black bean and cheese arepas

Arepas

- 2 cups (10 ounces) masarepa blanca
- 1 teaspoon table salt
- 1 teaspoon baking powder
- 2½ cups warm water
- ¼ cup vegetable oil

Filling

- 1 (15-ounce) can black beans, rinsed
- 4 ounces Monterey Jack cheese, shredded (1 cup)
- 2 tablespoons minced fresh cilantro
- 2 scallions, sliced thin
- 1 tablespoon lime juice
- ¼ teaspoon chili powder

WHY THIS RECIPE WORKS Arepas are a type of corn cake popular in Venezuela and Colombia, though iterations exist in other Latin countries. This Venezuelan variety is served split open and stuffed with anything from meat and cheese to corn, beans, or even fish. The arepa itself is made using masarepa (a precooked corn flour) along with water and salt, but getting the consistency right can be a challenge. In the end, using just a half-cup more water than masarepa produces a dough that is easy to shape, and a small amount of baking powder lightens its texture just enough. We shape the dough into rounds, brown them in a skillet with some oil, and finish them in the oven. To stuff our arepas, we make a filling of mashed black beans mixed with Monterey Jack cheese. Cilantro brings freshness, lime juice injects a bit of acidity, and chili powder adds a hint of heat. Masarepa is also called harina precocida and masa al instante and is available in the international aisle of well-stocked supermarkets and specialty Latin markets.

1 **For the arepas** Adjust oven rack to middle position and heat oven to 400 degrees. Whisk masarepa, salt, and baking powder together in large bowl. Gradually add water and stir until combined. Using generous ⅓ cup dough for each round, form eight 3-inch rounds on the counter, each about ½ inch thick.

2 Heat 2 tablespoons oil in 12-inch nonstick skillet over medium-high heat until shimmering. Add 4 arepas and cook until golden on both sides, about 4 minutes per side. Transfer arepas to wire rack set on rimmed baking sheet. Wipe out skillet with paper towels and repeat with remaining 2 tablespoons oil and remaining 4 arepas; transfer to wire rack.

3 Bake arepas on wire rack until they sound hollow when tapped on bottom, about 10 minutes.

4 **For the filling** Meanwhile, using potato masher or fork, mash beans in bowl until most are broken. Stir in Monterey Jack, cilantro, scallions, lime juice, and chili powder and season with salt and pepper to taste.

5 Using fork, gently split hot, baked arepas open. Stuff each with generous 3 tablespoons filling. Serve.

Variation

Avocado, Tomato, and Bell Pepper Arepas
Omit black beans and cheese. Increase cilantro to ¼ cup, scallions
to 4, lime juice to 3 tablespoons, and chili powder to ½ teaspoon.
Add to filling 2 halved and pitted avocados, 1 chopped and 1 mashed;
2 tomatoes, cored and chopped into ½-inch pieces; and 1 yellow bell
pepper, stemmed, cored, and cut into ¼-inch pieces.

Head Start

Refrigerate fried arepas for up to
3 days. Alternatively, freeze for up
to 1 month. Increase baking time
in step 3 as needed; if frozen, do
not thaw before baking.

Perfect Pair

Farro Salad with Sugar Snap Peas
and White Beans (page 192) or
Green Olive Tapenade (page 84)
are flavorful alongside.

Serves 10 (makes 10 buns) | **Active Time** 1 hour
Total Time 1 hour, plus 1½ hours rising and cooling

lop cheung bao

¾ cup whole milk, warm

3 tablespoons sugar

1 teaspoon instant or rapid-rise yeast

1 tablespoon vegetable oil

2 cups (10 ounces) all-purpose flour

2 tablespoons cornstarch

1 teaspoon baking powder

⅛ teaspoon table salt

10 lop cheung

WHY THIS RECIPE WORKS Lop cheung bao (sometimes called lap cheong bao) is one of the best pigs in a blanket the world has to offer. A snow-white yeasted dough is twirled around a cured Chinese sausage (lop cheung), and the buns are steamed until the dough turns fluffy and firm. The snap of the rich sausage when you bite into the pillowy, slightly sweet bun is heavenly, says Jacqueline Church, who developed this recipe. It is best made in a stacking bamboo steamer basket set inside a skillet. Using bleached all-purpose flour creates the bright-white color that is traditional and prized for these buns; you can also use unbleached all-purpose flour, though the bao will be less bright white. Avoid sausage containing liver here.

1 Whisk milk, sugar, and yeast together in 2-cup liquid measuring cup until sugar has dissolved, then let sit until foamy, about 5 minutes. Whisk in oil. Pulse flour, cornstarch, baking powder, and salt in food processor until combined, about 3 pulses. With processor running, slowly add milk mixture and process until no dry flour remains, about 30 seconds.

2 Transfer dough to lightly floured counter and knead by hand to form smooth, round ball, about 30 seconds. Transfer dough to lightly oiled large bowl, turning to coat dough ball in oil, arranging dough seam side down. Cover with plastic wrap and let rise until doubled in size, about 1 hour.

3 While dough rises, place plate in bamboo steamer basket and arrange sausages in single layer on plate. Set steamer basket over simmering water in skillet and cook, covered, until sausages are plump and color is muted, 10 to 15 minutes. (Add boiling water to skillet as needed while steaming.) Set aside plate with sausages and let cool completely. Remove basket from simmering water and set aside.

4 Cut ten 6 by 4-inch rectangles of parchment paper; set aside. Press down on dough to deflate. Transfer dough to clean counter and portion into 10 equal pieces (about 2 ounces each); cover loosely with plastic. Working with 1 piece of dough at a time (keep remaining pieces covered), form into rough ball by stretching dough around your thumbs and pinching edges together so top is smooth. Place ball seam side down on clean counter and, using your cupped hand,

drag in small circles until dough feels taut and round. Cover dough balls with plastic while rolling remaining dough.

5 Working with 1 dough ball at a time (keep remaining pieces covered) and starting at center, gently and evenly roll and stretch dough into 10-inch-long rope. Wrap dough around 1 cooled sausage, starting 1 inch from 1 end of sausage (dough should wrap around sausage at least 3 times and sausage should be roughly centered on dough) and place in basket on 1 prepared parchment rectangle, tucking ends of dough underneath sausage. Cover with damp dish towel while forming remaining bao, spacing bao about 1 inch apart. Let bao sit until slightly puffy, about 20 minutes.

6 Remove dish towel and set covered steamer basket over cold water in skillet. Bring water to simmer over high heat and, once steam begins to escape from sides of basket, reduce heat to medium and steam until bao are puffy and firm, 10 to 15 minutes. (Add boiling water to skillet as needed while steaming.) Remove basket from simmering water and let bao cool for 5 minutes before serving.

Finish Line

Serve with chili crisp and Spicy Peanut Dipping Sauce (page 15).

Perfect Pair

Serve with popcorn (see pages 30–31), Horiatiki Salata (page 182), or Chilled Marinated Tofu (page 41).

french bread pizzas

Pizzas

- 1 (24 by 4-inch) loaf soft French bread
- 1 tablespoon extra-virgin olive oil
- 8 tablespoons unsalted butter, melted
- 2 teaspoons garlic powder
- ¼ teaspoon red pepper flakes
- 12 ounces mozzarella cheese, shredded (3 cups)
- 1 ounce Parmesan cheese, grated (½ cup)
- 2 ounces thinly sliced pepperoni

Sauce

- 1½ cups canned crushed tomatoes
- 1 tablespoon extra-virgin olive oil
- 1½ teaspoons Italian seasoning
- ½ teaspoon sugar
- ½ teaspoon table salt

WHY THIS RECIPE WORKS Making fresh pizza is simple when soft supermarket French bread replaces pizza dough. (Baguettes can be substituted but will result in a slightly tougher crust.) We give the loaf a garlic-bread treatment before topping it, brushing the cut side with a spicy garlic butter and the crusty side with olive oil, then baking it until toasty brown and crispy. Crushed tomatoes, olive oil, Italian seasoning, and sugar make a pantry-friendly, bright pizza sauce. Mozzarella and Parmesan provide the perfect balance of melty creaminess and nutty depth.

1 **For the pizzas** Adjust oven rack to upper-middle position and heat oven to 450 degrees. Line rimmed baking sheet with aluminum foil. Cut bread in half crosswise, then halve each piece horizontally to create 4 equal pieces. Arrange pieces cut side down on prepared sheet. Brush crust with oil.

2 Combine melted butter, garlic powder, and pepper flakes in bowl. Flip bread cut side up and brush cut side evenly with melted butter mixture. Bake, cut side up, until browned around edges, about 5 minutes.

3 **For the sauce** Meanwhile, combine all sauce ingredients in bowl.

4 Spread sauce evenly over toasted bread, then top with mozzarella, followed by Parmesan and pepperoni (in that order). Bake until cheese is melted and spotty brown, about 15 minutes. Let pizzas cool for 5 minutes. Slice and serve.

Variations

Supreme French Bread Pizzas
Decrease pepperoni to 1½ ounces. Add 2½ ounces sweet Italian sausage, casings removed, meat pinched into ½-inch pieces; ½ cup thinly sliced red onion; ½ cup thinly sliced green bell pepper, cut into 2-inch lengths; and ½ cup sliced black olives with pepperoni.

Pineapple and Bacon French Bread Pizzas
Substitute ¾ cup crumbled cooked bacon and ¾ cup canned pineapple tidbits, drained and patted dry, for pepperoni.

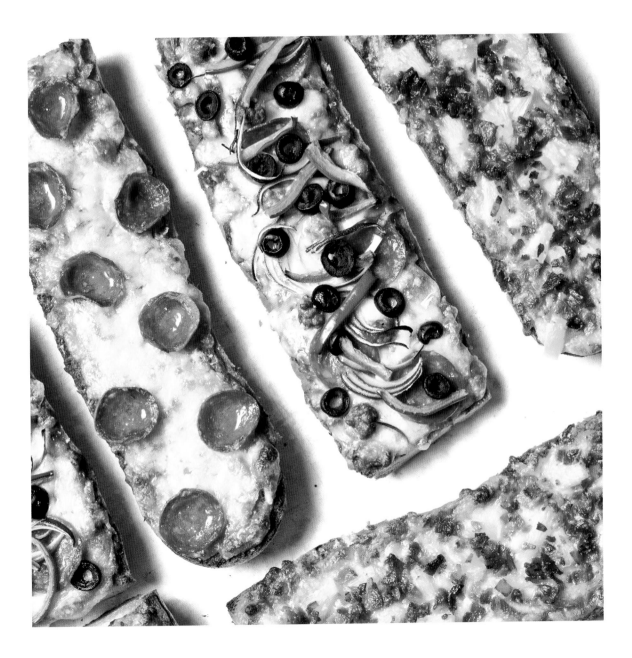

Head Start

Substitute one-and-a-half
18-inch baguettes for a loaf, if
you like. Cut baguettes into six
equal pieces and distribute the
toppings evenly. Refrigerate
sauce for up to 1 day.

Finish Line

Tear some basil leaves and
sprinkle them over pizzas
before serving. Cut pizzas into
finger food–size strips.

Perfect Pair

Pizzas are delicious
accompanied by Citrus
and Radicchio Salad with
Dates and Smoked Almonds
(page 166). Add Quick Pickled
Chard Stems (page 77) and,
if you have time, make Olives
all'Ascolana (page 36).

kataifi-wrapped feta with tomatoes and artichokes

1 (8-ounce) block feta cheese, cut into eight 3-inch-long by ¾-inch-thick fingers

7 tablespoons extra-virgin olive oil, divided

½ teaspoon dried oregano

¼ teaspoon red pepper flakes

6 ounces kataifi, thawed, unwrapped, and covered with damp towel

1½ pounds grape tomatoes, halved

1½ cups jarred whole artichoke hearts packed in water, rinsed, patted dry, and quartered

3 garlic cloves, minced

¼ teaspoon table salt

¼ teaspoon pepper

1 cup fresh parsley, dill, or mint leaves, torn

Perfect Pair

For a host of Middle Eastern flavors, serve with Ultracreamy Hummus (page 95), Butternut Squash and Apple Fattoush (page 185), and Lamb Fatayer (page 340).

WHY THIS RECIPE WORKS Thin, delicate strands of Greek kataifi pastry are most frequently used for baklava-style desserts, wrapped tightly around nut fillings, or broken into pieces and pressed into layers to encase a sweet cheese filling in the sugar syrup–soaked dessert knafeh. Here we use kataifi in a savory application, showcasing the unique crispy quality of the pastry by wrapping it around soft baked feta. We like to round out the plate and serve the bundles with barely cooked tomatoes and artichoke hearts, which make a juicy contrast to the pastry. Thaw kataifi in the refrigerator overnight or on the counter for 4 to 5 hours; do not thaw it in the microwave. Allow kataifi to come to room temperature before using for the easiest handling.

1 Adjust oven rack to upper-middle position and heat oven to 400 degrees. Line rimmed baking sheet with parchment paper. Brush feta with 1 tablespoon oil and sprinkle with oregano and red pepper flakes. Set aside.

2 Unspool kataifi so that strands lay flat in straight line, then cut into 8-inch lengths, discarding excess. Divide strands of kataifi into eight 8-inch-long by 3-inch-wide rectangles with short side parallel to edge of counter. Gently dab and brush rectangles with 3 tablespoons oil.

3 Place 1 feta finger at narrow end of kataifi rectangle, parallel to edge of counter, and roll kataifi around feta into tidy bundle. Place on prepared baking sheet. Repeat with remaining feta and kataifi rectangles, spacing feta bundles evenly apart on sheet. Bake until pastry is golden brown, about 25 minutes.

4 Meanwhile, heat remaining 3 tablespoons oil in 12-inch nonstick skillet over medium-high heat until shimmering. Add tomatoes, artichoke hearts, garlic, salt, and pepper and cook until tomatoes release their juices and just begin to break down, about 5 minutes. Off heat, stir in parsley. Serve kataifi-wrapped feta with tomato-artichoke mixture.

sweets and sips

financiers

5 tablespoons unsalted butter

¾ cup (3 ounces) finely ground almond flour

½ cup plus 1 tablespoon (4 ounces) sugar

2 tablespoons all-purpose flour

⅛ teaspoon table salt

⅓ cup (3 ounces) egg whites (3 to 4 large eggs)

WHY THIS RECIPE WORKS These buttery, nutty, two-bite treats leave a lasting impression. Yet for all their elegance, they're incredibly easy to whip up, making them a cook's secret weapon for rounding out a spread of small plates. We simply stir together almond flour, all-purpose flour, egg whites, and granulated sugar before baking the cakes in a mini-muffin tin. The granulated sugar doesn't entirely dissolve in the egg whites, giving the cakes a rustic, open crumb. Browned butter bolsters the almond flour's nuttiness. You will need a 24-cup mini-muffin tin for this recipe. Because egg whites can vary in size, measuring the whites by weight or volume is essential here. Baking spray with flour ensures that the cakes bake up with appropriately flat tops; we don't recommend substituting vegetable oil spray in this recipe.

1 Adjust oven rack to middle position and heat oven to 375 degrees. Generously spray 24-cup mini-muffin tin with baking spray with flour. Melt butter in 10-inch skillet over medium-high heat. Cook, stirring and scraping skillet constantly with heat-resistant rubber spatula, until milk solids are dark golden brown and butter has nutty aroma, 1 to 3 minutes. Immediately transfer butter to heatproof bowl.

2 Whisk almond flour, sugar, all-purpose flour, and salt together in second bowl. Add egg whites. Using rubber spatula, stir until combined, mashing any lumps against side of bowl until mixture is smooth. Stir in butter until incorporated. Distribute batter evenly among prepared muffin cups (cups will be about half full).

3 Bake until edges are well browned and tops are golden, about 14 minutes, rotating muffin tin halfway through baking. Remove tin from oven and immediately invert wire rack on top of tin. Invert rack and tin; carefully remove tin. Turn cakes right side up and let cool for at least 20 minutes before serving.

Variations

Nut Financiers
After distributing batter among muffin cups, sprinkle with lightly toasted sliced almonds.

Raspberry Financiers

After distributing batter among muffin cups, place 1 small raspberry on its side on top of each cake (do not press into batter).

Chocolate Chunk Financiers

After distributing batter among muffin cups, place one ½-inch dark chocolate chunk on top of each cake (do not press into batter).

Plum Financiers

Pit 1 small plum and cut into 6 wedges. Slice plum wedges crosswise ¼ inch thick. After distributing batter among muffin cups, shingle 2 plum slices on top of each cake (do not press into batter).

Head Start

Store financiers in airtight container at room temperature for up to 3 days; note that after storage edges won't be as crisp as on day 1.

Serves 8 to 10 (makes 18 cookies) | **Active Time** 20 minutes
Total Time 35 minutes

pine nut macaroons

1⅔ cups slivered almonds

1⅓ cups (9⅓ ounces) sugar

2 large egg whites

1 cup pine nuts

WHY THIS RECIPE WORKS These classic Italian cookies pack plenty of rich, almondy flavor and crunchy pops from pine nuts in a little package. Egg whites give these naturally flour-free cookies a pleasantly chewy texture. Coating the cookies in pine nuts maximizes their nutty flavor and creates their signature craggy-crunchy exteriors. Since the pine nuts gently roast while baking on the surface of the cookies, there's no need to toast (and risk burning) them separately. The food processor makes quick work of deftly grinding the almonds, sugar, and egg whites into cookie dough in less than a minute.

1 Adjust oven racks to upper-middle and lower-middle positions and heat oven to 375 degrees. Line 2 rimmed baking sheets with parchment paper.

2 Process almonds and sugar in food processor until finely ground, about 30 seconds. Add egg whites and process until smooth, about 20 seconds. (Dough will be sticky.) Transfer dough to large bowl. Place pine nuts in separate shallow bowl.

3 Spray 1-tablespoon measuring spoon with vegetable oil spray. Working with 1 rounded tablespoon dough at a time, shape into balls and roll balls in pine nuts until evenly coated. Place 9 balls on each prepared sheet, spaced 2 inches apart.

4 Bake cookies until light golden brown, 14 to 16 minutes, switching and rotating sheets halfway through baking. Let cookies cool completely on sheets. Serve.

Head Start
Store cookies in airtight container for up to 5 days.

Finish Line
Dust cookies with confectioners' sugar after removing them from oven.

chocolate-toffee bites

1½ cups (7½ ounces) all-purpose flour

½ teaspoon table salt

10 tablespoons unsalted butter, softened

⅓ cup packed (2⅓ ounces) dark brown sugar

⅓ cup (1⅓ ounces) confectioners' sugar

½ cup plain toffee bits, divided

1 cup (6 ounces) milk chocolate chips

¾ cup whole almonds, toasted and chopped coarse

Head Start

Store bars in airtight container at room temperature for up to 2 days.

Finish Line

For an invitingly rustic presentation, break bars into rough triangles; alternately, cut into neat squares.

WHY THIS RECIPE WORKS The classic combination of toffee and chocolate is sure to be a crowd pleaser. Toffee bits give the crisp-but-tender shortbread base of these easy bar cookies extra crunch. We sprinkle milk chocolate chips onto the still-hot base, where they melt and can be spread into a thin layer just substantial enough to hold on to toasted almonds and even more toffee bits. There are two kinds of toffee bits sold at the market; be sure to buy the ones without chocolate. Note that the squares need to cool for about 3 hours in order to set the chocolate. If you're in a hurry, you can put the bars in the refrigerator for 1 hour, but don't store them in the fridge for much longer than that because the crust can become too hard.

1 Adjust oven rack to middle position and heat oven to 350 degrees. Make foil sling for 13 by 9-inch baking pan by folding 2 long sheets of aluminum foil; first sheet should be 13 inches wide and second sheet should be 9 inches wide. Lay sheets of foil in pan perpendicular to each other, with extra foil hanging over edges of pan. Push foil into corners and up sides of pan, smoothing foil flush to pan. Spray lightly with vegetable oil spray.

2 Combine flour and salt in bowl. Using stand mixer fitted with paddle, beat butter, brown sugar, and confectioners' sugar on medium-high speed until light and fluffy, about 3 minutes. Reduce speed to low and add flour mixture in 3 additions, scraping down bowl as needed, until dough becomes sandy with large pea-size pieces, about 30 seconds. Add ¼ cup toffee bits and mix until combined.

3 Transfer dough to prepared pan and press into even layer using bottom of dry measuring cup. Bake until golden brown, about 20 minutes, rotating pan halfway through baking.

4 Remove crust from oven, sprinkle with chocolate chips, and let sit until softened, about 5 minutes. Spread softened chocolate into even layer over crust using small offset spatula. Sprinkle almonds and remaining ¼ cup toffee bits evenly over chocolate, then press gently into chocolate. Let bars sit at room temperature until chocolate is set, about 3 hours.

5 Using foil overhang, lift bars out of pan. Cut into 24 pieces and serve.

easy chocolate truffles

¼ cup (¾ ounce) unsweetened cocoa powder

1 tablespoon confectioners' sugar

8 ounces bittersweet chocolate, chopped fine

½ cup heavy cream

Pinch table salt

WHY THIS RECIPE WORKS Bite-size chocolate truffles are an easy yet sophisticated choice for rounding out a small plates menu, especially since they can be made considerably in advance. The truffles are made with a thick chocolate-and-cream ganache; after melting the chocolate and combining it with the cream, we pop the mixture into the refrigerator to thicken up. Once the ganache is scoopable, we shape it into bite-size balls, coat them with cocoa powder and/or flavorful additions such as spices, nuts, or citrus zest, and then refrigerate them again to firm the truffles back up before serving. Wear latex gloves when forming the truffles to keep your hands clean.

1 Sift cocoa and sugar through fine-mesh strainer into pie plate. Microwave chocolate, cream, and salt in bowl at 50 percent power, stirring occasionally with rubber spatula, until melted, about 1 minute. Stir ganache until fully combined; transfer to 8-inch square baking dish and refrigerate until set, about 45 minutes.

2 Using heaping teaspoon measure, scoop ganache into 24 portions, transfer to large plate, and refrigerate until firm, about 30 minutes. Roll each truffle between your hands to form uniform balls (balls needn't be perfect).

3 Transfer truffles to cocoa mixture and roll to coat evenly. Lightly shake truffles in your hand over pie plate to remove excess coating; transfer to platter. Refrigerate for 30 minutes. Let sit at room temperature for 10 minutes before serving.

Variations

Chocolate-Almond Truffles
Substitute 1 cup sliced almonds, toasted and chopped fine, for cocoa mixture coating. Add ½ teaspoon almond extract to chocolate mixture before microwaving.

Chocolate-Cinnamon Truffles

Sift ¼ teaspoon ground cinnamon with cocoa powder and sugar for coating. Add 1 teaspoon ground cinnamon and ⅛ teaspoon cayenne pepper to chocolate mixture before microwaving.

Chocolate-Lemon Truffles

Add 1 teaspoon grated lemon zest to chocolate mixture before microwaving.

Chocolate-Ginger Truffles

Add 2 teaspoons ground ginger to chocolate mixture before microwaving.

Head Start

Refrigerate truffles in airtight container along with excess cocoa mixture for up to 1 week. Shake truffles in your hand to remove excess coating and let sit at room temperature for 10 minutes before serving.

buckeye candies

1 cup creamy peanut butter

8 tablespoons unsalted butter, cut into 8 pieces, softened but still cold

¼ teaspoon table salt

2½ cups (10 ounces) confectioners' sugar

12 ounces bittersweet chocolate, chopped fine, divided

Head Start

Refrigerate candies in airtight container for up to 1 week.

WHY THIS RECIPE WORKS Each one of these bite-size candies is a soft, creamy, and balanced peanut butter–chocolate treat. The dough is a tender confection of sugar, softened butter, and peanut butter; we incorporate a full cup of peanut butter, so each candy is absolutely stuffed with nutty flavor. Starting with softened but still cold butter and mixing the ingredients until the dough just comes together before refrigerating the dough makes the candies easier to roll. Spearing each dough ball on a toothpick keeps your fingers clean as you dip them in the chocolate coating. You can substitute bittersweet chocolate chips for the bar chocolate, but be sure to finely chop the chips. Do not use natural peanut butter here. The butter should be about 67 degrees and give slightly when pressed; it should not be so warm that it loses its shape. You will need 32 toothpicks for this recipe.

1 Using stand mixer fitted with paddle, mix peanut butter, butter, and salt on medium speed until mixture is nearly combined with some visible pieces of butter remaining, about 30 seconds. Reduce speed to low and slowly add sugar. Mix until just combined, scraping down bowl as needed. Refrigerate for 15 minutes.

2 Line 2 large plates with parchment paper. Divide dough into 32 pieces (about 1 tablespoon each). Using your hands, gently roll dough into balls and transfer to prepared plates. Insert 1 toothpick three-quarters of the way into each ball. Freeze balls until firm, about 1 hour.

3 Microwave 10 ounces chocolate in 4-cup liquid measuring cup at 50 percent power, stirring with rubber spatula every 30 seconds, until nearly melted, 2 to 3 minutes (chocolate should still be slightly lumpy). Remove measuring cup from microwave and stir in remaining 2 ounces chocolate until melted and smooth.

4 Tilt measuring cup slightly so chocolate pools on 1 side. Working with 1 plate of balls at a time (keeping second plate in freezer), grasp toothpicks and dip balls in chocolate until covered by two-thirds. Return balls to prepared plate. Refrigerate balls, uncovered, until chocolate is set and dough is no longer frozen, about 30 minutes.

5 Remove toothpicks and serve.

fruit bites

Fresh fruit has been served as a lightly sweet finish to meals since time immemorial. A selection of fresh, unadulterated fruit is still a solid way to round out a spread, but for something just a little more elevated, try serving these small fruit bites at your next gathering.

turkish stuffed apricots with rose water and pistachios

Serves 8 to 12 (makes 24 stuffed apricots)
Active Time 1 hour
Total Time 1 hour

Rose water can be found in Middle Eastern markets as well as in the international food aisle of many supermarkets; if you cannot find it, simply omit it. Look for whole dried apricots that are roughly 1½ inches in diameter.

½ cup plain Greek yogurt

¼ cup sugar, divided

½ teaspoon rose water

½ teaspoon grated lemon zest plus 1 tablespoon juice

Pinch table salt

2 cups water

4 green cardamom pods, cracked

2 bay leaves

24 whole dried apricots

¼ cup shelled pistachios, toasted and chopped fine

1 Combine yogurt, 1 teaspoon sugar, rose water, lemon zest, and salt in small bowl. Refrigerate filling until ready to use. (Filling can be refrigerated for up to 2 days).

2 Bring water, cardamom pods, bay leaves, lemon juice, and remaining sugar to simmer in small saucepan over medium-low heat and cook, stirring occasionally, until sugar has dissolved, about 2 minutes. Stir in apricots, return to simmer, and cook, stirring occasionally, until plump and tender, 25 to 30 minutes. Using slotted spoon, transfer apricots to plate and let cool completely. (Apricots can be refrigerated in airtight container for up to 1 day. Let come to room temperature before continuing with step 3.)

3 Discard cardamom pods and bay leaves. Bring syrup to boil over high heat and cook, stirring occasionally, until thickened and measures about 3 tablespoons, 4 to 6 minutes; let cool completely.

4 Place pistachios in shallow dish. Place filling in small zipper-lock bag and snip off 1 corner to create ½-inch opening. Pipe filling evenly into opening of each apricot and dip exposed filling into pistachios; transfer to serving platter. Drizzle apricots with syrup and serve.

strawberries with balsamic vinegar

Serves 6
Active Time 30 minutes
Total Time 30 minutes

If you don't have light brown sugar on hand, sprinkle the berries with an equal amount of granulated white sugar. Portion the berries and syrup into small glass cups or 4-ounce wide-mouthed Mason jars and serve as is or with lightly sweetened mascarpone cheese.

⅓ cup balsamic vinegar

2 teaspoons granulated sugar

½ teaspoon lemon juice

2 pounds strawberries, hulled, sliced lengthwise ¼ inch thick if large, halved or quartered if small (5 cups)

¼ cup packed light brown sugar

   Pinch pepper

1 Bring vinegar, granulated sugar, and lemon juice to simmer in small saucepan over medium heat and cook, stirring occasionally, until thickened and measures about 3 tablespoons, about 3 minutes. Transfer syrup to small bowl and let cool completely.

2 Gently toss strawberries with brown sugar and pepper in large bowl. Let sit at room temperature, stirring occasionally, until strawberries begin to release their juice, 10 to 15 minutes. Pour syrup over strawberries and toss gently to combine. Serve.

warm figs with goat cheese and honey

Serves 8 (makes 16 fig halves)
Active Time 25 minutes
Total Time 25 minutes

1½ ounces goat cheese

8 fresh figs, halved lengthwise

16 walnut halves, toasted

3 tablespoons honey

1 Adjust oven rack to middle position and heat oven to 500 degrees. Spoon heaping ½ teaspoon goat cheese onto each fig half and arrange in parchment paper–lined rimmed baking sheet. Bake figs until heated through, about 4 minutes; transfer to serving platter.

2 Place 1 walnut half on top of each fig half and drizzle with honey. Serve.

Perfect Pair

These fruit bites can be served as a sweet finish to nearly any small plates gathering; they're excellent whether paired with a simple charcuterie or cheese board or served alongside cocktails such as Champagne Cocktails (page 391) or one of its variations. Instead of treating them as dessert and saving them for last, try putting them out at the same time as the rest of your small plates so they can act as mildly sweet punctuation for the savory dishes.

sweet glazed peaches

2 tablespoons lemon juice

1 tablespoon sugar

¼ teaspoon table salt

6 firm, ripe peaches, peeled, halved, and pitted

⅓ cup water

¼ cup red currant jelly

1 tablespoon unsalted butter

¼ cup pistachios, toasted and chopped

Finish Line

For a more substantial dessert, serve warm peaches with vanilla ice cream or frozen custard.

WHY THIS RECIPE WORKS This warm, velvety-textured dessert has just enough added sweetness to amplify the peaches' floral and fruity flavors. Just 1 tablespoon of sugar is all it takes to create a warm, caramelized glaze for the peaches when combined with a splash of water and baked under the broiler. To boost the flavor, we brush the peaches with a mixture of melted butter and red currant jelly partway through broiling. With a bit more glaze drizzled on top, plus a few nuts for texture, this simple fruit dessert is ready to wow. Use a serrated peeler to peel the peaches.

1 Adjust oven rack 6 inches from broiler element and heat broiler. Combine lemon juice, sugar, and salt in large bowl. Add peaches and toss to combine, making sure to coat all sides with sugar mixture.

2 Transfer peaches, cut side up, to 12-inch broiler-safe skillet. Pour any remaining sugar mixture into peach cavities. Pour water around peaches in skillet. Broil until peaches are just beginning to brown, 11 to 15 minutes.

3 Combine jelly and butter in bowl and microwave until melted, about 30 seconds, then stir to combine. Remove peaches from oven and brush half of jelly mixture over peaches. Return peaches to oven and continue to broil until spotty brown, 5 to 7 minutes.

4 Remove skillet from oven, brush peaches with remaining jelly mixture, and transfer peaches to serving platter, leaving juices behind. Bring accumulated juices in skillet to simmer over medium heat and cook until syrupy, about 1 minute. Pour syrup over peaches. Sprinkle with pistachios and serve.

raspberry mini cheesecakes

12 round shortbread cookies,
   2 inches in diameter and
   ½ inch thick

½ cup seedless raspberry jam,
   divided

1 (8-ounce) package
   cream cheese, softened

½ cup sweetened condensed
   milk

2 large eggs

12 fresh raspberries (optional)

WHY THIS RECIPE WORKS These adorable miniature cheesecakes, dressed up with a raspberry and a dollop of jam, can be put together with minimal fuss and yield enough to serve a large group. Using sweetened condensed milk in the filling streamlines the ingredient list, removing the need for additional sugar, sour cream, and even vanilla. For the crusts, we simply drop a shortbread cookie into each muffin cup. Lining a muffin tin with cupcake liners makes the individual cheesecakes easy and mess-free to extract. As for the raspberry flavor, a double dose of raspberry jam (one layer spread over the cookie and one layer on top) plus a fresh raspberry do the trick. We like to use Keebler brand Sandies for our crusts, since they fit perfectly into a muffin tin. If you use a thinner cookie, your mini cheesecakes will be slightly more mini. Be sure to use sweetened condensed milk, not evaporated milk, here. To soften cream cheese quickly, microwave it for 20 to 30 seconds.

Head Start

Refrigerate unglazed cheesecakes for up to 2 days.

1 Adjust oven rack to middle position and heat oven to 300 degrees. Line 12-cup muffin tin with cupcake liners. Place cookies in cupcake liners. Dollop with 1 teaspoon jam each.

2 With electric mixer on medium-high speed, beat cream cheese until light and fluffy, about 2 minutes. Gradually beat in condensed milk, scraping down sides of bowl as necessary, until incorporated. Add eggs, 1 at a time, and beat until smooth, 2 to 3 minutes.

3 Divide batter evenly among cupcake liners. Bake until set, about 20 minutes. Transfer to wire rack and let cool completely, about 20 minutes. Refrigerate until set, about 1 hour.

4 Remove cheesecakes from muffin tin. Microwave remaining ¼ cup jam until thinned slightly, about 15 seconds, and use it to glaze cheesecakes. Top each cheesecake with fresh raspberry, if using. Serve.

individual summer berry puddings

12 slices potato bread, challah, or hearty white sandwich bread

1¼ pounds strawberries, hulled and sliced (4 cups)

10 ounces (2 cups) raspberries

5 ounces (1 cup) blueberries

5 ounces (1 cup) blackberries

¾ cup (5¼ ounces) sugar

2 tablespoons lemon juice

Head Start

Refrigerate puddings for up to 1 day before unmolding and serving.

Finish Line

Serve puddings with a dollop of whipped cream.

WHY THIS RECIPE WORKS Slices of hearty, lightly dried bread greedily soak up the juices from fresh sweetened berries in this summery English pudding. For this recipe, you will need six 6-ounce ramekins and a round cookie cutter of a slightly smaller diameter than the ramekins. If you don't have the right size cutter, use a paring knife and the bottom of a ramekin (most ramekins taper toward the bottom) as a guide for trimming the rounds. If using challah, slice it about ½ inch thick.

1 Adjust oven rack to middle position and heat oven to 200 degrees. Place bread in single layer on rimmed baking sheet and bake until dry but not brittle, about 1 hour, flipping slices once and rotating baking sheet halfway through baking. Set aside to cool.

2 Combine strawberries, raspberries, blueberries, blackberries, and sugar in large saucepan and cook over medium heat, stirring occasionally, until berries begin to release their juices and sugar has dissolved, about 5 minutes. Off heat, stir in lemon juice; let cool completely.

3 Spray six 6-ounce ramekins with vegetable oil spray and place on rimmed baking sheet. Use cookie cutter to cut out 12 bread rounds that are slightly smaller in diameter than ramekins.

4 Using slotted spoon, place ¼ cup fruit mixture in each ramekin. Lightly soak 1 bread round in fruit juice in saucepan and place on top of fruit in ramekin; repeat with 5 more bread rounds and remaining ramekins. Divide remaining fruit among ramekins, about ½ cup per ramekin. Lightly soak 1 bread round in juice and place on top of fruit in ramekin (it should sit above lip of ramekin); repeat with remaining 5 bread rounds and remaining ramekins. Pour remaining fruit juice over bread and cover ramekins loosely with plastic wrap. Place second baking sheet on top of ramekins and weight it with heavy cans. Refrigerate puddings for at least 8 hours.

5 Remove cans and baking sheet and uncover puddings. Loosen puddings by running paring knife around edge of each ramekin, unmold by inverting into individual bowls, and serve immediately.

lemon posset with berries

2 cups heavy cream

⅔ cup (4⅔ ounces) sugar

1 tablespoon grated lemon zest plus 6 tablespoons juice (2 lemons)

7½ ounces (1½ cups) blueberries or raspberries

WHY THIS RECIPE WORKS This chilled British dessert with the plush texture of a mousse comes together almost by magic with little more than cream, sugar, and lemons. Using just the right proportion of sugar to lemon juice is the key to a smooth, luxurious consistency and a bright enough flavor to balance the richness of the cream. Lemon zest makes the lemon flavor even more prominent. We pair the dessert with fresh, seasonal berries for textural contrast and to keep it from feeling overly rich. Reducing the cream mixture to exactly 2 cups creates the best consistency. Transfer the liquid to a 2-cup heatproof liquid measuring cup once or twice during boiling to monitor the amount. Do not leave the cream unattended, as it can boil over easily.

Head Start

Refrigerate chilled possets, wrapped in plastic wrap, for up to 2 days; unwrap and let sit at room temperature for 10 minutes before serving.

Finish Line

Lemon Possets are fairly rich; to feed more people or yield smaller portion sizes, serve in demitasse cups or miniature jam jars.

1 Combine cream, sugar, and lemon zest in medium saucepan and bring to boil over medium heat. Continue to boil, stirring frequently to dissolve sugar, until mixture is reduced to 2 cups, 8 to 12 minutes. (If at any point mixture begins to boil over, remove from heat.)

2 Remove saucepan from heat and stir in lemon juice. Let sit until mixture is cooled slightly and skin forms on top, about 20 minutes. Strain through fine-mesh strainer into bowl; discard zest. Divide mixture evenly among 6 individual ramekins or dessert dishes.

3 Refrigerate, uncovered, until set, at least 3 hours. Let sit at room temperature for 10 minutes before serving. Garnish with blueberries and serve.

chocolate cream pies in a jar

2½ cups half-and-half

6 tablespoons plus 1 teaspoon sugar (2¾ ounces), divided

⅛ teaspoon table salt, divided

6 large egg yolks

2 tablespoons cornstarch

6 tablespoons unsalted butter, cut into 6 pieces

6 ounces semisweet chocolate, chopped fine

1 ounce unsweetened chocolate, chopped fine

2 teaspoons vanilla extract, divided

1 cup heavy cream, chilled

10 Oreo cookies, broken into coarse crumbs (1 cup), divided

Head Start

Refrigerate chocolate filling for up to 1 day before assembling pies.

WHY THIS RECIPE WORKS While it can be hard to please everyone when it's time for dessert, we're betting these individual-size chocolate cream pies served in mini Mason jars will get you pretty close. We make a rich chocolate custard with lots of semisweet (and a little bit of unsweetened) chocolate for deep, but not bitter, chocolate flavor. We then layer our chocolate cream over crumbled Oreos (for more chocolate flavor and an irresistible crunchy-creamy texture) and top it with whipped cream for mini desserts that taste as good—and chocolaty—as they look. We'd call that having your pie and eating it too. You will need twelve 4-ounce wide-mouthed Mason jars for this recipe.

1 Bring half-and-half, 3 tablespoons sugar, and pinch salt to simmer in medium saucepan over medium heat, stirring occasionally. Whisk egg yolks, cornstarch, and 2 tablespoons plus 1 teaspoon sugar together in medium bowl until smooth. Slowly whisk 1 cup of half-and-half mixture into yolk mixture to temper, then slowly whisk tempered yolk mixture back into remaining half-and-half mixture in saucepan.

2 Cook half-and-half mixture over medium heat, whisking constantly, until mixture is thickened and registers 180 degrees, about 30 seconds. Off heat, whisk in butter, semisweet chocolate, unsweetened chocolate, and 1 teaspoon vanilla until smooth. Strain mixture through fine-mesh strainer into clean bowl. Spray piece of parchment paper with vegetable oil spray and press directly against surface of filling. Refrigerate until chilled, at least 1 hour.

3 To make whipped cream, whip cream, remaining 1 tablespoon sugar, remaining 1 teaspoon vanilla, and remaining pinch salt in stand mixer on medium speed for 1 to 3 minutes, until soft peaks form. When ready to serve, divide ¾ cup cookie crumbs evenly among twelve 4-ounce wide-mouthed glass jars, then divide chocolate filling evenly among jars. Top with whipped cream and remaining ¼ cup cookie crumbs. Serve.

lemonade

1½ cups sugar

13 lemons (2 sliced thin, seeds and ends discarded, 11 juiced to yield 2 cups)

56 ounces cold water

WHY THIS RECIPE WORKS Casual outdoor dining and a tall pitcher of lemonade: It's hard to name a more iconic duo. The tart-sweet thirst-quencher offers a refreshing counterpoint to any number of summery small plates. We muddle the lemon slices with granulated sugar to extract the oils in the peel. We then combine the lemons with some water and freshly squeezed lemon juice—no simple syrup needed. Straining the mixture removes the solid bits of lemon for a smooth drink with sweet, lemony flavor. When purchasing lemons, choose large ones that give to gentle pressure; hard lemons have thicker skin and yield less juice. Lemons are commonly waxed to prevent moisture loss, increase shelf life, and protect from bruising during shipping. Scrub them with a vegetable brush under running water to remove wax, or buy organic lemons. Don't worry about the seeds in the extracted juice; the entire juice mixture is strained at the end of the recipe.

Using potato masher, mash sugar and half of lemon slices in large bowl until sugar is completely wet, about 1 minute. Add water and lemon juice and whisk until sugar is completely dissolved, about 1 minute. Strain mixture through fine-mesh strainer set over serving pitcher, pressing on solids to extract as much juice as possible; discard solids. Add remaining lemon slices to lemonade and refrigerate until chilled, at least 1 hour. Stir to recombine before serving over ice.

Variations

Cucumber-Mint Lemonade
Mash 1 thinly sliced peeled cucumber and 1 cup fresh mint leaves with sugar and half of lemon slices. Add 1 thinly sliced peeled cucumber and ½ cup fresh mint leaves to strained lemonade.

Raspberry Lemonade
Mash 2 cups raspberries along with sugar and half of lemon slices.

Strawberry-Lime Lemonade

Substitute 2 thinly sliced limes for thinly sliced lemons. Add half of lime slices and 1 cup sliced strawberries to large bowl and mash with sugar. Add remaining lime slices and 1 cup sliced strawberries to strained lemonade.

Watermelon Lemonade

Reduce water to 48 ounces. Mash 4 cups coarsely chopped seedless watermelon with half of lemon slices.

Head Start

Refrigerate lemonade for up to 1 week; stir to recombine before serving over ice.

watermelon-lime aguas frescas

8 cups 1-inch pieces seedless watermelon

16 ounces water

2 ounces lime juice (2 limes), plus extra for seasoning

2 tablespoons agave nectar or honey, plus extra for seasoning

¼ teaspoon table salt

Fresh mint leaves (optional)

WHY THIS RECIPE WORKS Agua fresca means "fresh water" in Spanish and is the catchall term for a variety of ultrarefreshing beverages made by combining fruits, grains, seeds, or flowers with sugar and water. To make a version with one of summer's favorite fruits—watermelon—that would be the perfect complement to a warm-weather fete, we whiz chunks of melon with water in a blender and strain out the pulp before accenting the mixture with lime juice, agave nectar, and a pinch of salt to bring out the sweet and tart flavors. Watermelons vary in sweetness, so adjust the amounts of lime juice and sweetener to your taste.

Working in 2 batches, process watermelon and water in blender until smooth, about 30 seconds. Strain mixture through fine-mesh strainer into 2-quart pitcher; discard solids. Stir in lime juice, agave nectar, and salt. Season with extra lime juice and extra agave to taste. Serve chilled over ice, garnished with mint, if using.

Head Start

Refrigerate agua fresca for up to 5 days; stir to recombine before serving.

Finish Line

If you like, you can garnish glasses with thinly sliced limes and extra watermelon pieces in addition to mint.

masala chai

Masala Chai Concentrate

- 6 cinnamon sticks
- 2 star anise pods
- 30 green cardamom pods
- 4 teaspoons whole cloves
- 1½ teaspoons black peppercorns
- 10 cups water
- ½ cup packed brown sugar
- 2 tablespoons finely chopped fresh ginger
- ⅛ teaspoon table salt
- 6 tablespoons black tea leaves

Masala Chai

- ½–⅔ cup Masala Chai Concentrate
- ⅓–½ cup milk

Head Start

Refrigerate concentrate for up to 1 week.

WHY THIS RECIPE WORKS Sweet and milky masala chai is equally great served at teatime with a variety of little bites or sipped as part of a light nighttime snack. We opted to create a concentrate that can be refrigerated for up to a week, so it's easy to enjoy a cup of hot (or iced) masala chai whenever the mood strikes—or to make in advance for stress-free entertaining. To avoid sediment in our tea, rather than grinding the spices we crush them, which results in bigger pieces. To ensure that the cinnamon, star anise, cardamom, cloves, and black peppercorns hold their own against a strong black tea, we simmer them for 10 minutes to extract their lively flavors before adding the tea leaves. Brown sugar and fresh ginger add caramelly and punchy notes, respectively. A boldly flavored tea such as Assam is ideal for this recipe; alternatively, use Irish or English breakfast tea. If you have one, a mortar and pestle can be used to crush the spices.

1 **For the masala chai concentrate** Place cinnamon sticks and star anise on cutting board. Using bottom of heavy skillet, press down firmly until spices are coarsely crushed; transfer to medium saucepan. Crush cardamom pods, cloves, and peppercorns and add to saucepan. Toast spices over medium heat, stirring frequently, until fragrant, 1 to 2 minutes.

2 Add water, sugar, ginger, and salt and bring to boil. Cover saucepan, reduce heat, and simmer for 10 minutes. Stir in tea, cover, and simmer for 10 minutes. Remove from heat and let tea and spices steep for 10 minutes. Strain mixture through fine-mesh strainer. Refrigerate until chilled, at least 1 hour. Stir before using.

3A **To make hot masala chai** Stir ½ cup concentrate and ½ cup milk together in saucepan and heat to desired temperature, or combine in mug and heat in microwave.

3B **To make iced masala chai** Add ⅔ cup concentrate and ⅓ cup milk to ice-filled glass. Gently stir to combine.

berbere-spiced bloody marys

Bloody Mary Mix

2 (24-ounce) jars passata

8 ounces cold water

8 ounces dill pickle juice

½ cup prepared horseradish

2½ ounces lime juice (4 limes)

2 ounces Worcestershire sauce

2 tablespoons kosher salt

1 tablepoon pepper

2 teaspoons berbere

Cocktails

2 tablespoons kosher salt

1 tablespoon berbere

12 ounces vodka

Lime wedges

WHY THIS RECIPE WORKS For a brunch-y small plates spread, Bloody Marys are a must. Loaded up with garnishes, the sweet-spicy-savory cocktail can practically be considered a small plate in its own right. In this version, we amp up the standard recipe with the addition of berbere (an Ethiopian and Eritrean spice blend with a sweet and spicy flavor profile), adding it to the cocktail mix as well as using it to rim the glasses. Passata, a bottled uncooked tomato puree with clean tomato flavor and a neither too thick nor too thin texture, provides the base of our cocktails, which we accent with the usual Worcestershire (for umami), horseradish (for that pungent, familiar warmth), pickle juice (for brininess), and fresh lime juice (for vibrant acidity). If you can't find berbere, you can substitute Old Bay, jerk seasoning, or garam masala, but the flavor profile of your drinks won't be the same.

1 **For the bloody mary mix** Whisk all ingredients in pitcher until combined. Cover and refrigerate until chilled, at least 2 hours.

2 **For the cocktails** Combine salt and berbere on small plate and spread into even layer. Moisten rims of 8 chilled highball glasses with lime wedge. Roll moistened rims in salt mixture to coat. Fill glasses with ice. Add 8 ounces Bloody Mary mix and 1½ ounces vodka to each glass and stir to combine. Garnish with lime wedges and serve.

Head Start

Refrigerate Bloody Mary mix for up to 1 week.

Finish Line

Garnish cocktails with anything you like, from Bloody Mary Pickled Asparagus Spears (page 79) and Cajun Pickled Okra (page 80) to candied bacon, shrimp, pickled vegetables, or salami and cheese skewers.

champagne cocktails

8 sugar cubes

2 teaspoons Angostura bitters

44 ounces (5½ cups)
   Champagne, chilled

8 lemon twists

WHY THIS RECIPE WORKS Fizzy cocktails made with Champagne or other sparkling wines are one of the easiest ways to make a small plates dinner or cocktail party feel festive. For Champagne cocktails that evolve from the first sip to the last, we start with an Angostura bitters–soaked sugar cube in the bottom of a chilled flute, which we then fill with Champagne and garnish with a lemon twist. We strongly prefer Champagne here, but you can use another quality sparkling wine as long as it's brut or extra brut. Tilt the glass to a 45-degree angle and pour the wine down the side of the glass to minimize foaming. The amount of Champagne called for here is slightly less than two full 750-milliliter bottles. Use a channel knife to make the lemon twist.

Place sugar cubes in small bowl. Add bitters to sugar cubes. Transfer soaked sugar cubes to 8 chilled champagne flutes. Add 5½ ounces champagne to each flute and garnish with lemon twists. Serve.

Variations

Mimosas
Use strained, fresh-squeezed orange juice here for the best flavor. We like Cointreau, but any orange liqueur will work here.

Add 2½ ounces strained and chilled orange juice and ¼ ounce orange liqueur to 8 chilled wine glasses or flute glasses and stir to combine using bar spoon. Add 3 ounces chilled sparkling wine to each glass and, using spoon, gently lift juice mixture from bottom of glass to top to combine. Garnish glasses with orange twists.

Bellinis
Either peach juice or nectar works well here.

Add 2½ ounces peach juice or nectar and ¼ ounce peach schnapps to 8 chilled wine glasses or flute glasses and stir to combine using bar spoon. Add 3 ounces chilled sparkling wine to each glass and, using spoon, gently lift juice mixture from bottom of glass to top to combine. Garnish glasses with fresh peach slices.

sangria for a crowd

Citrus Syrup

⅔ cup sugar

⅔ cup water

1 teaspoon grated lemon or lime zest plus 1 tablespoon juice

Sangria

2 (750-ml) bottles fruity red wine, such as Merlot

4 ounces orange liqueur

3 oranges (2 sliced thin, 1 juiced to yield 4 ounces)

2 lemons, sliced thin

Head Start

Refrigerate citrus syrup in airtight container for up to 1 month. Refrigerate sangria, prepared through step 3, for up to 8 hours.

WHY THIS RECIPE WORKS This amped-up chilled wine cocktail is the thirst-quenching accompaniment your tapas spread is craving. And not only is it make-ahead friendly, it actually gets smoother and mellower the longer it sits, making it the chef's secret weapon for avoiding hectic last-minute prep work (or at least for keeping guests content while that last-minute work occurs). A few ounces of orange liqueur enhance the flavors of the fresh citrus fruits (oranges and lemons) that are infused into the wine. An easy syrup brings a little extra sweetness and another hit of citrus flavor to the sangria.

1 **For the citrus syrup** Combine sugar, water, and zest and juice in 2- or 4-cup jar. Cover jar with lid and shake vigorously until sugar dissolves, about 2 minutes. Let syrup sit for 30 minutes to infuse flavor.

2 Strain syrup through fine-mesh strainer into bowl, pressing on solids to extract as much syrup as possible; discard solids.

3 **For the sangria** Combine wine, liqueur, oranges, orange juice, lemons, and syrup in serving pitcher or large container. Cover and refrigerate until flavors meld and mixture is well chilled, at least 2 hours.

4 Stir sangria to recombine, then serve in chilled wine glasses (over ice, if desired), garnishing individual portions with macerated fruit.

make-ahead recipes

Planning a menu and want to lighten your load by making some things a day, a week, or even an entire month in advance? We've got you. The recipes listed below will allow you to get a jump-start on your cooking, as either a major component of the recipe (such as a dough, a filling, or time-consuming vegetable prep) or the entire dish can be made ahead of time. For recipes that can be partially made ahead but require some last-minute work, we listed the make-ahead component in parentheses next to the recipe title. Specific make-ahead instructions are included on the page with the recipe.

3 to 5 Days Ahead

Marinated Olives • page 26

Toasted Almonds • page 33

Grilled Polenta with Charred Scallion and Gorgonzola Topping • page 52

Whole-Wheat Pita Chips • page 70

Stuffed Pickled Cherry Peppers • page 83

Tapenades • page 84

Whipped Feta Dips • page 88

Ultracreamy Hummus • page 95

Sweet Potato Hummus • page 96

Muhammaras • page 103

Skordalia • page 109

Smoked Trout Pâté • page 119

Easy Mushroom Pâté • page 120

Beet-Pickled Eggs • page 132

Brown Rice Salad with Fennel, Mushrooms, and Walnuts (cooked rice) • page 190

Farro Salad with Sugar Snap Peas and White Beans (cooked farro) • page 192

Kamut with Carrots and Pomegranate (cooked kamut) • page 195

Texas Caviar • page 196

Marinated Eggplant with Capers and Mint • page 209

Marinated Cauliflower and Chickpeas with Saffron • page 209

Espinacas con Garbanzos • page 256

Seared Tempeh with Tomato Jam (tomato jam) • page 288

Financiers • page 360

Pine Nut Macaroons • page 363

Watermelon-Lime Aguas Frescas • page 385

1 to 2 Days Ahead

Olives all'Ascolana (filling) • page 36

Chilled Marinated Tofu • page 41

Jalapeño Poppers (uncooked poppers) • page 45

Pigs in Blankets (uncooked pigs) • page 46

Soccas (topping) • page 50

Spinach Squares • page 56

Spinach and Edamame Brown Rice Cakes • page 64

Green Chile Cheeseburger Sliders (uncooked patties) • page 66

Classic Pub Plant-Based Sliders (uncooked patties, sauce) • page 68

Chunky Guacamole • page 92

Bean Dips • page 98

Baba Ghanoush • page 106

Sikil P'ak • page 112

Buffalo Chicken Dip (uncooked) • page 115

Chicken Liver Pâté • page 116

Frico Friabile • page 124

Soy-Marinated Eggs • page 131

Cheese Logs • page 134

Goat Cheese Log with Hazelnut-Nigella Dukkah • page 136

Baked Goat Cheese (uncooked) • page 139

Spanish Tortilla • page 148

Moroccan-Style Carrot Salads • page 159

Apple-Fennel Rémoulade • page 162

Fennel, Orange, and Olive Salad • page 165

Fava Bean and Radish Salad (fava beans) • page 178

Butternut Squash and Apple Fattoush (toasted pita) • page 185

Fingerling Tomato Salad with Sun-Dried Tomato Dressing • page 186

Sweet Potato Salad with Cumin, Smoked Paprika, and Almonds (cooked sweet potatoes, dressing) • page 188

nutritional information for our recipes

To calculate the nutritional values of our recipes per serving, we used The Food Processor SQL by ESHA research. When using this program, we entered all the ingredients, using weights wherever possible. We also used our preferred brands in these analyses. Any ingredient listed as "optional" was excluded from the analyses. If there is a range in the serving size, we used the highest number of servings to calculate nutritional values. We did not include additional salt or pepper for food that's seasoned to taste.

	CALORIES	TOTAL FAT (G)	SAT FAT (G)	CHOL (MG)	SODIUM (MG)	TOTAL CARB (G)	DIETARY FIBER (G)	TOTAL SUGAR (G)	ADDED SUGAR (G)	PROTEIN (G)
Getting Started										
Pineapple Salsa (per ¼ cup)	43	2	0	0	153	7	1	5	0	0
Spicy Peanut Dipping Sauce (per 1 tbs)	55	4	1	0	121	4	1	2	1	2
Romesco Sauce (per 1 tbs)	50	5	1	0	84	1	0	1	0	1
Red Wine–Miso Sauce (per 1 tbs)	68	2	1	5	312	4	0	2	1	1
Browned Butter–Lemon Vinaigrette (per 1 tbs)	73	8	5	20	113	1	0	1	1	0
Aioli (per 1 tbs)	113	15	2	32	50	1	0	0	0	1
Maple-Chipotle Mayonnaise (per 1 tbs)	74	8	1	4	76	1	0	1	1	0
Creamy Blue Cheese Dip (per 1 tbs)	35	3	1	5	96	0	0	0	0	1
Yogurt-Tahini Sauce (per 1 tbs)	16	1	0	1	33	1	0	1	0	1
Cilantro-Mint Chutney (per 1 tbs)	9	0	0	1	39	1	1	1	0	0
Scallion Dipping Sauce (per 1 tbs)	11	0	0	0	315	2	0	1	0	0
Soy-Vinegar Dipping Sauce (per 1 tbs)	8	0	0	0	440	1	0	1	1	1
Sichuan Chili Oil (per 1 tbs)	101	11	2	0	127	2	1	0	0	1
Quick Pickled Red Onion (per ¼ cup)	37	0	0	0	143	6	0	5	4	0
Quick Pickled Cucumber and Bean Sprouts (per ¼ cup)	13	0	0	0	304	3	0	2	1	1
Pistachio Dukkah (per 1 tsp)	13	1	0	0	87	1	0	0	0	0
Everything Bagel Seasoning (per 1 tsp)	9	1	0	0	250	1	0	0	0	0
Za'atar (per 1 tsp)	6	0	0	0	40	1	0	0	0	0
Shichimi Togarashi (per 1 tsp)	5	0	0	0	0	1	0	0	0	0

	CALORIES	TOTAL FAT (G)	SAT FAT (G)	CHOL (MG)	SODIUM (MG)	TOTAL CARB (G)	DIETARY FIBER (G)	TOTAL SUGAR (G)	ADDED SUGAR (G)	PROTEIN (G)
Bar Snacks and Finger Foods										
Blistered Shishito Peppers	57	6	1	0	1	2	1	1	0	0
Marinated Green and Black Olives	209	22	3	0	527	2	1	0	0	0
Southern Cheese Straws	178	12	8	35	246	12	0	0	0	6
Buttered Popcorn	114	9	3	9	79	7	1	0	0	1
Coriander-Turmeric Roasted Chickpeas	102	6	1	0	226	9	3	0	0	3
Firecracker Party Mix	384	23	7	17	637	38	3	4	0	9
Cinnamon-Ginger Spiced Nuts	360	25	2	0	275	28	7	19	17	11
Quick Toasted Almonds	217	19	2	0	346	7	4	1	0	7
Caprese Skewers	137	11	4	16	174	4	0	1	0	6
Olives all'Ascolana	310	17	4	79	442	26	1	2	0	0
Fried Pickles	286	9	1	0	1024	45	2	1	0	4
Chilled Marinated Tofu	116	4	0	0	847	10	2	7	3	9
Prosciutto-Wrapped Figs with Gorgonzola	137	4	2	20	594	20	3	16	0	7
Jalapeño Poppers	128	11	7	35	345	4	1	2	0	5
Pigs in Blankets	202	22	9	75	1309	21	1	4	3	31
Pakoras	405	35	3	0	359	19	4	3	0	5
Socca with Caramelized Onions and Rosemary	219	14	2	0	537	18	3	4	0	6
Grilled Polenta with Charred Scallion and Gorgonzola Topping	193	11	4	15	350	19	1	2	2	5
Pajeon	215	13	2	0	472	22	2	1	0	3
Spinach Squares	229	13	7	90	530	14	1	1	0	15
Karaage	270	12	2	91	520	18	0	0	0	20
Oven-Baked Buffalo Wings	224	15	5	121	1225	2	0	2	2	18
Easy Egg Rolls	269	15	3	23	557	24	2	3	1	10
Spinach and Edamame Brown Rice Cakes	133	5	0	0	465	19	3	2	0	5
Green Chile Cheeseburger Sliders	416	22	6	39	638	38	2	4	0	17
Classic Pub Plant-Based Sliders	255	15	4	1	448	22	3	3	1	11
Whole Wheat Pita Chips	35	0	0	0	111	7	1	0	0	2
Parmesan, Rosemary, and Black Pepper French Fries	321	14	4	12	414	43	3	1	0	9
Asparagus Fries with Yogurt Sauce	329	16	4	79	662	34	3	4	0	12
Ricotta Tartlets with Tomato-Basil Topping	58	4	1	6	47	4	0	1	0	2
Lemon-Pepper Chicken Wings	197	13	4	113	160	1	0	0	0	18

	CALORIES	TOTAL FAT (G)	SAT FAT (G)	CHOL (MG)	SODIUM (MG)	TOTAL CARB (G)	DIETARY FIBER (G)	TOTAL SUGAR (G)	ADDED SUGAR (G)	PROTEIN (G)
Pickles, Dips, and Spreads										
Quick Carrot Pickles	35	0	0	0	550	8	1	6	0	0
Quick Pickled Chard Stems	44	0	0	0	453	9	2	5	4	2
Pink Pickled Turnips	10	0	0	0	109	2	0	2	0	0
Bloody Mary Pickled Asparagus Spears	15	0	0	0	75	3	1	1	0	1
Cajun Pickled Okra	11	0	0	0	236	3	1	1	0	1
Stuffed Pickled Cherry Peppers	146	13	3	8	642	3	0	0	0	3
Green Olive Tapenade	156	16	2	2	624	1	1	0	0	1
Pimento Cheese Spread	197	19	9	43	285	1	0	0	0	8
Whipped Feta Dip	113	10	5	26	263	2	0	1	0	4
Homemade Labneh	50	3	2	11	38	4	0	4	0	3
Chunky Guacamole	69	6	1	0	21	4	3	0	0	1
Ultracreamy Hummus	195	13	2	0	583	14	4	0	0	6
Sweet Potato Hummus	143	10	1	0	57	13	2	3	0	2
Butter Bean and Pea Dip with Mint	55	0	0	0	138	10	3	2	0	3
Baharat Beef Topping	142	11	2	24	305	3	1	1	0	8
Crispy Mushroom and Sumac Topping	89	5	1	0	258	8	3	1	0	4
Muhammara	267	22	3	0	350	15	2	7	4	3
Caponata	130	6	1	1	292	17	4	12	2	3
Baba Ghanoush	85	6	1	0	224	8	3	4	0	2
Skordalia	160	14	2	0	176	8	2	1	0	2
Spinach and Artichoke Dip	218	18	6	32	521	9	2	2	0	5
Chile con Queso	218	17	11	57	541	5	0	2	0	11
Sikil P'ak	164	14	3	6	66	5	2	2	0	6
Buffalo Chicken Dip	458	36	17	136	1203	5	0	2	0	27
Chicken Liver Pâté	173	14	8	201	107	3	0	1	0	9
Smoked Trout Pâté	156	9	5	60	285	2	0	1	0	15
Easy Mushroom Pâté	109	8	5	24	254	6	1	2	0	3

	CALORIES	TOTAL FAT (G)	SAT FAT (G)	CHOL (MG)	SODIUM (MG)	TOTAL CARB (G)	DIETARY FIBER (G)	TOTAL SUGAR (G)	ADDED SUGAR (G)	PROTEIN (G)
Cheese and Eggs										
Frico Friabile	162	13	7	37	398	1	1	1	0	9
Marinated Manchego	361	37	12	22	450	2	0	0	0	8
Easy-Peel Hard-Cooked Eggs	72	5	2	186	71	0	0	0	0	6
Curried Deviled Eggs	67	6	1	105	75	0	0	0	0	4
Smoked Trout Deviled Eggs	65	4	1	111	110	1	0	0	0	6
Soy-Marinated Eggs	77	3	1	117	1178	4	0	4	2	7
Beet Pickled Eggs	85	4	1	162	156	6	0	5	5	6
Cheddar Cheese Log with Chives	144	13	6	31	188	2	0	1	0	5
Goat Cheese Log with Hazelnut-Nigella Dukkah	87	8	4	19	94	1	0	0	0	3
Baked Goat Cheese	143	11	5	13	627	6	2	3	0	7
Baked Brie with Honeyed Apricots	126	7	4	25	221	11	0	9	0	5
Saganaki	154	13	6	25	344	2	0	0	0	7
Egg Roulade with Spinach and Gruyère	171	11	5	269	270	3	1	1	0	14
Breakfast Buttercups	272	13	6	194	258	22	1	1	0	15
Spanish Tortilla	194	13	3	151	350	15	2	2	0	7
Quesadillas for a Crowd	304	20	10	40	691	17	1	2	0	14
Salads for Sharing										
Tomato Salad	99	9	1	0	207	5	1	3	0	1
Shaved Zucchini Salad with Pepitas	119	10	2	7	388	5	2	3	0	5
Herb Salad	78	7	1	0	73	3	2	0	0	1
Pai Huang Gua	26	2	0	0	399	2	1	1	0	1
Moroccan-Style Carrot Salad	94	6	1	0	215	10	1	6	0	1
Gajarachi Koshimbir	116	6	2	0	288	14	3	9	6	3
Apple-Fennel Rémoulade	97	8	1	4	333	6	2	3	0	1
Fennel, Orange, and Olive Salad	93	8	1	0	60	6	1	4	0	1
Citrus and Radicchio Salad with Dates and Smoked Almonds	179	11	1	0	196	21	5	15	1	3
Peach Caprese Salad	190	15	7	30	380	7	1	6	0	10
Tomato and Burrata Salad with Pangrattato and Basil	246	21	6	23	392	12	2	4	0	8
Watermelon Salad with Cotija and Serrano Chiles	117	7	2	10	419	11	1	8	2	5
Fresh Fig Salad	167	12	4	14	356	10	1	8	0	6
Esquites	193	12	4	16	412	18	3	4	0	6

	CALORIES	TOTAL FAT (G)	SAT FAT (G)	CHOL (MG)	SODIUM (MG)	TOTAL CARB (G)	DIETARY FIBER (G)	TOTAL SUGAR (G)	ADDED SUGAR (G)	PROTEIN (G)
Salads for Sharing (cont.)										
Horiatiki Salata	181	15	5	22	824	7	2	4	0	5
Butternut Squash and Apple Fattoush	235	15	2	0	374	26	3	4	0	3
Fingerling Potato Salad with Sun-Dried Tomato Dressing	229	12	1	0	693	28	3	0	0	4
Sweet Potato Salad with Cumin, Smoked Paprika, and Almonds	306	19	2	0	772	33	6	7	0	5
Brown Rice Salad with Fennel, Mushrooms, and Walnuts	312	17	2	0	21	36	3	3	0	6
Farro Salad with Sugar Snap Peas and White Beans	255	9	1	0	409	36	6	3	0	9
Kamut with Carrots and Pomegranate	174	7	1	0	107	26	5	4	0	5
Texas Caviar	142	7	1	0	594	17	4	3	2	5
Crispy Lentil and Herb Salad	235	18	3	3	172	14	2	3	0	7
Tuna and Heirloom Tomato Salad with Olives and Parsley	199	16	2	13	875	5	1	2	0	8
Crab and Mizuna Salad	249	21	3	41	508	6	2	3	1	12
Pinto Bean, Ancho, and Beef Salad	242	12	4	42	498	19	6	3	1	16
Dressed-Up Vegetables										
Marinated Zucchini	128	12	2	4	610	4	1	3	0	3
Marinated Eggplant with Capers and Mint	95	8	1	0	120	5	2	3	0	1
Marinated Cauliflower	133	11	2	0	580	7	2	2	1	2
Patatas Bravas	269	16	2	3	1367	28	2	2	0	4
Southern Corn Fritters	195	11	2	34	200	22	2	3	0	5
Fried Green Tomatoes	150	8	1	24	514	17	2	4	0	4
Sausage-and-Cheddar Stuffed Mushrooms	218	13	5	31	868	10	1	2	0	14
Roasted King Trumpet Mushrooms	82	7	4	17	180	4	0	3	0	2
Stir-Fried En Choy with Garlic	49	4	1	0	162	3	1	0	0	2
Pressure-Cooker Braised Radishes and Snap Peas	180	11	2	3	312	13	4	7	0	8
Skillet-Roasted Broccoli with Sesame and Orange Topping	205	19	3	0	285	7	3	1	0	4
Roasted Asparagus with Mustard-Dill Hollandaise	311	33	18	153	346	3	1	1	0	3
Roasted Carrots and Shallots with Chermoula	170	13	4	0	409	13	3	6	0	2
Grilled Radicchio	165	14	2	0	43	9	2	1	0	3

	CALORIES	TOTAL FAT (G)	SAT FAT (G)	CHOL (MG)	SODIUM (MG)	TOTAL CARB (G)	DIETARY FIBER (G)	TOTAL SUGAR (G)	ADDED SUGAR (G)	PROTEIN (G)
Dressed-Up Vegetables (cont.)										
Grilled Prosciutto-Wrapped Asparagus	128	9	2	20	765	3	1	1	0	9
Carciofi alla Giudia	199	3	3	0	78	9	4	1	0	3
Gobi Manchurian	184	12	2	0	794	18	1	3	2	2
Latkes	138	7	1	38	261	17	1	1	0	3
Samosas	345	16	2	0	546	45	3	2	0	7
Stuffed Tomatoes with Couscous and Spinach	352	16	4	16	350	43	6	10	2	12
Braised Eggplant with Soy, Garlic, and Ginger	73	3	0	0	402	10	2	5	3	2
Skillet-Roasted Brussels Sprouts with Chorizo and Manchego	263	19	6	23	880	14	5	4	2	11
Butternut Squash Steaks with Honey-Nut Topping	200	10	2	3	317	28	4	10	5	4
Loaded Sweet Potato Wedges with Tempeh	196	9	1	0	277	24	4	6	0	5
Spiralized Sweet Potatoes with Crispy Shallots, Pistachios, and Urfa	219	12	2	0	322	26	5	9	1	3
Pressure-Cooker Winter Squash with Halloumi and Brussels Sprouts	231	14	6	21	508	10	4	6	1	9
Proteins										
Espinacas con Garbanzos	282	15	2	0	382	277	7	4	0	10
Caramel Tofu	207	12	2	0	690	18	2	10	8	8
Gambas a la Plancha	93	4	1	114	569	2	0	0	0	12
Gambas al Ajillo	201	15	2	114	645	4	0	0	0	13
Pan-Seared Shrimp with Pistachios, Cumin, and Parsley	104	6	1	95	568	2	1	0	0	11
Cóctel de Camarón	153	4	1	107	1130	17	3	11	4	13
Shrimp Rémoulade	195	15	2	115	26	3	1	1	0	12
Tuna Poke	166	10	2	25	426	2	1	1	0	17
Peruvian Ceviche with Radishes and Orange	212	9	1	24	817	19	3	5	0	15
Crab Croquettes	458	26	8	93	687	40	2	4	0	14
Fritto Misto di Mare	179	8	1	153	343	10	0	0	0	16
Albóndigas en Salsa de Almendras	326	23	7	74	408	12	1	1	0	15
Pork and Ricotta Meatballs	440	30	11	115	1210	20	2	3	0	23
Keftedes	235	16	8	56	356	8	2	1	0	15
Lamb Rib Chops with Mint-Rosemary Relish	279	20	5	71	292	0	0	0	0	26

	CALORIES	TOTAL FAT (G)	SAT FAT (G)	CHOL (MG)	SODIUM (MG)	TOTAL CARB (G)	DIETARY FIBER (G)	TOTAL SUGAR (G)	ADDED SUGAR (G)	PROTEIN (G)
Proteins (cont.)										
Chickpea Cakes	318	17	2	0	426	35	7	1	0	9
Red Lentil Kibbeh	211	7	1	2	376	32	6	3	0	8
Seared Tempeh with Tomato Jam	217	13	3	0	185	14	1	7	5	14
Tempeh with Sambal Sauce	288	15	3	0	430	8	0	1	0	14
Shrimp Tostadas with Coconut and Pineapple Slaw	283	18	5	71	644	24	6	6	0	11
Pan-Seared Scallops with Asparagus-Citrus Salad	167	10	3	28	557	8	2	3	0	11
Sung Choy Bao	142	7	1	37	367	11	2	2	0	9
Dakgangjeong	478	31	8	189	272	16	1	5	4	32
Pretzel-Crusted Chicken Fingers with Honey Mustard	320	13	2	96	906	23	1	1	0	23
Chicken Satay	140	5	1	60	259	4	0	3	3	19
Kombdi, Jira Ghalun	262	11	2	102	886	7	2	2	0	33
Spicy Chicken Flautas	741	35	9	122	1337	63	7	5	0	45
Sizzling Beef Lettuce Wraps	274	20	6	61	555	5	1	4	2	18
Pinchos Morunos	231	14	3	84	397	2	1	0	0	24
Chile-Marinated Pork Belly	505	48	17	61	328	11	2	6	3	10
Chinese Barbecue Spareribs	337	14	4	132	645	13	0	9	7	39
Arrosticini	131	9	3	41	207	0	0	0	0	12
Breads, Dumplings, and Savory Pastries										
Easy Cheese Straws	161	10	5	6	334	13	1	1	0	6
Gochujang and Cheddar Pinwheels	148	10	5	30	148	12	1	1	0	5
Blini	65	3	2	20	114	7	1	2	1	2
Gougères	101	6	4	56	160	5	0	0	0	5
Baguette with Radishes, Butter, and Herbs	151	13	7	30	105	7	1	1	0	1
Blue Cheese and Chive Popovers with Blue Cheese Butter	397	25	15	170	619	27	1	3	0	14
Toast for Bruschetta	189	1	0	0	267	39	2	1	0	7
Bruschetta with Artichoke Hearts and Basil	289	14	3	9	824	30	2	1	0	11
Bruschetta with Arugula Pesto and Goat Cheese Topping	316	19	3	6	680	28	2	1	0	10
Molletes	240	18	12	56	447	11	3	3	0	10
Naan with Ricotta, Sun-Dried Tomatoes, and Olive Tapenade	296	20	5	17	434	22	1	2	0	8

	CALORIES	TOTAL FAT (G)	SAT FAT (G)	CHOL (MG)	SODIUM (MG)	TOTAL CARB (G)	DIETARY FIBER (G)	TOTAL SUGAR (G)	ADDED SUGAR (G)	PROTEIN (G)
Breads, Dumplings, and Savory Pastries (cont.)										
Grilled Onion, Pear, and Prosciutto Flatbread	372	20	7	36	1142	35	2	6	0	15
Easy Mini Chicken Empanadas	447	30	11	50	1094	33	1	2	0	13
Lamb Fatayer	332	16	5	28	535	33	1	2	1	13
Cabbage and Mushroom Dumplings	119	6	1	3	306	13	1	2	0	4
Pork and Cabbage Dumplings	204	11	3	62	581	13	2	2	0	13
Shu Mai	208	4	1	56	589	27	1	2	1	16
Potato-Cheddar Pierogi	506	25	14	119	860	56	3	3	0	14
Black Bean and Cheese Arepas	267	12	4	13	565	33	2	0	0	7
Lop Cheung Bao	233	10	3	18	352	28	1	6	4	7
French Bread Pizzas	411	26	13	60	965	30	2	5	0	17
Kataifi-Wrapped Feta with Tomatoes and Artichokes	283	19	6	25	465	20	3	4	0	8
Sweets and Sips										
Financiers	127	8	3	13	37	12	1	10	9	2
Pine Nut Macaroons	327	19	1	0	12	36	3	31	29	7
Chocolate-Toffee Bites	311	19	9	28	198	33	2	20	19	4
Easy Chocolate Truffles	169	14	8	14	17	14	2	1	1	2
Buckeye Candies	376	26	12	17	170	37	3	22	21	6
Turkish Stuffed Apricots with Rose Water and Pistachios	80	2	0	1	21	15	2	13	4	2
Strawberries with Balsamic Vinegar	86	0	0	0	5	20	3	16	7	1
Warm Figs with Goat Cheese and Honey	94	4	1	2	25	15	1	13	7	2
Sweet Glazed Peaches	65	2	1	3	55	11	1	10	1	1
Raspberry Mini Cheesecakes	242	13	8	65	148	27	1	19	0	4
Individual Summer Berry Puddings	313	3	1	1	282	69	8	37	25	6
Lemon Posset with Berries	380	29	18	90	22	30	1	28	22	3
Chocolate Cream Pies in a Jar	519	44	26	207	156	29	2	22	14	6
Lemonade	173	0	0	0	8	46	0	43	41	0
Watermelon-Lime Aguas Frescas	34	0	0	0	62	9	0	8	4	0
Masala Chai	26	0	0	1	15	6	0	6	5	0
Berbere-Spiced Bloody Marys	210	0	0	0	1750	20	4	10	0	3
Champagne Cocktails	144	0	0	0	8	7	0	4	2	0
Sangria for a Crowd	190	0	0	0	6	20	1	17	14	0

conversions and equivalents

Some say cooking is a science and an art. We would say that geography has a hand in it, too. Flours and sugars manufactured in the United Kingdom and elsewhere will feel and taste different from those manufactured in the United States. So we cannot promise that the loaf of bread you bake in Canada or England will taste the same as a loaf baked in the States, but we can offer guidelines for converting weights and measures. We also recommend that you rely on your instincts when making our recipes. Refer to the visual cues provided. If the dough hasn't "come together in a ball" as described, you may need to add more flour—even if the recipe doesn't tell you to. You be the judge.

The recipes in this book were developed using standard U.S. measures following U.S. government guidelines. The charts below offer equivalents for U.S. and metric measures. All conversions are approximate and have been rounded up or down to the nearest whole number.

example:
1 teaspoon = 4.9292 milliliters, rounded up to
          5 milliliters
1 ounce = 28.3495 grams, rounded down to
          28 grams

Volume Conversions

U.S.	metric
1 teaspoon	5 milliliters
2 teaspoons	10 milliliters
1 tablespoon	15 milliliters
2 tablespoons	30 milliliters
¼ cup	59 milliliters
⅓ cup	79 milliliters
½ cup	118 milliliters
¾ cup	177 milliliters
1 cup	237 milliliters
1¼ cups	296 milliliters
1½ cups	355 milliliters
2 cups (1 pint)	473 milliliters
2½ cups	591 milliliters
3 cups	710 milliliters
4 cups (1 quart)	0.946 liter
1.06 quarts	1 liter
4 quarts (1 gallon)	3.8 liters

Weight Conversions

ounces	grams
½	14
¾	21
1	28
1½	43
2	57
2½	71
3	85
3½	99
4	113
4½	128
5	142
6	170
7	198
8	227
9	255
10	283
12	340
16 (1 pound)	454

Conversions for Common Baking Ingredients

Baking is an exacting science. Because measuring by weight is far more accurate than measuring by volume, and thus more likely to produce reliable results, in our recipes we provide ounce measures in addition to cup measures for many ingredients. Refer to the chart below to convert these measures into grams.

ingredient	ounces	grams
flour		
1 cup all-purpose flour*	5	142
1 cup cake flour	4	113
1 cup whole-wheat flour	5½	156
sugar		
1 cup granulated (white) sugar	7	198
1 cup packed brown sugar (light or dark)	7	198
1 cup confectioners' sugar	4	113
cocoa powder		
1 cup cocoa powder	3	85
butter†		
4 tablespoons (½ stick or ¼ cup)	2	57
8 tablespoons (1 stick or ½ cup)	4	113
16 tablespoons (2 sticks or 1 cup)	8	227

* U.S. all-purpose flour, the most frequently used flour in this book, does not contain leaveners, as some European flours do. These leavened flours are called self-rising or self-raising. If you are using self-rising flour, take this into consideration before adding leaveners to a recipe.

† In the United States, butter is sold both salted and unsalted. We generally recommend unsalted butter. If you are using salted butter, take this into consideration before adding salt to a recipe.

Oven Temperatures

fahrenheit	celsius	gas mark
225	105	¼
250	120	½
275	135	1
300	150	2
325	165	3
350	180	4
375	190	5
400	200	6
425	220	7
450	230	8
475	245	9

Converting Temperatures from an Instant-Read Thermometer

We include doneness temperatures in many of the recipes in this book. We recommend an instant-read thermometer for the job. Refer to the table above to convert Fahrenheit degrees to Celsius. Or, for temperatures not represented in the chart, use this simple formula:

Subtract 32 degrees from the Fahrenheit reading, then divide the result by 1.8 to find the Celsius reading.

example:
"Roast chicken until thighs register 175 degrees."

to convert:
175°F − 32 = 143°
143° ÷ 1.8 = 79.44°C, rounded down to 79°C

index

O

Oil, Sichuan Chili, 19
Okra, Cajun Pickled, 80, *81*
Olive(s)
all'Ascolana, 36–37, *37*
Black, Tapenade, 84
Caponata, 104–5, *105*
Easy Mini Chicken Empanadas,
    338–39, *339*
Fennel, and Orange Salad, *164*, 165
Green, Tapenade, 84, *85*
Horiatiki Salata, 182, *183*
Marinated, with Baby Mozzarella, 26
Marinated Green, with Feta, 26
Marinated Green and Black, 26–27, *27*
and Parsley, Tuna and Heirloom
    Tomato Salad with, *200*, 201
and Red Onion, Cantaloupe Salad
    with, 172
Roasted Red Peppers, and Feta, Naan
    with, 334
Supreme French Bread Pizza, 354, *355*
Tapenade, Ricotta, and Sun-Dried
    Tomatoes, Naan with, 334, *335*
Onion(s)
Caramelized, and Rosemary, Socca
    with, 50–51, *51*
Grilled, Pear, and Prosciutto Flatbread,
    336–37, *337*
Pakoras, *48*, 49
Potato-Cheddar Pierogi, 348–49, *349*
Red, and Jalapeños, Quick-Pickled, 19
Red, and Olives, Cantaloupe Salad
    with, 172
Red, Quick Pickled, 19
Orange liqueur
Mimosas, 391
Sangria for a Crowd, 392, *393*
Orange(s)
-Cardamom Spiced Nuts, 33
Citrus and Radicchio Salad with Dates
    and Smoked Almonds, 166, *167*
Fennel, and Olive Salad, *164*, 165
-Fennel Almonds, 33
Mimosas, 391
Mint, and Poppy Seeds, Shishito
    Peppers with, 25
Moroccan-Style Carrot Salad, 159
Pan-Seared Scallops with Asparagus-
    Citrus Salad, 294–95, *295*
and Radishes, Peruvian Ceviche with,
    270–71, *271*

Orange(s) (cont.)
Sangria for a Crowd, 392, *393*
and Sesame Topping, Skillet-Roasted
    Broccoli with, 224–25, *225*
Shichimi Togarashi, 21, *21*
Oregano
Whipped Feta Dip, 88, *89*
Za'atar, 21
Oven-Baked Buffalo Wings, *60*, 61

P

Pai Huang Gua, 156, *157*
Pajeon, 54–55, *55*
Pakoras, *48*, 49
Pancakes
Blini, 322, *323*
Pajeon, 54–55, *55*
Socca with Caramelized Onions and
    Rosemary, 50–51, *51*
Socca with Swiss Chard, Apricots, and
    Pistachios, 51
**Pangratto and Basil, Tomato and
    Burrata Salad with, 170–71, *171***
**Pan-Seared Scallops with Asparagus-
    Citrus Salad, 294–95, *295***
**Pan-Seared Shrimp with Pistachios,
    Cumin, and Parsley, 264, *265***
Papaya
Som Tam, *180*, 181
Paprika
Coriander, and Yogurt, Braised
    Eggplant with, 243
Shichimi Togarashi, 21, *21*
Paprika, Smoked
Smoky Aioli, 16
–Spiced Roasted Chickpeas, 31
–Spiced Toasted Almonds, 33
Parmesan
Asparagus Fries with Yogurt Sauce,
    71–72
–Black Pepper Cheese Straws, 29
and Black Pepper Topping, Skillet-
    Roasted Broccoli with, 225
Easy Cheese Straws, 320, *320*
-Garlic Chicken Wings, 73
Marinated Zucchini, 208, *208*
-Pepper Popcorn, 30
Rosemary, and Black Pepper French
    Fries, *70*, 71

Parsley
Baguette with Radishes, Butter, and
    Herbs, 326, *327*
Crispy Lentil and Herb Salad,
    198–99, *199*
and Dill, Whipped Feta Dip with, 88
-Garlic Sauce, Saganaki with, 143
Herb Salad, *154*, 155
and Olives, Tuna and Heirloom Tomato
    Salad with, *200*, 201
Pink Bean and Lima Bean Dip with, 99
Party Mix, Firecracker, 32
Patatas Bravas, 210–11, *211*
Pâté
Chicken Liver, 116, *117*
Easy Mushroom, 120, *121*
Smoked Trout, *118*, 119
Peach(es)
Bellinis, 391
Caprese Salad, 168, *169*
Sweet Glazed, 372, *373*
Peanut butter
Buckeye Candies, 368, *369*
Spicy Peanut Dipping Sauce, 15
Peanuts
Caramel Tofu, *258*, 259
Gajarachi Koshimbir, 160–61, *161*
and Lime, Honeydew Salad with, 173
Soy Sauce, and Sriracha, Sweet Potato
    Salad with, 188
**Pear, Grilled Onion, and Prosciutto
    Flatbread, 336–37, *337***
Pea(s)
and Butter Bean Dip with Mint,
    98–99, *99*
Samosas, 238–39, *239*
Snap, and Radishes, Pressure-Cooker
    Braised, *222*, 223
Spanish Tortilla, 148–49, *149*
Sugar Snap, and White Beans, Farro
    Salad with, 192, *193*
Texas Caviar, 196, *197*
**Pecorino Romano and Oregano,
    Tomato Salad with, 154**
**Pepitas, Shaved Zucchini Salad
    with, 155**
Pepper Jack cheese
Green Chile Cheeseburger Sliders,
    66–67, *67*

S

U

V

W

Y

Z